Victor Duruy
& French Education

21ᵉ Bataillon
6ᵉ Cⁱᵉ

Victor Duruy.— 1870-1871.—

Duruy guarding the Ministry of Public Instruction during the Franco-Prussian War.

He was at the ministry what he would have been in the army: a good soldier.—Anonymous

Victor Duruy
& French Education

Liberal Reform in the Second Empire

Sandra Horvath-Peterson

Louisiana State University Press
Baton Rouge and London

Designer: Albert Crochet
Typeface: Linotron Sabon
Typesetter: G&S Typesetters, Inc.
Printer and binder: Vail-Ballou Press, Inc.

Publication of this book has been assisted by a grant from
the Andrew W. Mellon Foundation.

The author gratefully acknowledges permission to reprint
portions of Chapter VI, which appeared in "Victor Duruy and
the Controversy over Secondary Education for Girls," *French
Historical Studies*, IX (Spring, 1975), 83–104. The author also
wishes to thank Mme Albert Duruy for permission to print the
frontispiece and to quote from the letters of Victor Duruy.

LIBRARY OF CONGRESS CATALOGING IN PUBLICATION DATA

Horvath-Peterson, Sandra.
    Victor Duruy and French education.

    Bibliography: p.
    Includes index.
    1. Duruy, Victor, 1811–1894.   2. Educators—France—
Biography.   3. Education—France—History—19th century.
4. Education—Philosophy.   I. Title.
LB675.D842H67   1984   370'.92'4   [B]   83-23896
ISBN 0-8071-1157-0

To Morris, Courtney, and Brittany
To my parents
And to Joseph N. Moody

Contents

Illustrations

Abbreviations

AN   Archives Nationales, Paris

BHVP Bibliothèque de l'Hôtel de Ville de Paris

AIP   *L'Administration de l'instruction publique de 1863 à 1869*

BAIP *Bulletin administratif de l'instruction publique*

JGIP   *Journal général de l'instruction publique*

RIP   *Revue de l'instruction publique*

Preface and Acknowledgments

Victor Duruy, French minister of public instruction from 1863 to 1869 and liberal reformer, has long been acclaimed by historians as an important nineteenth-century education minister. His name is frequently linked with those of the other two great nineteenth-century education ministers—François Guizot and Jules Ferry. There are even some historians, Antoine Prost among them,[1] who consider Duruy the most important education minister in all of French history. Whatever the case, historians who question Duruy's importance would be difficult to locate. The purpose of this book is to take a close look at this famous education minister and to understand him in the context both of the history of French education and of that politically intriguing regime he served—the liberalizing Second Empire.

Politics are close to the heart of the story. In addition to being called an important educator, Duruy has also been variously called a leading liberal and a leading anticlerical of the Second Empire.[2] If these estimates are accurate, how did Duruy influence the changing Church-state relationship in the 1860s? Was he in any way responsible for inflaming the oftentimes noisy clerical-anticlerical conflict of the day? And did his appointment in any way mollify or attenuate the liberal and republican opposition to the regime? The answers to these questions, joined with evidence on Duruy's motives—political, social, economic, and cultural—for various actions will help clarify the role he played in Napoleon III's empire. It will be important to look at politics, additionally, because the budget of the education ministry and all

1. Personal interview with Antoine Prost, author of *Histoire de l'enseignement en France, 1800–1967* (Paris, 1968), October, 1968.
2. *L'Ordre et la liberté*, the legitimist paper of Evreux (Caen), referred to Duruy in its February, 1868, issue as "the second liberal in the empire" (clipping in F[19] 3972, Archives Nationales [hereinafter cited as AN]).

proposed major changes in the educational system had to be submitted for the approval of the legislature. Political considerations, therefore, circumscribed what Duruy was able to do. Comments by certain contemporary journalists that Duruy had autocratic power over all that transpired in French education or that he held virtual "power of life or death over the nation" are, of course, immediately suspect; but it will be helpful to see just how much—or how little—truth there may have been to these allegations. Finally, keeping in mind that the Second Empire was still essentially authoritarian in Duruy's day, it will be instructive to explore what it meant to be a liberal education minister in an authoritarian government.

Although educational reform and politics will be major concerns in this book, attention must also be given to the interaction between socioeconomic change and education because the Second Empire was a period of rapid industrialization and urbanization. Consequently, the book will scrutinize Duruy's sensitivity to socioeconomic needs and his reactions to the pleas and recommendations of concerned Frenchmen.

When, as a young graduate student, I first began work on this project, there was very little in the way of scholarly literature on Duruy.[3] Since that time, however, the field of education history has blossomed and Duruy has received much greater attention. Nevertheless, only one monograph with Duruy as its central focus has appeared, and that book, like most other recent publications that touch on Duruy's work, draws mainly on the printed sources for his period.[4] The present book, in contrast, relies heavily on archival sources and particularly on the F(17) series of the Ministry of Public Instruction at the Archives Nationales.[5] I have used for the first time the collection of confidential circulars in the F(17) series and the collection of private papers in possession of Mme Albert Duruy. Furthermore, for added perspective, I have drawn on a broad sample of press opinion that was published in

3. This literature is discussed in Sandra A. Horvath, "Victor Duruy and French Education, 1863–1869" (Ph.D. dissertation, Catholic University of America, 1971), iii–iv.

4. Jean Rohr, *Victor Duruy, ministre de Napoléon III: Essai sur la politique de l'instruction publique au temps de l'Empire Libéral* (Paris, 1967), 8.

5. A complete listing of the archival cartons used and their titles is given in the bibliography to Horvath, "Victor Duruy and French Education," 503–506.

the *Journal général de l'instruction publique* and the *Revue de l'instruction publique* during Duruy's tenure.[6]

Initial research on Duruy was made possible by a Fulbright Fellowship and a Woodrow Wilson Dissertation Grant. Additional research in Paris was facilitated by a Georgetown University Faculty Summer Research Stipend. I am most grateful to the institutions that awarded these grants. I am also deeply indebted to the kind archivists and librarians in Paris who assisted me over the many years; to Antoine Prost, who was my Fulbright adviser; to Mme Albert Duruy, who shared with me her collection of the minister's unpublished papers; to Jack Jackson of the library of the Boston Athenaeum, who loaned me volumes of the *Journal général de l'instruction publique*; to the editors of *French Historical Studies* for permission to draw on material from my article, "Victor Duruy and the Controversy Over Secondary Education for Girls," in the spring, 1975, issue of that journal; to the editors of the Louisiana State University Press for their many kindnesses and their patience through a period during which I had to juggle revisions on this manuscript, full-time teaching, and family responsibilities; to my typist, Mary Dyer, whose critical eye has spared me many an error or inconsistency; and finally, to the numerous historians, colleagues, and friends who have offered advice, encouragement, and assistance. Among the latter, I must particularly mention, first, my beloved mentor, Joseph N. Moody, and then, Guillaume de Bertier de Sauvigny, John Zeender, James Malloy, Thomas West, Doris Goldstein, and Denis Blum. I can never sufficiently thank my parents, my husband, and my in-laws for their support and constant encouragement. To my parents and my husband I owe special thanks for giving me uninterrupted blocks of time to write or rewrite portions of this book while they attended to babies and baby bottles. Finally, I would

6. The *Journal général de l'instruction publique* and the *Revue de l'instruction publique* (hereinafter cited as *JGIP* and *RIP*) were invaluable sources of information. The *JGIP*, known for its basic hostility to Duruy, and the *RIP*, known for its fundamental sympathy for Duruy, both excerpted from the contemporary press all significant opinion on education whether or not that opinion matched their own. They also offered texts of the legislative debates on education, reviews of relevant books, and communiqués which various other newspapers received for having criticized ministerial actions and programs. Although both of these papers, and especially the *JGIP*, had to be sensitive to government censorship, it was not difficult for them to speak freely about the minister of public instruction and his programs.

like to thank our daughters, Courtney and Brittany. They are much too young at present to understand how they have contributed, but someday, I would like them to know that they made life while I was completing this book more joyful and meaningful.

Victor Duruy
& French Education

I · Duruy's Early Life

No existence was more honorable than that of M. Duruy.
—Ernest Legouvé, *Dernier travail, derniers souvenirs*

Victor Duruy's lifetime spanned almost the entire nineteenth century. Born September 10, 1811, in one of the Gobelins factory apartments, he lived in Paris and its vicinity until his death in 1894. The ideas he was exposed to as a child and as a student of history had an enormous impact on his life, greatly influencing his later activities as a man, historian, professor, citizen, and minister. To trace his origins and his early experiences is to develop an understanding of the motivations that would guide all of his subsequent actions.

Jean Victor Duruy was the son of Charles Duruy and Suzanne Legendre. Almost nothing is known about Suzanne Legendre. It is thought that she emanated from the peasantry, but there is no certain proof. She died when Duruy was only eight years old, and he had little to say about her in his memoirs, *Notes et souvenirs*. Somewhat more is known about Charles Duruy. A highly respected master craftsman and foreman at the Gobelins factory, he was from a family of specialists in a tapestry technique known as *haute lisse* (high warp weaving) that had been brought from Arras by Colbert seven generations earlier.[1]

Charles Duruy was the truly formative influence in his son's early life. Since Victor Duruy was sickly as a child and family finances had been strained by his mother's illness, Charles Duruy assumed responsibility for his son's elementary schooling. In the process of educating the boy, he inculcated in him faith in liberalism and patriotism (what Donald G. Charlton has called the "secular religions"), the principles of 1789, and the glories of the First Empire.[2] In the gardens near the

1. *Acte de naissance*, 6314, in the archives of the department of the Seine, France; Victor Duruy, *Notes et souvenirs, 1811–1894* (2 vols.; Paris, 1901), I, 2.
2. Donald G. Charlton, *Secular Religions in France, 1815–1870* (London, 1963).

Gobelins factory this proud commander of a local National Guard unit taught his son the songs of the republican Pierre Jean de Béranger and often allowed him to listen to his animated political conversations with his co-workers. At the age of eleven, Victor Duruy, following in his father's footsteps, became an apprentice at the Gobelins factory. He took a course in industrial design and began weaving in the workshop while simultaneously furthering his elementary studies in a small school on the rue Pôt-au-Fer run by the Bonapartist and anticlerical Monsieur Hénon.

Information on Duruy's contacts with religion during these early years is sparse. The register of baptisms for the local parish church, Saint-Médard, shows that Duruy was baptized promptly after he was born and that his godparents were his maternal grandfather and his paternal grandmother. It is impossible to determine whether at this time Duruy's parents might have been what Gabriel Le Bras has called "seasonal Catholics" (those who sought out church services only for the great "seasons" of life—baptism, marriage, and death), but a fair guess is that Charles Duruy's anticlericalism dominated the household.[3]

Duruy remembered the local church in his memoirs with mixed sentiments. He noted that a religious order had "established itself in *our* little church of Saint-Médard." (The congregation is not identified.) Their "pompous" ceremonies and "passionate" sermons were used to gain from "tender" souls what the "austere" gospel could not. The clerics, enveloped in the smoke of the censers, processed through the streets of the quarter, while choir boys scattered rose petals along the route. "This was the triumph of the Church over honest but naive individuals who could be attracted by the glamour of religion from the depressing realities of daily life," Duruy recounted. Duruy implied that he merely watched these processions. Ernest Lavisse, however, asserts that Duruy was one of the young boys who marched in the processions. Whatever the case, Duruy's later memories of the processions were negative.[4]

3. Baptismal register of the Eglise Succursale de Saint-Médard, Paris, 1811–14, no. 348 (Microfilm 312981 of the Genealogical Society of the Church of Latter Day Saints, Salt Lake City, Utah). For "seasonal Catholics," see Gabriel Le Bras, *Etudes de sociologie religieuse* (2 vols.; 1955, rpr. New York, 1975), I, 5.

4. Duruy, *Notes et souvenirs*, I, 4, 7, emphasis added; Ernest Lavisse, *Association des anciens élèves de l'Ecole Normale Supérieure* (Paris, 1895), 11–12.

To be sure, Duruy's formative experiences with the Church were mixed. The religious ceremonies in the relatively anticlerical fifth arrondissement may have invited some mockery, as Duruy claims, but he enjoyed more positive associations with the Church in his teen years at the Collège Sainte-Barbe. He did not enter the *collège* immediately after he completed primary school because for a time during his twelfth year he was a full-time apprentice at the Gobelins factory. But then a close friend of the family, Baudemont, became aware that Duruy often took a history book to work to read during intervals while he was weaving, and he convinced Charles Duruy that his son's true interests were academic. Baudemont secured a partial scholarship for Victor at the Collège Sainte-Barbe, and Charles Duruy had to pay the rest of the tuition, a crushing 800 francs (about $160) annually for the first two years until tuition was reduced.[5]

Although Sainte-Barbe was run by the clergy, it was liberal in religious matters. Duruy reported in his memoirs that it was impossible to detect any specific sympathies in his teachers. The Abbé Faudet, who directed the school, and the Abbé Sénard, a teacher on the faculty, were "two very distinguished souls" who respected students' doubts, and among the lay members of the faculty, it was "impossible to say [whether the] professors were Catholic, Protestant, or freethinkers." Once, a student who expressed publicly the difficulties he was experiencing with belief was summoned by the chaplain for an amiable tête-à-tête. Duruy relates that this student was never pressed by the chaplain because the chaplain realized that "one can have a Christian soul without having the faith of the Church." The same principle was, Duruy continues, "what a minister [of public instruction] practiced forty years later." Evidence from Charles, comte de Montalembert, one of Duruy's classmates, corroborates these recollections. Students were permitted to sing the songs of Béranger in the courtyard between classes, and on one occasion they were allowed to vote on the existence of God. God won by one vote.[6]

5. Duruy, *Notes et souvenirs*, I, 4. Roger Williams, *The World of Napoleon III* (New York, 1957), 173, notes, rightly, that Baudemont was an *économe* at Saint-Barbe but incorrectly translates *économe* as economist; he was the bursar.

6. Victor Duruy to Mme Jules Michelet, July 1, 1884, in Jules Michelet Papers, I.5.A. (3), Bibliothèque de l'Hôtel de Ville de Paris (hereinafter cited as BHVP); Albert duc de Broglie, "Victor Duruy," *Revue des deux mondes*, February 1, 1898, p. 525.

These were good years for Duruy. He enjoyed the students, teachers, and studies at Sainte-Barbe. He worked diligently under the tutelage of Jules Michelet, who became his favorite teacher. Duruy described later to Mme Michelet her husband's magnetic attraction as a professor: "His speech, vibrant, forceful, inflamed, stirred one from the bottom of his soul and always made one more enlightened. Never at that time did his courses tell us whether he was legitimist, Orleanist, or republican, Catholic or freethinker. In spite of his rich and powerful personality, his teaching, his conversation had an absolutely impersonal character. He did not at all propagandize for a faction or for a doctrine; but he did make ardent propaganda for what he believed to be historical truth. . . . It was precisely for him and by him that history was brought alive."[7] Duruy always regretted school vacations because they meant an interruption in the happiness of academic life and a separation from classmates who returned home to the countryside.

The years at Sainte-Barbe drew to a close for Duruy just as the July Revolution erupted in the streets. On the night of July 26, 1830, against his father's orders, Duruy left the bed where he was supposed to be sleeping, donned a uniform, and joined his father in the reconstituted National Guard. The contingent was moving toward the center of Paris when word came that the prisoners of Saint-Pelagie were rioting. Faced with a conflict of interests, the unit ultimately decided to return to its quarters to restore order. Once the prisoners were secured safely in their cells, a command from an unknown source directed the unit to guard the porte d'Italie for the remainder of the night. Thus Duruy was prevented from taking a direct part in the protest against Charles X.[8] But his experiences during the July Days left him with great optimism because ultraroyalism had been overthrown and the principle of legality had been restored. Liberty, he was convinced, was the promise of the new regime.

Once the political turmoil subsided, Duruy began to prepare for the October 3 entrance examination to the recently revived Ecole Normale Supérieure. Given the smallness of the classes and the keenness of the competition, however, he fully expected that he would not be admitted to the school. If that happened, he promised himself he would enter the army. But his score on the examination was just good

7. Duruy to Mme Michelet, April 28, 1884, Michelet Papers, I.5.A. 3756 (1), BHVP.
8. Ernest Lavisse, *Un ministre—Victor Duruy* (Paris, 1895), 7–8.

enough to qualify him for the next entering class, although he was at the very bottom of that class. Not lacking in determination, Duruy worked indefatigably after school began, and within a few months he won the reputation of being a "beast of burden." This was a notable distinction, according to Jules Simon, because at Normale everyone worked hard.[9] Michelet, now a professor at the school, recorded in his journal that Duruy was "intelligent and hardworking; [and that he had a] remarkable aptitude for historical study." Surely Duruy's industry was due in part to his excellent professors—not only Michelet but also Théodore-Simon Jouffroy, Eugène Burnouf, and André-Marie Ampère. Some of his willingness to work hard might have been born of sheer ambition. But more likely, it came from a conviction the idealistic Duruy confided to his diary at this time: that human liberty is proportionate to intelligence and knowledge. In any event, Duruy redeemed himself academically. Three years after entering Normale, he emerged at the top of his class.[10]

Despite his seriousness toward immediate responsibilities, Duruy did spend time daydreaming about his future. One of the ambitions he shared with his friends was his desire to marry a beautiful woman, have children, and buy a nice home. Another was to write history books that would be lively and interesting because he had long been frustrated by the style and aridity of the books he had been forced to read as a student. He resolved that his first book would be dedicated to France.[11]

Upon finishing at the Ecole Normale in 1833 Duruy took the *agrégation* in history and won first place. He then accepted a job teaching history at the *collège* of Reims and, not unpredictably, found life there dull. After just a few weeks, he wrote to Michelet and begged him to

9. Simon did not know Duruy there because he entered the school the day Duruy left. He did, however, hear immediately about the latter's reputation. Later, when Duruy was minister, Simon criticized him for trying to make *universitaires* too "savant." "We do not need to know everything," he told Duruy. "Scholars who try to talk to children make the mistake of trying to teach them everything." "I would be very upset to have all your information. But you must possess it because you are M. Duruy" (Jules Simon, "Notice historique sur la vie et les travaux de Victor Duruy," *Journal des débats*, Supplément, November 30, 1895).

10. Note dated 1831–32, Michelet Papers, I.5.A. 3952 (189), BHVP; Duruy, *Notes et souvenirs*, I, 22; note in Victor Duruy's hand, undated, in possession of Mme Albert Duruy; Louis Planté, "Une rencontre de César: Victor Duruy, ministre de l'instruction publique," *Revue bleue*, May 2, 1931, p. 271.

11. Octave Gréard in Institut de France, *Inauguration du monument élevé à la mémoire de Victor Duruy à Villeneuve-Saint-Georges* (Paris, 1900), 12–13.

help him return to Paris. There were some "excellent businessmen" in Reims but few people who could stimulate his intellect. "Each month I stay here puts me one step behind," he complained.[12]

Despite his dissatisfactions, however, Duruy took his duties seriously. He worked on his teaching diligently, reminding himself daily that his students' minds were like a book on which he was writing in indelible ink. And he refrained from involving himself in a controversy that had erupted at the *collège* between the professor of philosophy, an abbé, and the professor of physics, a layman, over the existence of miracles. As he related later in his *Notes et souvenirs*, he believed that teachers had no right to enmesh themselves in religious or political disputes. Such altercations were alien to formal education.[13]

Duruy was rescued from Reims three months later by the king. Louis-Philippe, wishing to engage as tutor for his sons the man who had won top honors in the recent *agrégation*, invited Duruy to return to Paris. A jubilant Duruy accepted. Along with his tutorial responsibilities, he was given a supplementary position at the Collège Henri IV.

Happiness during the next years was to be found in a renewed association with Michelet. Duruy continued his tutoring at the Tuileries and his teaching at Henry IV, but he also assisted Michelet at the Sorbonne as a lecturer and aided the master in his historical research. Duruy's lectures at the Sorbonne were geared not toward historical comprehensiveness but toward propagating his immense faith in human progress and science, a faith this heir of the Enlightenment believed he shared with all rational men. Lavisse, a student in his class at the time, who became a lifelong friend, relates that Duruy "spoke of science with a religious respect. One day, at the end of a lecture at the Sorbonne, he proclaimed that science would be a 'second revelation' for mankind." As research assistant to Michelet, Duruy was given small daily tasks to complete at local Parisian libraries. For one month during the summer of 1835, he traveled in the southwest of France with Michelet in search of historical materials.[14]

But then, although Duruy served as a teaching assistant for Michelet again from December, 1836, to October, 1837, both the research as-

12. Victor Duruy to Jules Michelet, November 29, 1833, Jules Michelet Correspondence, XIV, 4722 (1), BHVP.

13. Duruy, *Notes et souvenirs*, I, 20–23.

14. Ernest Lavisse in Institut de France, *Inauguration du monument élevé à la*

sistantship and friendship seem to have come to an abrupt end. The evidence suggests that the two men had a dispute over religious matters.[15] In any event, the rupture was not repaired until 1848.

In the meantime, Duruy married Adele de Graffenreid, daughter of a Berne notable. Over the next seventeen years, they had five children—three sons and two daughters. Duruy installed his family in an apartment at 5, rue de Medicis in Paris, across the street from the home of Ernest Lavisse. Later, after he began to receive royalties from his history books, Duruy purchased a large house at Villeneuve-Saint-Georges, overlooking the Seine. There he loved to watch his children romp in the grassy meadows along the banks of the river.[16]

Duruy was now busy writing and publishing. The first two volumes of his multivolume *Histoire Romaine*, which had been undertaken in the 1830s on Michelet's encouragement and would help stimulate an interest in ancient history among serious historians, appeared in 1843 and 1844.[17] These volumes earned Duruy the attention of the academic world, a *croix de chevalier* from the Legion of Honor, and a promotion to titulary professor at the Lycée Saint-Louis in 1845. In that same year, Duruy published his *Histoire sainte d'après le Bible*, an orthodox interpretation by a man who had read the Bible many times. "The Bible is the book par excellence," Duruy wrote, "that of the wise and the simple, that which for two thousand years has nourished the young generations. . . . The Bible, history of God himself . . . develops and exalts the religious sentiment, but also [pleads earnestly] for domestic and social virtues. It calls for prayer; but even more [emphatically] perhaps, it entreats action, i.e., charity toward one's neighbors and devotion to the state. God, family, and fatherland, these are, in effect, the great ideas the sacred books teach." Above all else, the Bible, with its Jewish legacy of reverence for justice, equality, and monotheism in the face of polytheistic superstition, was, for Duruy, one of the greatest books on morality ever written.[18]

---

mémoire de Victor Duruy, 17; Duruy to Mme Michelet, May 2, 1884, Michelet Papers, I.5.A. 3756 (5), BHVP; Voyages I.A. 3722, ibid.

15. The evidence is reviewed in Horvath, "Victor Duruy and French Education," 49–52.

16. Institut de France, *Inauguration du monument élevé à la mémoire de Victor Duruy*, 63.

17. Michelet Papers, I.5.A. 4882 (20), BHVP; James Westfall Thompson and Bernard J. Holm, *A History of Historical Writing* (2 vols; New York, 1942), II, 509.

18. Victor Duruy, *Histoire sainte d'après la Bible* (Paris, 1863), 1, ii–vi.

Two years after *Histoire sainte* was published, the minister of public instruction, Narcise, comte de Salvandy, offered Duruy the vacant rectorate in the academy of Algeria. Duruy immediately enrolled in an Arabic course and began studying Islamic civilization. But when he was called before the Royal Council of Public Instruction for an interview, he upset his candidacy by asserting: "Our civil code is incompatible with the customs of the Arabs, and Islam is absolutely opposed to Catholicism. There is only the book, namely science, which can morally conquer these three million men whose hostility is a continual danger for us."[19] Council members were outraged. Victor Cousin and François Saint-Marc Girardin led the opposition, and Duruy was denied the post.

Embittered by what he judged to be the narrow-mindedness of the Royal Council and convinced, according to his memoirs, that all men should take stock of their convictions halfway through life (he was then thirty-six), Duruy retreated into a review of his values and beliefs. In a full chapter in *Notes et souvenirs* entitled "Mon examen de conscience," Duruy discussed religion, society, and history as he saw them in 1847. He revealed, as Roger Williams has put it so well, that his mature views were "a curious mixture of eighteenth-century rationalism, skepticism and idealism."[20]

Theologically, Duruy was a Deist.[21] He believed that on earth man has only to concern himself with the pursuit of truth. Although justice is not always accorded to men individually in their temporal life, it is always rendered to humanity or nations at large. Nevertheless, all intelligent men should seek truth and justice in life. "The theologian," he stated, "looks for these in the Gospel, the philosopher in man, the historian in humanity." In order to live an intelligent and a good life, a person has to be well-educated. How reminiscent these ideas were of

19. As quoted in Marguerite Schwab, "Victor Duruy et les premiers pas de l'enseignement laique," *Cahiers laïques*, no. 73 (January–February, 1963), 4–5.
20. Williams, *World of Napoleon III*, 175.
21. In an interview in 1969, Mme Albert Duruy (the daughter of Victor Duruy's only child by Mme Redel and the wife of Albert Duruy, the son of Victor Duruy's last child by his first wife, Mlle de Graffenreid) claimed that her grandfather was an agnostic. But my own reading of Duruy's sympathies, especially those expressed in *Notes et souvenirs*, persuades me that Duruy firmly believed in the existence of a supernatural being. This view is corroborated by the duc de Broglie and Emile Ollivier, who call Duruy "a convinced Deist" (de Broglie, "Victor Duruy," 561, and Ollivier, *L'empire libéral* [18 vols.; Paris, 1903], VI, 603).

the Victorian Englishman, who proclaimed, "Virtue is the child of knowledge, vice of ignorance."[22]

Education, however, would never assist man in proving the existence of God; that required an act of faith. "Man would be . . . more than God if he could analyze and define Him." Here Duruy emerges as the model Deist: religions were created by "men of superior talent who ranged themselves between God and the masses."[23] Every culture that had ever existed had some form of religion which answered the fears and hopes of its people. Duruy, the ancient history scholar, had studied many. Religion was the inevitable result of deficiencies in scientific knowledge. Ultimately, however, science would be able to explain everything, everything, that is, except the existence of God. The age of full human enlightenment was nearing, and when it was attained, man-made religion with its myths, miracles, cosmologies, ceremony, and pageantry would be a thing of the past. Enlightened humanistic philosophy would be its substitute.

Duruy had a positivist frame of mind, but like several others of his generation—Claude Bernard, Charles-Adolphe Wurtz, and Claude-Louis Berthelot for example[24]—he did not simultaneously subscribe to the positivist "faith." He always retained a belief in God, the soul, and some form of afterlife. If an afterlife did not exist, he often argued, there would be no reason for man to be moral, and it was obedience to the law of morality that made man superior to all other living creatures. Interestingly, his reverence for morality propelled him to reject the notion of Providence for it coincided too closely with the Calvinist doctrine of predestination. Similarly, Duruy rejected notions of Divine omniscience and omnipotence because he could not reconcile them with his belief in free will.[25]

Duruy's differences with institutional religion did not make him an unbridled foe of the churches. He abhorred religious polemic and

22. Duruy, *Notes et souvenirs*, I, 33; Peter Stearns, *European Society in Upheaval: Social History Since 1750* (New York, 1975), 132.
23. Duruy, *Notes et souvenirs*, I, 34, 36. The full argument is in Victor Duruy, *Italie ancienne* (2 vols.; Paris, 1851), II, 346–467. It would not have been uncharacteristic for Duruy to have attempted to jolt a believer by querying whether God was a Catholic, Protestant, Jew, or Moslem.
24. William Arthur Bruneau, "The French Faculties and Universities, 1870–1902" (Ph.D. dissertation, University of Toronto, 1977), 196.
25. Duruy, *Notes et souvenirs*, I, 40–44.

garish ceremonies, but as a historian and a moderate man he remained respectful of the positive contributions of the established churches, a distinction, unfortunately, most of his religious critics later chose to ignore. Duruy believed the churches had performed an enormous service in synthesizing moral ideas for the masses. Jesus, only a man, was nevertheless one of the greatest moral prophets who had ever lived. Duruy was more than just tolerant of religion: he respected all honest believers, and he believed so completely in freedom of conscience that he excoriated intolerance whenever it was expressed. Indeed, he would later allow his first wife to convert to Catholicism.[26]

Pierre Corneille's admonition, "Do your work, and leave the gods alone," was one of Duruy's favorite maxims. Salvation could be earned on earth by anyone who dedicated his life to the expansion of morality among the masses. All human progress was dependent on making knowledge, morality, taste, and well-being the property of a great number. As Duruy put it, "Man has been given powers, it is our *duty* to develop them."[27]

The notion of progress and evolution that so affected Duruy's views derived from his study of history, although his knowledge of science and scientific advancements certainly reinforced his convictions. "Each era has its miseries," he declared, "[but] everything heals itself, and, in spite of detestable incidents, humanity follows its route toward a greater well-being and security which is the ambition of our terrestrial life. What generation has seen more misfortune than ours (Sedan and the Commune!), more threats to its peace! However, I always have hope."[28]

These ideas decidedly colored his political beliefs. Politics were transitory, a question of conformity and convenience. There were no absolutes in politics: "All governments except the violent are good when they accord with the interests and ideas of the moment." They are bad when they contradict those contemporary needs. The needs and de-

---

26. *Ibid.*, 45–46, 67. Duruy spoke of "tolerance" for all honest believers, but it is clear he meant "respect."

27. As quoted in Williams, *World of Napoleon III*, 176. No source is given. I have italicized the word "duty" in this excerpt to emphasize a concept that was a critical part of Duruy's value system.

28. Duruy, *Notes et souvenirs*, I, 19.

sires of a society could best be determined through a study of its history.[29]

The social and economical problems of the lower classes also concerned Duruy because, as he phrased it, the grandeur of France was his "religion" and because, like Michelet, he had a sincere affection for the classes from which he had risen. He was convinced that poverty and misery were relative conditions. They could never be fully eradicated from society, but they were mitigated, in the nineteenth century, by constant material improvements and a leveling of the social classes. Duruy spurned utopian socialistic schemes and communism because he believed that private property was absolutely essential to human liberty. Beyond that, education was the answer to the social problem, and a *disciplined* capitalistic system the solution to proletarian discontent.[30]

A few months after this "examination of conscience" was made, while Duruy was occupied with his writing, the revolution of 1848 erupted. The February Revolution came as no surprise to him; it was part of the natural evolution toward republicanism and democracy.[31] Louis-Philippe and Guizot had precipitated the coup d'etat by their complacency and insensitivity to political and economic grievances. Unlike most teachers at the time, Duruy did not take sides. Nonetheless, he was disturbed by the violence that accompanied the coup, and, according to Lavisse, he foresaw the catastrophes of May and June. Utopian formulas only led the lower classes to tragedy. No amount of shouting "Vive la République" would bring the republic into existence. A republic would be established in France, Duruy was convinced, only when all other forms of government proved impossible.[32]

That spring, the minister of public instruction, Hippolyte Carnot, offered Duruy a position as a people's lecturer, "a utopian scheme" that Duruy refused. After the bloodbath of June, Duruy supported order and General Louis-Eugène Cavaignac. The Bonapartist loyalties he

---

29. *Ibid.*, 52, 49; see also 240. Duruy often reminded Napoleon that "the best of politics is the wise administration of national interests." He claimed that this was his rule as minister of public instruction.

30. *Ibid.*, 52, 57–59.

31. Ernest Lavisse in *Femmes diplômes*, special no. 43, 3rd trimester (1962), 11.

32. Thompson and Holm, *History of Historical Writing*, II, 265; Ernest Lavisse, "Victor Duruy," *Revue de Paris*, January 15, 1895, pp. 232–33.

had imbibed as a youngster from his father had been neutralized by his study of Roman history, and he now feared the rise of a new Caesar in the person of Louis-Napoleon. In 1860, he would bravely explain this anxiety to the emperor. In the meantime, he voted "No" in both of the plebiscites.

In 1849, Duruy attempted to fulfill a lifelong ambition by applying for a vacant chair in history at the Ecole Normale. But the minister of public instruction, Hippolyte Fortoul, was busy purging liberals from the University, and he refused to entertain Duruy's candidacy. A bitter Duruy, now twice rejected by the University, returned to his writing. Fortunately, at about the same time, he received from Louis Hachette an opportunity to direct a universal history series for the secondary schools.[33] Sensitive to the unsuitability of Michelet's textbooks, which were generally considered too theoretical for the young, and troubled by the mediocre quality and boring presentations of other textbook authors, Duruy readily accepted the offer.[34] Over the next decade he would publish in this series several historical texts, which became known popularly as "Les Duruys." The first, *Histoire grecque*, published in 1851, prompted a reprimand from the minister of public instruction because it displayed preference for Athens over Sparta.[35] Another, the *Abrégé de l'histoire de France*, won a stinging attack by the Abbé Brulebois, headmaster of a private school at Chalon-sur-Saône, because it allegedly contained certain "dangerous" interpretations, especially in the sections on the Civil Constitution of the Clergy. Unhappily, the *Journal général de l'instruction publique* (*JGIP*) in its April 2, 1853, issue allied itself with the abbé. Fortoul soon agreed, telling Duruy that his *Histoire de France* contained "regrettably hasty thoughts," even though a moderate Catholic inspector general assigned to investigate Duruy's text reported that it contained no major errors. Duruy was despondent. He wrote to the director of personnel: "From one end of France to another, I am a kind of excommunicate with whom contact is dangerous. At Saint-Louis, where my books cannot be placed at the disposition of candidates to Saint-Cyr, I have given twelve copies

33. Victor Duruy, ed., *Histoire universelle: Publiée par une société de professeurs et de savants, sous la direction de M. V. Duruy* (Paris, various dates).
34. A. Macé to Victor Duruy, November 1, 1863, Victor Duruy Papers, 114 AP-2-IV, AN; Lavisse, *Un ministre—Victor Duruy*, 65.
35. *JGIP*, 1853, p. 190.

of my books to students at my own expense. These volumes have just been taken from them as bad books, dangerous works. . . . This is where I am after twenty-three years laboriously filled by functions or work exclusively for the University." But more dispassionately, Duruy believed that such a judgment was to be expected from a "clerical period." In October, 1854, Duruy took some revenge by reporting to Fortoul that in spite of the abbé's attack, his *Abrégé* was being used in both public and religious schools. The minor seminary of Saint-Nicholas in Paris, for example, had just purchased seventy-two copies.[36]

Duruy wrote a total of seventy-four books for Hachette, more than sixty of which treated ancient history. All were written in a lively style; all were pervaded by Duruy's strong sense of morality; and all contained, in simple form, the latest historical findings. E. Zévort said that Duruy had a magical style and that as a writer he was without peer. Gustave Ducordray, commenting on the moral tone in Duruy's writings, called his books *livres-missionaires*. And Jules Simon and the duc de Broglie asserted that although Duruy's books did not impress some of the "pontiffs of the time" and earned for him among those "pontiffs" a reputation as a "*faiseur de petits livres*," they were a distinct cut above the usual pedestrian textbooks. Indeed, whenever Duruy re-edited his books, he always revised them to include the most recent scholarship. It was no surprise to Duruy's friends that he was the first nineteenth-century French historian to make history texts exciting for schoolchildren. These books would become standard fare in the French schools for the remainder of the century and on into the twentieth century.[37]

Work on the popular histories was balanced by more scholarly pursuits. The third and fourth volumes of *Histoire des Romains* were completed at this time but not published because Duruy feared that their favorable interpretation of Caesar and the Roman Empire would be misused by the authoritarian government. Duruy could condone dictatorship in ancient times but not in an enlightened age. The two volumes would remain in manuscript until after the fall of the empire,

36. Lavisse, *Un ministre—Victor Duruy*, 23–25; Duruy, *Notes et souvenirs*, I, 72–77; Williams, *World of Napoleon III*, 180.

37. E. Zévort, "Victor Duruy," *Revue pédagogique*, XXV (1894), 481; *RIP*, 1863, p. 85; Lavisse's essay in *Femmes diplômes*, 11; de Broglie, "Victor Duruy," 526; *Cinquantenaire du Lycée Victor Duruy (1912–1962)* (Paris, 1963), 22.

when they were published. Duruy worked simultaneously on his doctorate, preparing the two required dissertations. The first analyzed the
transition of ancient Rome from republic to empire, arguing that the
republic was irreparably decayed by Caesar's time. This thesis reflected Duruy's general political philosophy that new governments
arise when the old ones are no longer tenable. The second dissertation,
inspired by remarks Michelet had made when Duruy was his student
at the Ecole Normale, revised the original historiography of Tacitus
and Suetonius, both members of the Roman aristocracy, on Tiberius.
Without exonerating Tiberius for his faults and travesties, Duruy portrayed him as a wise and economical administrator, who had har-
nessed the Roman nobility for the good of the state. This revisionist
interpretation is considered Duruy's most original contribution to historical literature.[38] Duruy's other historical works were simply good
syntheses of contemporary scholarship.

Defended at the Sorbonne in July, 1853, Duruy's thesis on Tiberius
was the occasion of a famous "affair of the two moralities." The incident developed when one of the examiners on the committee, Victor
Le Clerc, dean of the faculty of letters and author of *Histoire des em-
pereurs*, attacked the morality of the Caesars. Duruy held respectful
silence, but Desiré Nisard attempted to defend Duruy by asserting that
two moralities existed. Pandemonium erupted in the hall, and police
had to be called in to restore order. Several arrests were made before
the session ended. In 1856, Nisard would write Duruy, requesting that
he refresh his memory: Nisard admitted that the incident had been unfortunate but denied having stated that there were two moralities. Duruy, however, could not agree to this prevarication and refused to ab-
solve Nisard.[39]

If Nisard held a grudge against Duruy for this refusal, he did not
hold it for long. Shortly thereafter, Nisard, in his capacity as general
inspector, visited one of Duruy's classes and was charmed by his
knowledge and imaginative teaching. Duruy had originally planned to
speak on Voltaire, Rousseau, and Mme de Pompadour, but when he
discovered that Nisard would be attending his class, he switched to a

38. Gabriel Monod, *Portraits et souvenirs* (Paris, 1897), 121.
39. Desiré Nisard, *Souvenirs et notes biographiques* (2 vols.; Paris, 1888), I, 83;
Monod, *Portraits et souvenirs*, 121, affirms that Nisard did indeed assert in 1853 that
there were two moralities.

lecture on the development of European colonialism. "During more than an hour and a half," Duruy later wrote, "I took my inspector to the Indies, America, [and] Canada, reopening for him the history of Leatherstocking Tales, the length of the Caribbean, and not for an instant placing foot in Europe."[40] Nisard was won over, and thereafter he had only good words about Duruy's teaching ability. Duruy's reward finally came in February of 1855, when he was promoted to full professor at the Lycée Napoléon, the former Collège Henri IV.

Four years later, Duruy accepted a project that would lead him to the Ministry of Public Instruction. In 1859, Marshal Jacques Randon, who had been governor of Algeria, was replaced by Prince Jerome Napoleon, the new minister of colonies. Fearing his removal would imply that he had been a poor colonial administrator, Randon sought the services of Duruy to chronicle his achievements, and Duruy was delighted because he prided himself on being a *cocardier* (a flag-waver). After convincing Randon that the brochure should have no political overtones, Duruy went to Algeria for three months to collect the necessary documents. Some time later, they issued *L'administration de l'Algérie de 1852 à 1858*, although as the result of an earlier agreement, its authorship was attributed to Randon's former aide-de-camp.[41]

Randon proved to be Duruy's key to the ministry for he introduced Duruy to Napoleon III. Not long after Randon was named minister of war in 1859, he noticed a copy of Duruy's *Histoire romaine* on the emperor's desk. When questioned, Napoleon remarked that he was impressed by the book and desired to meet the author. Napoleon was writing his biography of Caesar at the time, and he hoped that Duruy might supply him with additional information. A meeting was arranged for that very evening. During the course of an hour and a half, Duruy related to the emperor his views on Roman politics, including his judgment that "to seize sovereign power [in Rome] . . . one had only to pierce the chest of a man." Duruy later regretted the remark because he wanted the emperor to understand that he was a political moderate.[42] Napoleon, however, apparently was not troubled by the comment. He reported subsequently to Randon that he had been im-

40. Duruy, *Notes et souvenirs*, I, 85–86.
41. Lavisse, "Victor Duruy," 238.
42. Duruy, *Notes et souvenirs*, I, 109–10. It was at one of his early meetings with the

pressed by Duruy's intelligence and erudition but could not accept all of Duruy's interpretations. Thus Duruy was relieved of his worst fears.

Duruy now became involved in the Roman Question. In 1860, Gustave Rouland, possibly on Napoleon's orders, commissioned Duruy to prepare an essay on the temporal power of the papacy. Duruy, planning to leave for Greece four days later, enclosed himself at Villeneuve-Saint-Georges and drafted an essay on temporal power, which he submitted to Rouland. Upon his return from Greece, he was summoned to Rouland's office and shown galley proofs of his essay. The astonished Duruy was told that it had been printed because it had been reviewed by someone (obviously Napoleon III) who did not care to read manuscripts.

Originally, Rouland planned that Duruy's essay would be published as a series of articles in *La Patrie*. But after the revolt of the insurgents at Romagna, the French government decided the publication would be untimely. According to Lavisse, Duruy insisted that his essay still be published, and Rouland was willing to approve as long as the publication was anonymous and at Duruy's expense. Consequently, the essay appeared as an unacknowledged pamphlet with the title *Les papes, princes italiens*. Within a few days, it had sold more than ten thousand copies. It was countered by a violent rebuttal published shortly thereafter by Joseph d'Avenel, the author of several histories of the Church and Catholic figures.[43]

What is most interesting about Duruy's brochure is that although it was not ultimately published by the government, it reflects the evolution in imperial policies from 1859 to 1860. Throughout this time, the government had launched a number of trial balloons in the press and elsewhere to determine public opinion on Rome.[44] Perhaps the most famous was the pamphlet *Le pape et le Congrès*, written by Arthur de La Guéronnière in December, 1859, which argued that the papacy need maintain only limited temporal power to continue as an independent power. Duruy's pamphlet, written for a more highly educated au-

---

emperor that he confessed he had voted for Cavaignac in 1848 and against the authoritarian empire in 1851 and 1852.

43. *Ibid.*, 110–12; Joseph d'Avenel, *Le pape, prince italien, réponse à la brochure Les papes, princes italiens* (Paris, 1860).

44. Natalie Isser, *The Second Empire and the Press: A Study of Government Inspired Brochures on French Foreign Policy in Their Propaganda Milieu* (The Hague, 1974).

dience than La Guéronnière's, advanced a more daring thesis. The papal states, which had been acquired "through war and treaties, ruses and farce, craftiness and perfidy—all very human means," and which were once an asset to the pope, were now a handicap. The political dissension in those territories was jeopardizing the spiritual independence of the papacy. Duruy proposed that the pope limit himself to the Vatican and establish a civil list for all Catholic countries that would donate funds in proportion to their Catholic populations.[45] Such views were certainly more acceptable to the republicans the government hoped to appease, and Napoleon's approval of Duruy's thesis shows how the emperor's politics were evolving during these critical months.

The emperor was greatly pleased with Duruy's work. When in 1861 a vacancy occurred in the inspector general corps, he tried to persuade Rouland to appoint Duruy over Pierre Chéruel, the logical nominee for the post. Duruy, however, intervened to save Rouland from embarrassment.[46] As a compromise, Duruy was named lecturer at the Sorbonne and inspector of academy at Paris.

In his new capacity as inspector, Duruy worked conscientiously. He prepared a general list of necessary reforms in the academy of Paris, and, on the rector's request, a specific report on primary instruction. Although his colleagues requested action on his suggestions, they were ignored at the ministry. But Randon, at the Ministry of War, was interested in Duruy's ideas, and in July he asked Duruy to review the curriculum of the military schools. The result was a detailed report that greatly pleased Randon. Yet surprisingly, Rouland accused Duruy of insulting the minister of war. Duruy wrote a hasty riposte to Rouland: at Normale, where Chéruel had offered only one course, he had given two; as inspector of academy, normally a sinecure, he was actively filing well-researched reports; no one at the University had anything but praise for his suggested reforms of military school curricula; at the same time, he was discreetly pursuing an inquiry on the teaching of history at the primary level and the reform of modern languages.[47]

45. [Victor Duruy], *Les papes, princes italiens* (Paris, 1860); see esp. chap. XV.
46. E. Levasseur, "L'enseignement des jeunes filles et M. Duruy," *Revue internationale de l'enseignement*, XXX (1895), 550, claims Duruy told the emperor that the appointment would be too abrupt. He wished to follow normal advancement procedures and gain experience first as an inspector of academy.
47. Duruy, *Notes et souvenirs*, I, 118–19.

Rouland was caught in the middle because Duruy was an imperial favorite. In February of 1862 he felt compelled to name Duruy inspector general, and this time Duruy accepted. Because the new duties required that he tour schools in the provinces for four months out of the year, Duruy resigned from Normale. But in compensation, he was appointed to the new chair of history at Polytechnique. Arrangements were made so that his teaching and inspection duties would not conflict.

The eager reformer now applied his energies to the history curriculum at Polytechnique. Instead of offering to its elite student body another survey of French history, which was a more sophisticated version of what they had had at the secondary level, Duruy proposed a course on the great historical problems of Europe that would emphasize contemporary affairs. "Here are young men of intelligence," he wrote General Gregoire Coffinières de Nordeck. "They will soon enter public service, yet they know nothing of recent history and the current interests of the society in which they will become active members." Such a course would be suspect to men who feared that the podium could be used for political propaganda, but Duruy insisted that his course would be objective. Certainly, he argued, the conversations of the students in the barracks or the cabarets of the Latin Quarter were no less political because the students spoke out of ignorance.[48]

Duruy's course was finally approved, and his first lecture, an elaboration of his general philosophy, became a classic. The lecture began with a survey of the tremendous advances in the contemporary world. The creation of savings bank accounts, the rise of the working class, progress in education, freedom of religion, and the improvement of public morality, Duruy told his students, were as important as material gains. He attributed ameliorations in public morality to the spread of education, and, ignoring studies done in the 1830s which disputed a correlation between illiteracy and criminality, Duruy stated that the prison population displayed the highest illiteracy rates in France. Moral progress could ultimately eradicate war, and if a better world was to be created, all energies should be focused on the schools.

The sciences, Duruy professed, had played an enormous role in human progress, but they had to be balanced and complemented by stud-

48. *Ibid.*, 121–25.

ies in letters and the arts. Pure science alone was insufficient, as the Greeks had realized when they constructed the Parthenon. The beauty of the Parthenon owed not to scientific precision but to departures from rigid scientific principles. Truth and beauty were often a mixture of the scientifically true and false.

Such appreciations were important for educators and students. Overspecialized training in any one field, a growing tendency of modern civilization, was fraught with dangers unless men were firmly grounded in general education. A scientist, for example, could not make valuable contributions to society unless he understood its goals. Similarly, logic, by itself, was dangerous. "History is full of the monstrosities and deplorable errors of men who thought poorly but reasoned well." Just consider the Inquisition, St. Bartholomew's Day, Marat, and the September Massacres, Duruy advised his students. "All those violent people who said 'Perish the world rather than my thought or belief,' started from an idea that they thought just; they rigorously deduced from this thought terrible consequences: the one, in the God of the Gospel saw the implacable divinity of the auto-da-fé; the other, in the doctrine of human fraternity found the logical necessity of immense murder." [49]

All life, Duruy asserted, was a process of making value judgments: "There is for the soul a . . . work, by certain regards superior to the deductive judgments of the mathematicians; it is first to conceive, then to judge the infinite variety of things which compose the intellectual and moral world, the effects and causes, the ends and means, the beautiful and the ugly in art, the good and bad in morality, the just and unjust in life and society, customs, religions, political and civil institutions, etc." Historical knowledge could especially supply men with the essentials for making these value judgments. [50] "History is still the treasure of the universal experience." History alone appeases political passions for it demonstrates that ideas take time to mature and that societies are inevitably compensated for injustices done to them. "His-

49. The text of the lecture is in *ibid.*, I, 128–57; quotation on p. 148. Both editions of the lecture were printed as V. Duruy, *Leçon d'ouverture du cours d'histoire à l'Ecole Polytechnique pour les deux divisions réunies* (Paris, 1862).

50. For Duruy, no history was more important than the history of France, that of "the most enlightened people." Duruy's chauvinism prevented him from being a complete liberal—a universal humanitarian. See Adrien Dansette, "Un grand ministre méconnu," *Revue de Paris*, December, 1967, p. 53.

tory comes then to complete and extend the principles of individual morality that God has placed in us. . . . It is the conscience of the human species. It teaches . . . the noble and austere doctrine of work which is its own reward . . . ; [through work] we repay our debt of life to the Creator by increasing the intelligence and moral force which He has given us; this work is the common labor of humanity."[51] Duruy's uplifting comments made a great impression on his students. His lecture was published shortly thereafter, and it would go through two more editions.

While Duruy was in Paris giving his lectures at Polytechnique during the winter of 1862–1863, the emperor continued to consult with him on Caesar. Duruy was invited to join the imperial family at Compiègne for Christmas, but he declined because he felt uncomfortable in court society. At the end of December, when the court returned to the Tuileries, Duruy was called to assist Jean-François Mocquard, the emperor's ailing chief secretary. Thinking this would mean helping Napoleon with the writing of the biography of Caesar, he accepted, although he insisted that the assignment be kept a secret and that he earn no compensation for his labors. At first, however, Duruy was disappointed; Mocquard gave him only official letters to edit. But then, on the third day, Napoleon visited him in the secretary's chambers and showed him galley proofs of the *Vie de Caesar.*

An enlightening episode occurred after Duruy perused the preface of the biography. Toward the end of the preface there was a section in which the emperor asserted that Providence creates men such as Caesar, Charlemagne, and Napoleon when it wishes "to fulfill several centuries of work in a few years." Duruy felt compelled to advise the emperor that the concept of Providence had been used in the past to explain the inexplicable but that it was no longer taught by most educators in the nineteenth century. Men were not slaves but masters of their fortune. The emperor, however, was not moved; he insisted on retaining the passage. Duruy also protested unsuccessfully against the emperor's assertion in the book that when public order was in danger, usurpation of authority was often necessary. Duruy bravely lectured Napoleon: "Violations of law are never justifiable. There have been

51. Duruy, *Notes et souvenirs,* I, 149–50, 153–54, 156.

coups d'etat, but we should try to forget them." Duruy never concealed his sentiments, particularly not before the emperor. He would later allege to his friends: "I was a poor courtier, but I did my job as a good citizen." [52] For his part, Napoleon III respected Duruy's independence of thought. Frequently he answered Duruy's critics with the terse rejoinder: "Duruy is an *honnête homme.*"

In the spring, Duruy went on his inspection tour. Arriving at Lorient in April, he noticed that the general education program he had outlined for the military schools had not been implemented uniformly and that the curriculum at Lorient had no humanities courses yet. He promptly wrote a complaint to Rouland: "Before giving a special direction to the forces of the mind, it is necessary to develop these forces through general education [*culture générale*]." He even supplied Rouland with a simile to relay to the minister of the navy—"A young man trained in general education is like a ship whose seaworthiness has been proven and whose furnaces are filled with coal. The captain has only to give the signal for full steam ahead and the ship will move quickly and well through the water." [53]

At Coutances (Manche), Duruy found another problem. He saw a young boy who was twice the size of his classmates struggling hopelessly with Latin and Greek. This boy, however, was destined to follow his father's occupation in farming; a classical education was inappropriate for him. It was this experience, Duruy claimed later, that convinced him of the need for a technical and scientific program in the secondary schools. [54]

By June 23, 1863, Duruy, traveling with inspector Roustan, was at Moulins. Word reached them that a telegram was waiting for Duruy. At first, Duruy feared that his son, seriously ill with a sore throat, had died. Roustan later recounted:

> Imagine the anxiety we had while he tore open the dispatch. I lowered my head, as I feared seeing the sadness that would cover his face. "Take it," he told me, throwing the letter on my plate after having read it with no change in the gravity expressed on his face. The dispatch from his son-in-law

52. *Ibid.*, I, 183–84; *M. Victor Duruy* (n.p., 1876).
53. Victor Duruy to Gustave Rouland, April 26, 1862, in Lavisse, "Victor Duruy," 241.
54. Duruy, *Notes et souvenirs,* I, 167.

[Charles Glachant] read only, "You have been named our minister." We ate very little of our lunch; he was surprised not to be able to express any joy. He was immediately taken by the crushing weight of this [new] burden, but it was also not difficult to see that he sensed the honor of this charge and indication of [imperial] confidence, because many times during the next few hours, he repeated with tears in his eyes, "Ah, my father, my father." [55]

Duruy's surprise at his appointment is evident here and elsewhere. All of his associates who wrote and spoke of him later confirm that Napoleon III had never discussed the ministry with Duruy before the appointment in June. Earlier, Duruy had admitted, on a query from the emperor, that his highest ambition was to be a general inspector of education. Yet the appointment was not illogical. Napoleon III was familiar with Duruy's ideas from their many conversations. He knew Duruy's thoughts on religion and politics, as well as those on the problems of the University. [56] According to Desiré Nisard, what the emperor liked most about Duruy was his "liberalism mixed with a little daydreaming." [57] Perhaps the emperor saw a bit of himself in Duruy. At any rate, Duruy was just the man Napoleon III believed he needed as minister of public instruction in 1863. Duruy had an impressive set of academic credentials, experience as a school inspector, and the reputation of being both a scholar (his work would soon inspire Ernest Lavisse, Alfred Rambaud, and Gabriel Monod), [58] and an *honnête homme*. Indeed, Duruy was well known for his reliability; as Jules Simon put it: "From professor to minister, he always thought the same things and he always said what he thought." Furthermore, Duruy was a reformer, a liberal, a man who could pledge loyalty to the liberalizing regime, and a moderate anticlerical. Duruy's anticlericalism would be just strong enough to sting the clergy without causing it substantial damage. To be sure, it was far removed from the resolute anticlericalism or vehement antichristianity of the republican generation. [59]

Back in Paris on the twenty-fourth of June, Duruy traveled to Fon-

55. Inspector Roustan to his daughter, June 25, 1863, *Le centenaire de Victor Duruy, 1811–1911* (Cahors et Alençon, 1911), 18.

56. Duruy, *Notes et souvenirs*, I, 189.

57. Nisard, *Souvenirs et notes biographiques*, I, 283. Duruy's lively imagination became well known. See *JGIP*, 1868, p. 227.

58. Thompson and Holm, *History of Historical Writing*, II, 264.

59. Roger Marlin, "Le dernière tentative électorale de Montalembert aux elections législatives de 1863," *Revue d'histoire moderne et contemporaine*, XVII (1970), 1012–13.

tainebleau to meet with the emperor. Asking Napoleon why he decided to make him minister, Duruy was told simply, "Ça ira bien."[60] Duruy claimed in his memoirs that the emperor never gave him any guidance on what he should do as minister. Yet it is obvious that Duruy had a good sense of the emperor's wishes because he outlined what he thought they were in a letter to the emperor soon thereafter:

> 1. To govern the University neither with timidity nor undue force . . . but in the [liberal] spirit of the times, placing it in the broad current of ideas and needs of a new society;
>
> 2. To develop instruction in every area so that it will keep pace with all other vigorous areas of national activity, especially industry and commerce; and
>
> 3. To contain both the authorized and nonauthorized male teaching congregations, not by harassing or persecuting them, but by forcing them to comply with the law and especially by revitalizing laic education.[61]

Victor Duruy, born to be an artisan at the Gobelins factory, seemed destined to follow his father's profession. But his early interest in serious books caught the eye of a family friend, and he was soon immersing himself in classical studies and embarking on a career as a teacher and a historian. As a result of his reputation for hard work and his interest in reform, he eventually drew the attention of the emperor. Enchanted by Duruy's liberalism and impressed by Duruy's devotion to principle, Napoleon III could find no better man than Victor Duruy to be his minister of public instruction in 1863.[62]

---

60. Duruy, *Notes et souvenirs,* I, 192.

61. Victor Duruy to Napoleon III, April 21, 1866, copy of a letter in possession of Mme Albert Duruy.

62. Some historians have boldly asserted that Duruy was the best ministerial appointment of Napoleon III's reign. See Paul A. Gagnon, *France Since 1789* (New York, 1964), 187; and Thompson and Holm, *History of Historical Writing,* 266.

II · Education, Society, and Politics Before 1863

Education represents the most sustained and far reaching attempt of a
society or sections of it to reproduce itself and shape its future.
—Gillian Sutherland, "The Study of the History of Education."

When Victor Duruy became minister of public instruction in 1863, he
came to preside over a system of education that was highly elitist and
centralized. The elitism was typical for the day and the result of traditional opinion about who should be educated. The centralization was
particularly French and the result of both late eighteenth-century demands for a more rational system of education and Napoleonic political designs. Hippolyte Taine later immortalized the centralization in
his quip that during the Second Empire a minister of education could
draw out his watch and know that *lycée* students all around France
were studying the same page of Virgil.[1] But centralization meant more
than just a state-specified set of schools and curriculum at each level. It
also meant that the minister exercised considerable power over the
schools and the educational personnel and that the most important
educational facilities were, by virtue of the circumstances, concentrated at Paris. The elitism of the system was especially obvious in that
there were schools for the popular classes (regular elementary schools)
and schools for the middle and upper classes (*lycées* and *collèges*,
which had elementary and preparatory classes within their walls, and
higher professional schools). Elitism was also manifest in the differing
school tuition levies, the stiff entrance examinations for the higher
professional schools, and the rigorous national examinations for the
major academic degrees. Yet centralization and elitism were never absolute (Taine notwithstanding). Exceptions and modifications in school
and curricular requirements were fairly widely tolerated throughout

---

1. Carlton Hayes, *France: A Nation of Patriots* (New York, 1930), 36–63; Hippolyte Taine, *The Modern Regime* (2 vols.; New York, 1931), II, 162.

the better part of the nineteenth century, and municipally run or private institutions offered further diversity in curricula and methods.[2] Also, it was possible for talented boys from the lower classes to rise through the system by dint of their intellect, as Duruy had done. But *in relative terms*, centralization and elitism were still dominant characteristics of French education. To understand the origins of this system with which Duruy had to deal, it is necessary to review the main developments in French education from 1789 to 1863.

During the Revolution, legislators, politicians, and theorists spent an impressive amount of time discussing various proposals for French education, even though they were preoccupied with preparing fundamental law, writing civil legislation in areas other than education, and waging war against both internal and external enemies. For the most part, they took their ideas from Rousseau and the Encyclopedists, but they also borrowed heavily from the Old Regime.[3] The task they set for themselves was nothing less than to replace the old Church-dominated educational structure with a new public and state-run system. Intended to be explicitly national, this system was expected to help forge a sense of national unity, produce an enlightened and rational-minded citizenry, and create a nationwide republican consensus. Ultimately, lack of sufficient time, resources, and money kept the revolutionaries from realizing the totality of their plans. But by 1799 they had taken a number of noteworthy steps. At the primary level they created a secular school system by establishing a limited number of state-directed laic schools and by subjecting all schools, public and private, to the control of lay authorities. At the secondary level, they created a system of public "central" schools (that is, they were to be located in the center of each department, one to a department), which emphasized, in contrast to the classical *collèges* of the Old Regime, modern languages and the physical sciences. And at the highest level, they established a number of professional schools of applied arts such as the Ecole Normale for the training of teachers, the Ecole Polytechnique for the training of engineers, and the Ecole des Langues Orien-

2. Historians have been justly careful of late in their characterization of the French education system as "centralized." Some even speak of centralization as an ideal, not to be confused with reality. A good discussion of the situation can be found in Robert Fox and George Weisz (eds.), *The Organization of Science and Technology in France, 1808–1914* (Cambridge, 1980), 1–28.
3. Robert J. Vignery, *The French Revolution and the Schools* (Madison, 1965), 141.

tales for the training of students in Eastern languages. It is instructive
that the revolutionaries made no attempt to revive the old universities,
which were abolished early in the Revolution; instead, they allocated
some higher education subjects—for example, law and anatomy—
to the curriculum of the central schools and confided the remaining
higher subjects to the new professional schools.

Napoleon I, ever the synthesizer, borrowed extensively from both
the Revolution and the Old Regime but molded schools under the empire to suit his own political needs. In 1802 he suppressed the central
schools and put in their place a system of secondary schools, which
consisted of local public and private *écoles secondaires* (*collèges*) and
imperial *lycées*. He then subordinated all the secondary schools to
state control by requiring them to have government authorization to
operate and by subjecting them to the direct surveillance of the local
prefect. Furthermore, Napoleon determined that all secondary schools
would return henceforth to the classical curriculum of the prerevolu-
tionary period. Science, however, was given a relatively larger place in
the curriculum, and religion, omitted in his initial plans, was reinte-
grated, Napoleon having decided that it was better to try to control
religion than ignore it.[4]

The *lycées* were Napoleon's prized creation. At the beginning, there
were twenty-seven of them; by 1865, there would be seventy-seven.
Intended to be exclusive institutions that would provide general education in the liberal arts for the nation's elite, the *lycées* were also designed to produce young men who would be loyal supporters of the
regime. Napoleon specified that the *lycées* should be boarding schools,
but like the *collèges* of the Old Regime they could also accept some
day students. The routine in the *lycées* was to be strict and militaristic.
Students were required to wear uniforms, to participate in military exercises, and to follow a detailed daily schedule. Classes were begun
and ended with the beat of a drum. To supervise both the curriculum
and the discipline in the *lycées*, a small corps of three general inspectors was created.

Napoleon's law of March 17, 1802, on secondary schools men-

---

4. Robert Palmer, "The Central Schools of the First Republic: A Statistical Survey,"
in Donald N. Baker and Patrick J. Harrigan (eds.), *The Making of Frenchmen: Current
Directions in the History of Education in France, 1679–1979* (Waterloo, Ont., 1980),
229; Alphonse Aulard, *Napoleon 1ᵉʳ et le monopole universitaire* (Paris, 1911), 95.

tioned primary and higher education but made no changes in the schools. Higher education was still to be offered in the special state schools established during the Revolution, and primary education was still to be the responsibility of the local communes under state supervision. Napoleon exhibited no apparent concern that primary education had deteriorated since the Revolution because of the disappearance of the religious orders, the lack of training facilities for lay teachers, the lack of adequate funding, and the lack of even subsistence-level salaries to attract competent teachers. Instead, he relied on private and municipal efforts and the Brothers of the Christian Schools, who were just beginning to return to France, to rejuvenate primary education. In 1812, he gave the Brothers a 25,000 franc subsidy, but this was the sole expense the regime made for primary education.[5]

Napoleon had hoped that the *lycées* would thrive. But the results of their first few years were not encouraging. Although the *lycées* had a guaranteed student body in sixty-four hundred scholarship boys, they were failing to attract paying students from the middle classes in significant numbers. Most bourgeois families preferred the private and Catholic schools in which their sons got more religion and less Bonapartism and militarism. Napoleon decided, consequently, to tilt the system further in his favor by creating a vehicle to control all of public and private education. This vehicle was called the Imperial University.

The Imperial University was created by the law of May 10, 1806, and given more definitive organization by the decree of March 17, 1808, and other regulations that followed. Alphonse Aulard relates that the idea for the University originated in a plan advanced by the president of the Parlement of Paris, Barthélemy-Gabriel Rolland d'Erceville, in 1768, and that there were many historical precedents and reasons for Napoleon's creation. But he also claims that the immediate and special reason for the University was Napoleon's desire to save the *lycées* from the ruinous competition of the Catholic secondary schools.[6]

In establishing the University, Napoleon allocated control over all teachers and schools in the nation to the state. Thus all existing

5. The state required a certificate of good conduct, a certificate of teaching ability (*brevet de capacité*), and a rectoral authorization from all *instituteurs* (Prost, *Histoire de l'enseignement en France*, 91–92).

6. Aulard, *Napoleon Ier et le monopole universitaire*, 140–45.

schools at the primary and secondary levels were brought under the direction of the University. The principle of freedom of teaching (*liberté de l'enseignement*) promulgated during the Directory was tacitly abolished. Henceforth the state alone had the power to certify teachers, authorize the granting of degrees, and sanction the opening and operation of schools. Furthermore, Napoleon revived remnants of the old universities but not the universities themselves. The medical and law schools became known as faculties, and to their number were added theology, letters, and science. Each of these faculties, brought under the auspices of the University, was, however, an entity unto itself. Unlike previously, there were no means for communication between them. And while Napoleon endowed Paris with a full complement of the five kinds of faculties, other cities were given only one, two, three, or four kinds, depending on the academic traditions of the locality and the perceived needs of the nation. The theology faculties were created in the hopes that they would become another vehicle for controlling the Catholic Church in France. Ultimately, however, the bishops foiled Napoleon by choosing to train priests in their own seminaries. The letters and science faculties were created to collate the three main academic degrees—the baccalaureate, the *licence*, and the doctorate—and to engage in research, although the research function would rapidly disappear from the provincial letters and science faculties, which would generally become little more than degree-granting institutions, subordinate to the purposes of the *lycées*.

Finally, at the highest level, in 1810 Napoleon reestablished the Ecole Normale, which had lasted only a year during the Revolution. Now the Ecole Normale was to be a pedagogical institute attached to the faculties of letters and sciences at Paris. And instead of training *instituteurs* as it was designed to do, it was given the job of training professors for the imperial *lycées*.[7]

To supervise the educational system and to give it a sense of order such as he knew in the army, Napoleon hierarchized the educational administration and teaching and administrative personnel. The University was, according to the law of 1806, a corporation of teachers. The decree of 1808 put at the head of this corporation a grand master

7. See Robert J. Smith, *The Ecole Normale Supérieure and the Third Republic* (Albany, N.Y., 1982).

with a modest-sized bureaucracy and an Imperial Council of Public Instruction at Paris to assist him. Outside of Paris, the University was divided into academies—one for each court of appeal or twenty-seven in 1812 for old metropolitan France. The decree put a rector in charge of each academy and established an academic council to assist each rector.[8] Routine supervisory responsibility for the schools was entrusted to a group of inspectors consisting of general inspectors assigned primarily to inspect the *lycées* and academic inspectors assigned to inspect all schools within one particular academy. At the last level of the hierarchy were the teaching personnel—professors, teachers, and instructors—who constituted Napoleon's "laic congregation."[9] And within this last level, especially in the secondary schools, there was another complete hierarchy of ranks and titles. All teachers in the University were specifically pledged to "obedience and the statutes of the teaching corps which have *as a goal the uniformity of instruction* and which help to form for the state citizens attached to their religion, their prince, their country, and their family."[10] They were required also to wear the *habit noir* (black robe) of the University. Money to operate this imposing system came partially from state funds as a subsidy but mainly from the University's own budget, which was established by Napoleon and was not dependent on the annual vote of the legislative body.

In constructing his University, Napoleon attempted to co-opt Catholicism. He directed that "all schools of the University take for the basis of their teaching the Catholic religion," and he insisted that all personnel from the grand master down be good Catholics. Thus the marquis de Fontanes was chosen over the comte de Fourcroy as first grand master, the first chancellor of the University was a bishop, and bishops and priests were designated by Napoleon as the "natural surveillants" of the schools. Napoleon reasoned that if the University had control over the appointment of advisers from the clergy and over reli-

8. Rectors were responsible for the financial affairs of each school and faculty, for the quality of instruction in every classroom, and for the maintenance of favorable public relations between the university community and local people.

9. Aulard, *Napoleon 1ᵉʳ et le monopole universitaire*, 180.

10. Article 38 of the decree of March 17, 1808. Pierre Chevallier, Bernard Grosperrin, and Jean Maillet, *L'enseignement français de la Révolution à nos jours* (2 vols.; Paris, 1968, 1971), II, 58; emphasis added. Volume II is by Chevallier and Grosperrin only.

gious teachers and chaplains, it would have a fair chance of ensuring that religion would be taught by moderate men. Furthermore, if the clergy were brought into the state system and given an important voice in its proceedings, it was likely that they would imbibe the *"esprit d'un corps laique"* and become "neutralized." [11]

Intentions, of course, are always one thing and realities another, and indeed Napoleon's main objective in devising the University—gradually to eliminate all Catholic schools at the secondary level and create a true monopoly for the public schools—was undermined by his first grand master, the loyal Catholic Fontanes. [12] But for the most part, at the end of the empire, the University reflected fairly faithfully the educational specifications that Napoleon had elaborated in the various imperial decrees and regulations.

When the Bourbon monarchy returned to France in 1814, plans were immediately made to destroy the University. The post of grand master was suppressed, and the University was divided into seventeen smaller systems. A national education council was constructed at Paris to coordinate the programs of the regional universities. This education system was overthrown when Napoleon returned to power in 1815, and the Imperial University and its subordinate academies were restored. But when the Bourbons reclaimed their throne later that spring, the existence of the University was once again cast in doubt. This time, however, the Bourbons did not hasten to dismantle the University. At first, they retained the structure on a provisional basis. Eventually, despite some strenuous opposition to the University from the left and right, they decided to leave it in place. The major reason for the change or evolution in Louis XVIII's sentiments seems to have been his awareness of the utility of the centralized University in a politically divided nation. The one modification made in the University structure was a reorganization of the post of grand master: the post was given ministerial status under the aegis of the minister of the interior. This change diminished the autonomy of the University, but for all intents and purposes the structure was left intact. [13]

11. Aulard, *Napoleon Ier et le monopole universitaire*, 200, 250, 366–67.

12. *Ibid.*, 305–12. Aulard (368–69) reminds us that the University never had a true monopoly because private schools always existed. At most, the monopoly meant that the state possessed the means of controlling private schools.

13. Felix Ponteil, *Histoire de l'enseignement en France, 1789–1965* (Paris, 1966), 157–62.

Monarchists and clericals saw to it that the Church was given a more important role in French education under the Restoration. Article 30 of the ordinance of 1816 specified that the base of all education in the land was religion, respect for the laws, and love for the sovereign. Other articles of the same ordinance put archbishops, bishops, and priests in important inspection posts. After the assassination of the duc de Berry in 1820 and the ascendancy of the ultraroyalists (the Ultras) to power, a bishop, Monsignor Denis Frayssinous, was made grand master and minister of religion and public instruction, and significant numbers of ecclesiastics were named rectors, inspectors, secondary school officials (*proviseurs* and *censeurs*), and professors. Felix Ponteil notes that "out of thirteen *censeurs*, nine were ecclesiastics." At the same time in the communal *collèges*, the number of ecclesiastical principals, assistant principals, and professors increased notably.[14]

Few changes were made in higher education under the Restoration. A special professional school or *grande école*, the Ecole des Chartes, was established in 1821 to train librarians, archivists, and paleographers. The Ecole Normale Supérieure was suppressed in 1822 by the Ultras in an attempt to choke off laic and liberal teaching, and it would not be restored until 1826. Also, certain liberal professors at the Sorbonne such as the historian François Guizot and the philosopher Victor Cousin (both to become ministers of education under the next regime) were dismissed from their posts. Plans surfaced during the period of the Restoration—sponsored notably by Guizot and Cousin—to establish true universities at Rennes, Strasbourg, Toulouse, and Montpellier as counterweights to the faculties at Paris, but these never materialized.[15]

At the secondary level, *lycées* became royal *collèges*, and military exercises were abolished. The crowning degree of secondary studies, the baccalaureate, was made, by virtue of an ordinance in 1815, the essential requirement for access to all liberal careers. For students not destined to the liberal careers, special practical and technical courses oriented toward commerce and industry were attached to some secondary schools.

After 1822, the Church largely controlled secondary education. It

---

14. Chevallier, Grosperrin, and Maillet, *L'enseignement français de la Révolution à nos jours*, I, 59; Ponteil, *Histoire de l'enseignement en France*, 161.
15. Ponteil, *Histoire de l'enseignement en France*, 162–63.

had, of course, considerable influence over the royal and communal *collèges* (the latter supported by municipalities), but it also had its own religious schools—known either as *écoles ecclésiastiques* or *petites séminaires*—for the training of young men destined to the priesthood. Many of the young boys attending these schools had no intention of ever becoming priests, but their parents desired that they receive a solidly religious education. As it turned out, certain ordinances and regulations promulgated during the early years of the Restoration, especially the ordinance of 1814, had given the Church a virtual carte blanche in the operation of its ecclesiastical schools, and by the 1820s these schools were developing into a full-fledged religious school system, outnumbering the royal *collèges* by better than a three-to-one ratio, if only the authorized schools are considered, or by better than a five-to-one ratio if the unauthorized schools are included.[16] This system no doubt offered serious competition to the public secondary schools. In 1828, when Ultra power was momentarily compromised and a more liberal council of ministers under the direction of the vicomte Martignac was in place, efforts were made to limit the religious schools and especially the unauthorized Jesuit order, which was then operating eight minor seminaries in France. These efforts resulted in the closing of the Jesuit seminaries and the limiting of regular diocesan seminaries to a maximum of twenty thousand students for the whole of France, but in the long run little was actually accomplished because government officials were lax in enforcing the restrictions. The technically illegal system of Catholic secondary education, therefore, continued to grow.[17]

In primary education, there was an effort to compensate for the damage done during the Revolution and First Empire. In 1816, an ordinance was passed requiring each commune to maintain a primary school for boys and to ensure gratuity for those who could not pay tuition, and by the circular of June 3, 1819, and the ordinance of April 3, 1820, the provisions were extended to girls. In the following years, there was impressive growth in the number of primary schools

---

16. *Ibid.*, 174.

17. Louis Secondy, "Place et rôle des petits séminaires dans l'enseignement secondaire en France au XIXe siècle," *Revue d'histoire de l'église de France*, LXVI (1980), 243–59.

in the kingdom. But on balance, the law was not well enforced, and by the end of the regime, there were still thousands of communes (close to a quarter of the more than thirty-eight thousand communes in France) which pleaded that they were too poor to fulfill the requirement.

At about the same time the 1816 ordinance was passed, the duc de la Rochefoucauld-Liancourt translated into French and had published Joseph Lancaster's book on the monitorial or mutual method of education.[18] Soon the idea of using older children to teach younger ones as a means of compensating for the lack of teachers began to catch on, and mutual schools began appearing in Paris and other large cities of France. But they were opposed by many Catholic clergymen on the grounds that they neglected religious and moral formation and, by virtue of their "democratic" teaching, tended to give young students too great a taste for republicanism.[19] A few hostile priests even saw the mutual schools as a dangerous Protestant import. Despite the opposition, however, the mutual schools perdured until 1840, by which time the supply of teachers had increased significantly.

The major development in primary education under the Restoration was the expansion of the Catholic religious teaching orders. This expansion was made possible by the ordinance of 1819, which exempted the Christian Brothers from the *brevet de capacité* or teacher's license in recognition of the fact that they already had certification in the form of a letter of obedience (*lettre d'obédience*) from their teaching order. The exemption became an issue of greater consequence when the provision was later extended to women's religious orders devoted to teaching.[20]

The dearth of a sufficient number of teachers and especially of qualified teachers—because many teachers were teaching without the approved teaching certificate in inexpensive clandestine or unauthorized schools throughout the country—was clearly one of the major

18. Prost, *Histoire de l'enseignement en France*, 103; Y. Pasquet, "L'alphabétisation dans le départment de la Vienne au XIXᵉ siècle," in François Furet and Jacques Ozouf, *Lire et écrire* (2 vols.; Paris, 1977), II, 264; Chevallier, Grosperrin, and Maillet, *L'enseignement français de la Révolution à nos jours*, I, 65.

19. Chevallier, Grosperrin, and Maillet, *L'enseignement français de la Révolution à nos jours*, I, 66.

20. *Ibid.*, 59.

problems in primary education. Fortunately, during the late Restoration and July Monarchy there was not only a great increase in the number of *congréganists* but also a significant growth in the number of independent courses on teaching (*cours normaux*) and normal schools for laymen. By 1832, there would be forty-seven *écoles normales d'instituteurs*. But there was no parallel development in normal schools for laywomen largely because the numerous religious orders were able to supply most of the necessary teachers. The first *école normale des institutrices* would not, in fact, be opened until 1838 (and by the time Duruy took office in 1863 there would be only eleven normal schools for women).[21]

Not surprisingly, these differences were reflected in the number of primary schools for girls and boys. By 1830, there were only ten thousand girls' schools, whereas in 1820 there had been two and one-half times that number for boys.[22] These numbers, however, are somewhat deceiving because indications are that close to a third of all girls going to school attended a coeducational school (*école mixte*). This was especially true in the northern half of France, north of a line that could be drawn between Saint-Malo and Geneva.[23] Still, the mixed school was viewed as undesirable, a stopgap measure to be gradually retired, and facilities for girls in both kinds of schools were much more meager than those for boys.

Under the July Monarchy, primary education continued to develop rapidly. Of special importance was the passage in 1833 of the Guizot Law, which revived at the elementary level the old principle of the freedom to teach (*liberté de l'enseignement*) and thus gave official sanction to the private primary schools. The law also promoted primary education by requiring all communes of more than eight hundred inhabitants to maintain an elementary school for boys, outlining a required curriculum for primary education, requiring the creation of higher primary schools (*écoles primaires supérieurs*) to offer a general

21. Furet and Ozouf, *Lire et écrire*, I, 120–25, 171; Chevallier and Grosperrin, *L'enseignement français de la Révolution à nos jours*, I, 64.

22. Chevallier, Grosperrin, and Maillet, *L'enseignement français de la Révolution à nos jours*, I, 64.

23. Claude Langlois, "Women, Religious Orders, and Education in Nineteenth-Century France," trans. Timothy Tackett, paper given at the Sixty-first Annual Meeting of the American Catholic Historical Association, December 28, 1980, p. 4.

technical education, and mandating the establishment of normal schools for *instituteurs* in each department.

Except in the Grand-Ouest studied by Gabriel Desert, the Guizot Law did not lead to a sudden increase in the number of boys' schools because many communes already had them; but it did force negligent communes such as Roger Thabault's Mazières-en-Gâtine to establish schools, and it did force all departments to maintain (as anticipated by the decree of 1808) a normal school.[24] The Guizot Law was thus the first state attempt to intervene in primary education in a serious way. It amounted to a "charter" of primary education for nineteenth-century France.

The Guizot Law also marked a turning point in attitudes toward primary education. In the past, the dominant classes had expressed considerable fear that education would distract the popular classes from manual labor and agriculture. By 1833, that fear continued to prevail in many quarters, but clearly it was beginning to give way to the conviction that men from the popular classes could not be efficient, reliable, and loyal or even docile workers unless they were given at least a minimal education. In short, more and more members of the governing classes were beginning to view primary education as an important means of social control and economic progress.

Although a few educators, and Guizot himself, had hoped that the Guizot Law would apply to girls' education as well, the majority of educators and legislators in 1832 and 1833 feared (unfortunately, with much justification) that including girls would only compromise efforts to get the education bill passed. Three years after the Guizot Law was passed, the legislature approved a primary education law for girls, the Pelet Law, which encouraged the creation of girls' schools and regulated the conditions under which they could be created. But notably the Pelet Law did not require that schools for girls be established.[25]

Nonetheless, while the number of schools for boys continued to

24. Gabriel Desert, "Alphabétisation et scolarisation dans le Grand-Ouest au 19ᵉ siècle," in Baker and Harrigan, *Making of Frenchmen*, 150; Roger Thabault, *Education and Change in a Village Community: Mazières-en-Gâtine, 1848–1914*, trans. Peter Tregear (New York, 1971), 55; Prost, *Histoire de l'enseignement en France*, 91.

25. Françoise Mayeur, *L'éducation des filles en France au XIXᵉ siècle* (Paris, 1979), 88; Paul Rousselot, *Histoire de l'éducation des femmes en France* (2 vols.; Paris, 1883), II, 362; Prost, *Histoire de l'enseignement en France*, 102–103.

grow, so did the number of schools for girls, if at a slower rate. In 1832, counting both public and private schools, there were 31,420 boys' and coeducational schools and at least 10,672 girls' schools. By 1843, there were 42,551 boys' and mixed schools and at least 17,287 girls' schools.[26] Viewed from another angle, in 1832, 10,400 communes out of more than 38,000 were without schools. By 1837, only 5,600 communes were deprived of schools, and by 1847, only 3,213 communes lacked schools. The most impressive gains in primary education during the July Monarchy were made in urban areas, where skilled workers were becoming especially interested in education. To supervise the expanding primary system, the government created in 1835 a permanent corps of primary school inspectors.[27]

With the principle of freedom of teaching established at the primary level through articles 3 and 4 of the Guizot Law, Catholics began gradually to work for an extension of the principle to the secondary level. By the 1840s, a full-fledged campaign was mounted, and several efforts were made to get bills passed by the legislature. None of these proved successful, however, because legislators were both reluctant to deprive the state of control over what was considered the most important level of education and fearful of the return of the Jesuits to French education. Many anticlerical Frenchmen were already angered by the proliferation of other religious orders in France. And the growth of the minor seminaries, which often competed vigorously with the regular secondary schools, did not help matters.[28]

Attitudes were to change dramatically with the revolution of 1848 and even more with the tumultuous, bloody days of June that followed. The threat of major social unrest convinced even the Voltarian bourgeoisie that the Church should play a larger role in education. Members of the conservative governing classes decided that certain schools and certain teachers had encouraged too many utopian visions during the 1840s. Also, according to Matthew Arnold, who had close contacts with French school officials, they were concerned about a re-

26. The figures are computed from Prost, *Histoire de l'enseignement en France*, 108. For girls' schools, Prost's estimate is conservative.

27. *Ibid.*, 97; Roger Price, *The French Second Republic: A Social History* (London, 1972), 77; Ponteil, *Histoire de l'enseignement en France*, 206.

28. Secondy, "Place et rôle des petits séminaires dans l'enseignement secondaire en France au XIXe siècle," 243–59.

cent report that crime was on the increase.[29] Thus the educational system needed modification, dangerous ideas and instructors would have to be rooted out, and education for the lower classes especially would have to be given a more solidly religious base, particularly by relying more fully on the resources of the Church.

But before the conservative reaction set in and during the ministry of the former Saint-Simonian Hippolyte Carnot (February 24–July 3, 1848), more moderate and liberal forces had a chance to make a few changes and propose a few reforms. Most noteworthy, the royal *collèges* became *lycées* again, the regime founded a *grande école* of public administration, and Carnot attempted to make primary education free and compulsory for both sexes. The *grande école* of public administration was able to hold classes for only one semester before conservatives and law faculty partisans managed to suppress the school by the law of August 9, 1848. The concept of a special higher school to train government functionaries would continue to have its supporters during the next two and a half decades, but it would not bear fruit again until 1872, when the Ecole Libre des Sciences Politiques was established. The democratic plan of making primary education free and compulsory was intended to help eradicate illiteracy and prevent the cascade of "*mauvais*" (conservative) votes that were registered in the election of April, 1848, and it was accompanied by various proposals to improve working conditions for lay elementary schoolteachers.[30] But it too was vetoed by conservatives.

The sole significant piece of education legislation to issue from the Second Republic was fashioned by conservative forces after Carnot left office. Known as the Falloux Law, it was passed by the legislature on March 15, 1850.

Ernest Lavisse would later call the Falloux Law "one of the most decisive events of the century." It brought an end to the "largely autonomous corporation" of the past and converted the Ministry of Public Instruction "into a closely managed bureaucracy." There was no reference to the University of France in the law, which meant that of-

29. Matthew Arnold, *The Popular Education of France* (London, 1861), 62.
30. The expression "*mauvais*" is that of Victor Clavel, professor at the faculty of letters of Lyons, in his preface to J. Janicot, *Monographie des écoles communales de Lyon, 1828–1891* (Lyons, 1891), as quoted in Furet and Ozouf, *Lire et écrire*, I, 147; Price, *French Second Republic*, 254–55.

ficially the University was abolished; in informal usage, however, the
term was continued, and, for all practical purposes, the basic administrative framework of the University was left in place although the sixteen great regional academies were abolished and eighty-seven departmental academies put in their stead. Also suppressed was the title
grand master of the University; henceforth, the head of the education
system in France was to be known simply as the minister of public instruction. The endowment and buildings belonging to the University
were restored to the state, the independent University budget was
abolished, and the Ministry of Public Instruction was forced to depend
on the legislature for its annual budget. Furthermore, the advisory
councils of public instruction, once exclusively controlled by *universitaires*, were reconstructed to include "a balance of social forces."
Thus, for example, the old Royal Council (known as the Imperial
Council under the First Empire) became the Superior Council of Public Instruction and included among its twenty-eight members only
eight representatives of public instruction (*universitaires*, as they continued to be known). The remaining twenty members included four
bishops or archbishops, two protestant ministers, a rabbi, three delegates from the Council of State, three members of the Cour de Cassation, three members of the Institut de France, and three representatives
of private education. (The twenty-eighth member was the minister.) A
similar "balance of social forces" was provided for on the academic
and municipal councils. Finally, among the changes that helped to destroy the old University, the Falloux Law established what had been
promised in article 69 of the charter of 1830—freedom of teaching at
the secondary level. This right to teach, however, was somewhat re-
strained, and conservative Catholic forces were disappointed that they
did not get full control over their own schools: anyone with the requisite teaching credentials could open or teach in a secondary school,
but the state retained control over the important baccalaureate examination and reserved the right to inspect all schools for violations of the
constitution, laws, or morality.[31]

31. Ponteil, *Histoire de l'enseignement en France*, 245; Roger L. Geiger, "Prelude to
Reform: The Faculties of Letters in the 1860s," in Baker and Harrigan, *Making of
Frenchmen*, 390; Louis Liard, *L'enseignement Supérieur en France, 1789–1893* (2
vols.; Paris, 1888–94), II, 236, n. 3; the law of March 15, 1850, reprinted in *JGIP*,

Beyond establishing freedom of secondary teaching, the Falloux Law made no other changes at the secondary level. The classical curriculum remained intact, and the baccalaureate as both the terminal degree for secondary studies and the essential ticket for entrance to the higher schools continued to be the "master-key" of education.[32]

The Falloux Law was silent on higher education. But this omission was because legislators in 1849 and 1850 planned to prepare a new organic law on higher education that would include its own provision for the freedom of teaching.

At the lowest level, freedom of teaching was reaffirmed, and members of female religious orders devoted to teaching were once again exempted from the *brevet de capacité*. Religious education was emphasized as one of the most important parts of the curriculum. The pressing tasks of the elementary school, especially as they were viewed after June, 1848, were to inculcate social deference, teach patience with economic conditions, and imbue respect for religion, the family, and a host of other bourgeois values. In short, the mission of the "schools of the people" was to "moralise" the masses.[33] The *écoles primaires supérieurs* were tacitly abolished because many conservatives believed they encouraged unrealistic social aspirations in the lower classes and *déclassement*, but the curriculum of the former higher primary schools was attached as optional curriculum to the regular primary schools.[34] The Falloux Law also recommended the establishment of preprimary schools (*salles d'asile*) and night school courses for adults and mandated, especially now that primary education was to be "turned over to the *congréganists*," the establishment of girls' schools in all communes of eight hundred or more residents which still did not have provisions for female primary instruction, but only " 'if their own

March 30, 1850; John K. Huckaby, "Roman Catholic Reaction to the Falloux Law," *French Historical Studies*, IV (1965), 203–13.

32. The term "master key" is from Geiger, "Prelude to Reform," 338.

33. Richard Johnson, "Educational Policy and Social Control in Early Victorian England," *Past and Present*, no. 49 (November, 1970), 119, gives a definition of "moralise" for nineteenth-century England which gives some additional concepts that were associated with the term in nineteenth-century France: to "moralise" the people meant to make them "respectful, cheerful, hard-working, loyal, pacific and religious."

34. C. R. Day, "The Development of Higher Primary and Intermediate Technical Education in France, 1800 to 1870," *Historical Reflections/Réflexions Historiques*, III (1976), 51.

resources furnished the means,'" which made the obligation largely il-
lusory.[35] Finally, the Falloux Law reconfirmed partial gratuity for indigent children as it had been institutionalized by the Guizot Law.

Not illogically, partisans of University education were bitter about
the Falloux Law. As Louis Liard put it later, the framers of the Falloux
Law "did everything to diminish it [public education]. . . . In contrast,
for private education, everywhere [they granted] privileges, exemptions." But as Felix Ponteil points out, the University was not actually
destroyed and it was not truly subordinated to the Church, even though
clergymen were given a considerable voice in its operation. The real
significance of the Falloux Law was that it allowed the Church to become the formidable rival of the University. It made the Church a veritable competitor for French youth, and it led to substantial fears
among anticlericals about the creation of "two youths" in France. It
also contributed significantly to the development of anticlericalism in
the second half of the nineteenth century.[36]

Nor was the Falloux Law the end of the political reaction. Under
the authoritarian government of the 1850s, most of the politically and
socially conservative aspects of the Falloux Law were continued and
strengthened. Napoleon III, anxious to consolidate the base of his political support in the country, took the lead in granting special privileges to Catholics. In September, 1852, shortly after religious education was made obligatory for all boarding students in *lycées*,[37] he
publicly reaffirmed his commitment to sustain and propagate religious
ideas. The following month he supported a decree that required students of normal schools to attend daily prayers and to be present at all
religious ceremonies. Additionally, he introduced cardinals into the
Senate, increased the budget of the Ministry of Religions, reinforced
the Index, and saw to it that authorizations for religious orders to
teach in France were liberally extended. Confessional education thrived
in this atmosphere. The moral influence of the clergy on the University
councils, the enthusiasm of the religious orders for opening new
schools, the advantages parents believed Catholic schools afforded

35. Mayeur, *L'éducation des filles en France*, 104.
36. Liard, *L'enseignement supérieur en France*, II, 238; Ponteil, *Histoire de l'enseignement en France*, 244–45.
37. Pierre Zind, "La religion dans les lycées sous le régime de la loi Falloux, 1850–
1873," in Baker and Harrigan, *Making of Frenchmen*, 251.

their children in the moral and pedagogical realm,[38] and the desires of municipalities to save money by giving their schools to the less costly religious teachers led to a tremendous expansion in the number of Catholic schools.

Napoleon III seriously considered dismantling the University because he deemed it too independent and a seedbed of radical and dangerous ideas. But Hippolyte Fortoul, his minister of education and religion beginning in December, 1851, persuaded him to yoke the University and its teachers instead. Thus the University was left in place, and Fortoul adopted a policy of salutory neglect toward the Church while tightening his personal control over the University. Taking advantage of article 2 of the Falloux Law, he dissolved the permanent section of the Superior Council, which had consisted of distinguished *universitaires*, and replaced it with a group of men selected from the general inspection corps directly under his control. Then, by the law of June 14, 1854, he abolished the departmental rectorships established by the Falloux Law and restored the great regional academies of the University, each encompassing four or five departments, over which he would have greater control.[39] These would still be in existence when Duruy became minister (see Appendix A). Fortoul also continued the policy of purging the University of outspoken liberals (thus retiring such men as Guizot, Cousin, Michelet, Edgar Quinet, Adam Michiewicz, and Jules Simon), eliminated certain suspect courses at higher institutions (for example, constitutional law and the history of philosophy), reduced the curriculum of the Ecole Normale Supérieure, and deprived municipal councils of their right to name and revoke *instituteurs*. By the time he completed his changes, the "Babylonian Captivity" of the University was complete.[40] *Universitaire* Louis Liard, looking back on this period, commented that the first years of

38. Many of the laic schools were still run by a single teacher who employed the mutual or Lancastrian method. The parochial schools, especially those of the Christian Brothers, usually had two teachers or more per school. See Octave Gréard, *Education et instruction* (4 vols.; Paris, 1904), I, 39.

39. *JGIP*, June 24, 1854 (law of June 14, 1854), and August 26, 1854 (decree of August 22, 1854).

40. These measures would leave an acid taste in the mouths of staunch *universitaires* for years. In his regular column on February 13, 1868, Edmond Goumy would call the era of the Falloux Law the era of "the Babylonian Captivity of the University" (RIP, 1868, p. 721).

Napoleon III's reign were the worst years of the century for public education. *Universitaires*, embittered by the coup d'etat of 1852, the requirement that they take an oath of loyalty to the regime or resign, and the mandate that they shave their mustaches, had now to labor under Fortoul's repressive measures.[41]

Fortoul virtually neglected primary and higher education. His major concern was secondary education. In 1852, largely in response to clerical demands, he eliminated the liberal eclecticism of Cousin from the philosophy course in the secondary schools, renamed the course logic, and reduced its program essentially to the teaching of a set of incontrovertible syllogisms. Then, to modernize the curriculum and make it more responsive to the needs of the time, he mandated the teaching of gymnastics and linear design in all of the *lycées*, ordered secondary professors to give more attention to the modern period in history courses, and introduced a new program of technical education, known as *bifurcation*, into the secondary schools. Although the technical program had the enthusiastic support of industrialists, liberal economists, and such eminent scientists as J.-B. Dumas, its veritable founder, it met staunch opposition from the University community, which believed, for the most part, that technical education had no place in the secondary schools. Thus when Fortoul introduced it in 1852, he had to impose it on an unwilling University.

When Fortoul died in 1856, he left behind a mixed record and reputation. He had strengthened the University but at the expense of greater centralization and political reaction. Bonapartists were generally pleased and Catholics had nothing to complain about, but *universitaires* and liberals were alienated. Despite the many positive contributions he made to education,[42] Fortoul became the most despised minister of education in the nineteenth century.

Although Fortoul had been neither ultramontane nor clerical and had never personally favored the ostentatious support the emperor had given to Catholicism during the early years of the regime, his cooperation with imperial wishes sealed his reputation among anticleri-

41. Liard, *L'enseignement supérieur en France*, II, 241–43.

42. Fortoul has been rehabilitated by Paul Raphael and Maurice Gontard, *Un ministre de l'instruction publique sous l'empire authoritaire: Hippolyte Fortoul, 1851–1856* (Paris, 1975).

cals, who were now grówing stronger in number and voice. They had, in fact, experienced a period of relative quiescence in 1848, when liberal Catholicism was a visible movement in the Church and Catholicism seemed to be tied to the success of the republic. But after 1849, when French troops were sent to protect the pope in Italy, when a revived ultramontanism began to drown out the voices of liberal Catholicism and win significant favors from the regime, and when the Church seemed to have "blessed" the coup d'etat of 1852 and the recourse to naked force, anticlericalism flared up again, this time in a more radical form.[43] By the 1860s, anticlericalism was becoming entwined with positivism, scientism, and materialism. As John McManners has noted, anticlericals, calling for the creation of a new laic morality, were assaulting the old Christian basis of morality, arguing that the Church was teaching immoral doctrines (original sin, intolerance) and recommending immoral behavior (humility, neglect of the body).[44] Neither anticlericalism nor clericalism, of course, was a monolithic position. There were as many shades of each as there were intellectual, political, and emotional reasons for them. Indeed, some Catholics supported the clergy simply because they were loyal to the Church, as in the case of the political candidate who was described as "more Catholic than clerical," and others refused to support *les clericaux*, not because they were anticlerical but because they were unclerical. In addition, large segments of the population remained untouched by the controversy.[45] But among the politicized portions of the population, grievances against both sides began to mount. As the press began to play a more important role in the politics of the empire, a polarization of positions began to appear which spilled over into the educational realm. It was against this background that Fortoul's successor, Gustave Rouland, took office.

Gustave Rouland, reared in Normandy and trained in law, was a moderate Gallican magistrate. Yet despite his background, he was a partisan of lay education as his much-maligned predecessor had been.

43. René Rémond, *L'anticléricalisme en France de 1815 à nos jours* (Paris, 1976), 124–25.
44. John McManners, *Church and State in France, 1870–1914* (New York, 1972), 16–17.
45. F(17) 2682, AN; Jacob Salwyn Schapiro, *Liberalism and the Challenge of Fascism: Social Forces in England and France, 1815–1870* (New York, 1964), 172.

But Rouland, unlike Fortoul, was able to foster state education more visibly because the shift in imperial foreign policies after 1858 and the disappearance of the revolutionary threat that had plagued the earlier years of the 1850s permitted, if not dictated, a reorientation in educational policies. Soon it became clear that the era of granting excessive privileges to the Church was coming to an end.[46]

After Napoleon III decided to abet Italian republicans in their efforts to overthrow Austrian domination and unite the northern states of Italy and it became apparent that the political base of imperial power had to be reoriented toward liberals and republicans, Rouland commissioned Léon Pillet, chief of his primary education division, to compile a set of proposals on countermanding the growth of the Church in education. Rouland was concerned that since the end of the July Monarchy, in primary education alone, the numbers of religious orders of men and women devoted to teaching had nearly tripled. At the secondary level, Catholic schools had made great gains since the Falloux Law. By the end of 1851, 257 private secondary schools (10 of them Jesuit) had opened their doors.[47] Pillet's proposals, presented in 1860 but made public only in 1873, recommended that the government refuse to authorize any more male congregations; constrict the conditions for authorization of female congregations; grant full support to laic schools without interfering with the freedom of choice of municipal councils; energetically support an increased budget for laic primary schools; apply the Organic Articles more strictly (49 unauthorized male congregations and nearly 250 unauthorized female congregations were functioning in France at the time); and suppress everywhere religious newspapers, especially Louis Veuillot's *L'Univers*.[48] Most of these proposals were ultimately approved by the emperor, and in the next few months several were implemented by Rouland.

46. Jean Maurain, *La politique ecclésiastique du Second Empire de 1852 à 1869* (Paris, 1930), 175.

47. Maurice Gontard, *Les écoles primaires de la France bourgeois (1833–1875)* (Toulouse, 1964), 137; Maurice Gontard, "Une réforme de l'enseignement secondaire au XIXᵉ siècle: 'La bifurcation' (1852–1856)," *Revue française de pédagogie*, no. 20 (1972), 6.

48. [Leon Pillet], *Mémoire remis à l'empereur par un de ses ministres des cultes sur la politique à suivre vis-à-vis de l'église* (Bourges, 1873), 16–17.

After 1860, no new male congregations and only a few female congregations were authorized to teach. The practice of granting private financial gifts (*dons et legs*) to confessional schools was greatly circumscribed, religious primary schools were forced to charge tuition to make them more competitive with the laic schools, and municipalities were pressured into favoring laic schools over confessional ones.[49] By late 1860, the process of granting or transferring primary schools to religious orders had virtually ended. Rouland, however, did not stop with the primary schools; he extended similar restrictions to the secondary schools. Thus the Jesuits were refused a school at Brest and, as an unauthorized (but previously tolerated) order, they were prevented from opening any more schools during the rest of the decade. Moreover, Rouland urged municipal authorities to regain control of *collèges* that had been entrusted to bishops, and he pumped additional funds into the renovation of public secondary schools, converting some of them into imperial *lycées*.

These Gallican strictures in education, enforced at a time when the external and internal political atmosphere for Catholics was being dramatically reversed, caused Catholics to sense that their cause was being abandoned. If a political barometer of reactions to these developments could be constructed, it would register the beginnings of a defensive clericalism that would characterize the response of the Church to all further reforms in education. This attitude would become part of the more serious struggle that developed between clericals and anticlericals after the national elections of 1863.

The Rouland years, however, were good for the University. These years constituted, as Paul Gerbod has described it, "the era of reparations," an era during which some of the damage Fortoul had done to the morale of the *universitaires* was reversed.[50] Rouland consistently demonstrated his sincere concern for the welfare of the teaching corps. He not only made many efforts to curb the influence of the Church on education but regularly consulted with his teachers on needs in their schools. A particular example of his effort to help *instituteurs* was the

49. Joseph N. Moody, *French Education Since Napoleon* (Syracuse, 1978), 67–68; Maurain, *La politique ecclésiastique du Second Empire*, 469.
50. Paul Gerbod, *La condition universitaire en France au XIXe siècle* (Paris, 1965), 355–416.

circular of August 26, 1862, which specified that the *instituteur* could not be asked to assist the curé after regular school hours; no longer was the *instituteur* to be a "docile servant of the curé." The best example of Rouland's consultations with his subordinates, however, was the 1860 essay contest he sponsored on the deficiencies of primary education in rural areas.[51] Rouland had few rewards to distribute to his teachers, but he did raise salaries for *instituteurs* from 600 to 700 francs after five years of service,[52] and he did reduce Fortoul's technical education program (*bifurcation*) somewhat, thus mollifying disgruntled *lycée* professors.

In the realm of higher education, Rouland, like most of his predecessors, accomplished little of significance. He failed to revive plans that had been advanced in the past for the construction of true universities, although he did create more faculties in law and medicine to ease the pressure of growing enrollments in those areas. And he did help to promote the prestige of the Ecole Normale Supérieure, and more generally the cause of scientific research, by placing Louis Pasteur in charge of its scientific section.[53]

When Victor Duruy was chosen to succeed Rouland in June, 1863, he was given only the portfolio of the minister of public instruction. The portfolio of the Ministry of Religions, which had been joined frequently to that of instruction, was given, along with the Ministry of Justice, to the Gallican Pierre Baroche. To be sure, had any effort been made to give Duruy the Ministry of Religions, it would have met strenuous resistance from Catholics. But Napoleon did not want to alienate Catholics; he simply wished to reorient education to the new political realities. And those realities included not only his promise to liberalize the empire but also his need to respond meaningfully to the results of the legislative elections of 1863.

The national elections of 1863, which were influential for Duruy's

51. These essays were collected and published in Charles Robert, *Plaintes et voeux présentés par les instituteurs publics en 1861* (Paris, 1864).

52. Moody, *French Education Since Napoleon*, 70, notes: "This salary which affected about one-half of the personnel was still below the cost of room and board in a *lycée*." The exchange rate at this time was roughly five francs to a dollar (*RIP*, 1867, p. 753).

53. Craig Zwerling, "The Emergence of the Ecole Normale Supérieure as a Centre of Scientific Education in the Nineteenth Century," in Fox and Weisz (eds.), *Organization of Science and Technology in France*, 31, 41–42, 45–50, 58–60.

appointment, were a decisive turning point in the history of the Second Empire. Liberals and republicans increased their representation in the Corps législatif from five to seventeen, while opponents of the regime on the right won fifteen seats.[54] Although these gains seem hardly significant numerically, given that there were 282 deputies in the lower house, they were nevertheless an ominous omen of growing dissent with imperial policies, particularly because the government was still attempting to manage elections. Furthermore, the thirty-two opposition deputies "were all popular men of great talent who could not fail to win converts."[55] Charles Seignobos claims that the results of the election persuaded Napoleon that he should renounce further political concessions for the moment and try instead to satisfy liberal and republican forces with social reform.[56] At any rate, there was a major reshuffling of important political personages: the duc de Persigny was dismissed from the Ministry of the Interior for his failure in the electoral campaign, the conservative Eugène Rouher was made president of the Council of State (Conseil d'État), and liberals of various degrees were moved to key posts in the cabinet: Adolphe Billault to the Ministry of State, Baroche to the Ministry of Religions and Justice, Louis-Henri-Armand Béhic, the great Orleanist industrialist, to the Ministry of Public Works, and Duruy to the Ministry of Public Instruction. Unfortunately for the emperor, these changes triggered the entrance of the old supporters of the authoritarian regime, the so-called Party of Order, into the opposition on the right.

This sketch of the chief developments in French education to 1863 has shown how the system came about and how it remained relatively centralized and elitist. What is left now is to review the main deficien-

54. It is useful to keep in mind that this era predates the period of more disciplined party formations and that the political opposition was composed of groups of loosely affiliated men. On the right, there were the Legitimists, Orleanists of the "fusionist" stripe, clericals, protectionists, and some authoritarian Bonapartists. On the left were Orleanists of the "nonfusionist" stripe, republicans, socialists, and anticlericals. For a discussion on the differences between the "fusionist" and "nonfusionist" Orleanists, consult Louis Girard, "Political Liberalism in France, 1840–1875," in Evelyn M. Acomb and Marvin L. Brown, Jr., *French Society and Culture Since the Old Regime* (New York, 1966), 19–32.

55. Antonin Debidour, *Histoire des rapports de l'église et de l'état en France de 1789 à 1870* (Paris, 1898), 581.

56. Charles Seignobos, *Le déclin de l'empire et l'établissement de la Troisième République*, p. 37, vol. VII of Ernest Lavisse (ed.), *Histoire de France contemporaine* (10 vols.; Paris, 1921).

cies and weaknesses in and the problems of French public education on the eve of Duruy's appointment to office.

To begin with, public education in France was too dependent on and too much a victim of politics. Of course, public education had been created with politics in mind; as Stephen d'Irsay has put it, "First and foremost, the University was an instrument of politics, power, and government."[57] Napoleon III certainly saw it in this light: the University was a vehicle not only for confirming political loyalties but also for changing them. And the granting of universal suffrage in 1848 had made use of the University as a political tool even more essential. Yet as a result, teachers often suffered from politically repressive or narrow-minded measures, as they did under Fortoul, and programs and reforms were not implemented unless they met the approval of the governing groups in Paris.

As a result of the centralization of the system and the development over the years of entrenched interest groups, the system was relatively inflexible, as was obvious, for example, when Rouland introduced his technical education program into the secondary schools in 1852. Professors of classical studies were unequivocally hostile to the program.

The French public school system was too elitist. Here, simple figures tell the story. In 1865, there were 2,307,000 boys in primary schools but only 140,253 boys in secondary schools. At the next level, French faculties awarded only about 1,800 degrees annually. And the results for the *grandes écoles* were even more meager; the Ecole Normale Supérieure, for example, which was under the jurisdiction of the Ministry of Public Instruction, admitted only about thirty students a year, while St. Cyr, which was under the Ministry of War, admitted only about 250–300 students a year. As Patrick Harrigan and others have shown, the secondary school was the true social hurdle in the system.[58] Its substantial tuition fees, the paucity of scholarships, and the rigorous classical curriculum discouraged untold numbers of families from sending their sons for an advanced education. Yet, at a time when new

57. Stephan d'Irsay, *Histoire des universités françaises et étrangères des origines à nos jours* (2 vols.; Paris, 1935), II, 172.
58. Enrollment figures for 1865 are from Prost, *Histoire de l'enseignement en France*, 108 and 45; computation of number of degrees is based on figures in Fritz Ringer, *Education and Society in Modern Europe* (Bloomington, Ind., 1979), 147; Patrick J. Harrigan, "Secondary Education and the Professions in France During the Second Empire," *Comparative Studies in Society and History*, XVII (1975), 349–71.

social classes were appearing, the *couches nouvelles* of which Léon Gambetta would later speak, and the working classes were developing a sense of class consciousness, the elitism in the system was becoming less and less acceptable.

The French educational system was slow in responding to the need for skilled workers and foremen in an economy that was undergoing rapid commercial, technological, and industrial change. As a result of the development of banks, credit facilities, railroads, the telegraph, canals, mining, and manufacturing during the 1860s, the French "index of industrial production rose from 40.4 to 44.4 while the labor force rapidly expanded and urbanized."[59] Businessmen and prominent members of the industrial and scientific communities were pressuring both the minister of public instruction and the minister of commerce to develop more appropriate and more complete programs of technical education.

But the French governing classes spent as little as possible on the public schools. Local, departmental, and especially the national budgets for the schools were notoriously low. There was, indeed, a tradition by 1863 that the state did not spend much money on education.

Moreover, teaching was still an insufficiently recompensed profession. Salaries were low, near or below subsistence level for elementary schoolteachers, and not very attractive at many higher levels; promotions were irregularly and sparingly granted; pensions were meager; and teacher education was deficient everywhere except at the Ecole Normale Supérieure.

In addition, although most French boys and a respectable and growing number of French girls (most French girls by the end of the 1860s) were attending elementary schools, elementary education in France was still plagued by many fundamental problems. Poor attendance of the schools, a dearth of adequate books, desks, and school buildings, and ill-equipped teachers were among those problems. One of the more popular indexes of the deficiencies in or lack of elementary education at the time was the rate of illiteracy, and in France in 1863 illiteracy (defined as the inability to read and write) was estimated at 28 percent for bridegrooms and 42 percent for brides.[60]

59. Bruneau, "French Faculties and Universities," 31.
60. Carlo M. Cipolla, *Literacy and Development in the West* (Baltimore, 1969),

The state, unfortunately, had yet to encourage women's education in any substantial way. At the primary level, the state still had not done as much for girls as it had for boys in the Guizot Law of 1833. And at the secondary level, it offered nothing for young women. Certainly cultural prejudices and economic realities determined the attitudes of legislators up to 1863. But two additional facts are important. First, the state had once recognized the existence of a higher form of education in private schools for girls in pronouncements in the late 1830s but had been curiously silent on this subject in the more recent statements and pieces of legislation, especially in the Falloux Law. And second, lay teachers in private schools and even the conservative religious orders had been offering at least some secondary education for women in the private *pensionnats* for decades, if not longer.

Higher education suffered from a serious lack of attention, in large part because of the overriding importance attached to secondary education, which offered liberal arts education to the upper classes and the prestigious baccalaureate degree as a capstone of studies for those who did not care to continue their education in a professional school. Higher education thus was still fragmented among the various faculties and *grandes écoles*, and it still lacked an organic law, even though it had been promised one in 1850. Research at higher institutions was neglected everywhere except in Paris. Science and letters faculties in the provinces were little more than degree-granting institutions because attendance at lectures in these faculties was not required for higher-level degrees. Some students wishing more sophisticated training in certain fields such as history were beginning to go to the German states.

Finally, there was a compelling need to improve the overall quality of education. The government wanted laic schools at the primary and secondary levels to compete effectively with Catholic schools; at the primary level, as we have seen, religious schools had made rapid gains, and at the secondary level, by 1860, Catholic schools were beginning to offer serious competition to the public schools.[61] In the *lycées* and

121–24. These figures are in line with the estimates produced by the census of 1866 and the Maggiolo report. Cf. Furet and Ozouf, *Lire et ècrire*, I, 28.

61. Patrick J. Harrigan, "Social and Political Implications of Catholic Secondary Education During the Second French Empire," *Societas*, VI (1976), 44–55.

municipal *collèges*, the curriculum would have to be modernized, the pedagogy improved, and the baccalaureate examination converted from an exercise in mnemonics to an exercise in real thinking and knowledge.[62] And at the higher level, where there was no freedom of teaching and hence no Catholic schools, as a matter of national pride the government wanted its *grandes écoles* and faculties to be able to compete effectively with the best foreign schools and universities. The very future of France, to paraphrase a telling comment of Paul Gagnon, seemed to depend on the schools.[63]

The system of education with which Duruy had to work, therefore, was essentially that bequeathed by Napoleon I. There were lay and religious schools at the elementary level, and, since 1850 especially, both lay and religious schools at the secondary level. The ability of the laic schools to hold their own against the religious schools was a major problem that Duruy had to contend with. But there were other towering concerns such as the poor attendance at primary schools in an era of universal suffrage, the quality of education everywhere, the state of the physical plant and scientific facilities, the fragmentation of faculties and higher education facilities, and the condition of teachers and professors in France. The agenda facing Duruy was, indeed, substantial.

62. Albert Duruy, *L'instruction publique et la démocratie, 1879–1886* (Paris, 1886), 201 and 206, points out that there were many calls for these reforms in the 1860s.

63. Gagnon's comment is, "Since the Revolution, the French have assumed that the course of their politics and their style of life depended upon the character of French education" ("The French Lesson: The Right to Culture," *Change*, VII [December–January, 1975–76], 39).

III · The Challenges of University Administration and Direction

He brought to the Ministry of Public Instruction love of people, a high and firm conception of the needs of democracy, a sentiment of professional duty, and an integrity that was peerless among the ministers of the Second Empire.
—E. Zévort, "Victor Duruy"

The appointment of Duruy to the Ministry of Public Instruction came as a surprise to practically everyone.[1] To many it seemed little more than the caprice of a despot. There was no evidence that Rouland had incurred the emperor's disfavor; indeed, despite his Catholic and conservative background, Rouland appeared to be implementing imperial policies quite well. Furthermore, no one would have guessed that Napoleon would appoint a man with no previous legal training or political experience. Both Fortoul and Rouland had made their mark in politics during their early careers, and although Rouland had not risen through the academic ranks as Fortoul had done, he had gained compensating experience in the magistracy. Duruy had only his experience as professor and general inspector. But by 1863, Duruy had proven himself to be hardworking, a liberal reformer, and a moderate anticlerical. And he had won imperial favor. That was all that really mattered.

Almost inevitably, when news of Duruy's appointment was announced in the *Moniteur*, a considerable stir occurred in University circles. Some *universitaires* were thrilled that one of their own had been appointed. Others, men with longer and more distinguished careers than Duruy's such as Urbain Le Verrier, director of the Imperial Observatory, Nisard, director of the Ecole Normale, and Dumas, the distinguished chemist and vice-president of the Imperial Council, were

1. Excerpt of an article by Edmond About in *La Presse*, *JGIP*, 1867, p. 25.

incensed that they had been passed over for the ministry. Le Verrier even threatened to resign from his post until Nisard dissuaded him. Eventually, however, most of those who were jealous of Duruy—but not Nisard or Le Verrier—reconciled themselves to the appointment.

Liberals everywhere approved of Duruy's appointment. The famous Saint-Simonian Michel Chevalier wrote Duruy and congratulated him on this victory for "true liberalism." Students at the Ecole Normale applauded what they termed the democratic coup against University mandarins. And Alfred Fouillée of Auxerre wrote to Charles Glachant, Duruy's son-in-law, "I dare tell you how much he is loved in our province and how everyone is concerned with the reforms by which he will improve the University." For once, there was a good chance that academic concerns would take precedence over politics; the appointment of a professor to head the University seemed to signal that the emperor was serious about educational reform. Republicans also welcomed Duruy's appointment.[2] Only clericals and conservatives had reason for dismay.

But the emperor's decision was a fait accompli, and Duruy went directly to the office of the ministry at 110, rue de Grenelle on the morning of June 24, 1863, even though he had traveled all night by train from Moulins and had visited Napoleon III early that morning at Fontainebleau. Before noon, he assembled his immediate staff for a short briefing. He told them: "All of you owe your position to M. Rouland. I will not disturb any of the advantages he accorded you, not even those granted just before he left office. . . . I hope you will serve me with the same enthusiasm as you have had for him. I place my trust in you, as if we had known each other a long time. But I arrive knowing my *métier*, or at least what should be accomplished here, and I intend to superintend everything."[3] Before the meeting terminated, he directed the division chiefs to pursue "law and justice" in the areas under their jurisdiction.

Some of the career service bureaucrats already in place would serve

2. Michel Chevalier to Victor Duruy, July 30, 1863, Duruy Papers, 114 AP-1-IX, AN; Lavisse in *Femmes diplômes*, 13; Alfred Fouillée to Charles Glachant, August 20, 1863, Duruy Papers, 114 AP-3-II, AN; Katherine Auspitz, *The Radical Bourgeoisie: The Ligue de l'enseignement and the Origins of the Third Republic, 1866–1885* (New York, 1982), 59.
3. Duruy, *Notes et souvenirs*, II, 230.

Duruy well. Léon Pillet, chief of the primary education division, was especially valuable because of his lengthy experience and his interest in forcing errant clergy to comply with education laws. Armand du Mesnil, chief of higher education, was a loyal supporter of Duruy's and would continue to champion his proposals and reforms for many years after Duruy left office. Du Mesnil's habit of working long hours at the ministry pleased Duruy greatly. The other division chiefs, according to Alfred Rambaud, lacked initiative, ambition, and professional dedication, forcing Duruy to deal even with the more minor details of their departments. But "in revenge, he took all responsibility and credit for his acts."[4]

The few new men Duruy brought into his administration were reliable and dedicated professionals. Charles Robert, who had already made his mark as a proponent of popular education during Rouland's administration, served as Duruy's secretary general from October, 1864, to December, 1866, and was especially involved in the development of plans for free and compulsory education.[5] Ernest Lavisse, who had been Duruy's student at Normale, served as secretary, confidant, and special assistant in the program for female secondary education. Duruy thought of Lavisse as one of his sons. Charles Glachant, Duruy's son-in-law and a highly respected professor of rhetoric at the *lycée* Louis-le-Grand, was variously Duruy's principal private secretary and director of personnel. Glachant later prepared a very important memorandum for Duruy on the reception of some of his reforms at the secondary level.

In appointing Glachant to his first position, Duruy was especially concerned about possible accusations of nepotism, even though it had been a fairly normal practice in government earlier. He wrote to the emperor, telling him that he did not see any reason why a man who was "approved by the whole University" should be barred from a high position just because he happened to be the son-in-law of the minister.

---

4. *Ibid.*, 229; Alfred Rambaud, "Victor Duruy (1811–1894)," *Journal des savants*, II (September, 1904), 489.

5. Robert had several reports and brochures to his credit: a report on vocational education, popular libraries, and primary education at the London Exposition of 1862; the analysis of *instituteurs*' 1860 essays on primary instruction in rural areas mentioned above; and a famous brochure, *De l'ignorance des populations ouvrières et rurales de la France et des causes qui tendant à la perpetuer* (Montbéliard, 1863).

But Duruy did promise to appoint Glachant on a trial basis for three months before regularizing his appointment. Later Duruy would name his sons Albert and Anatole to high posts at the ministry, without giving the matter special attention. He had already stated their academic qualifications to the emperor in a letter on July 10, 1863.[6]

Duruy wished to establish rigorous standards of professional probity for the bureaucracy as a whole. In his letter to the emperor on July 10, 1863, he gave an exact accounting of his own financial situation. He was determined that neither he nor any of his subordinates would profit personally from the offices they held; bribes and kickbacks or special favors, perhaps more notoriously a part of the Second Empire than the July Monarchy, would have no place in his administration. Shortly thereafter, he made public examples out of two cases of abuse he uncovered at the ministry.[7]

These same standards of discipline, professional probity, and loyalty to the new minister of public instruction were forced on the Imperial Council of Public Instruction. At his first meeting with the council, Duruy, sensing the hostility of some of its members, firmly asserted his authority: "The emperor wished, undoubtedly, that one of the old soldiers of the militant University, a person who has borne some of the greatest daily burdens in the system, be put to the test: it is the University being called to take care of itself and its future." At the end of that meeting, Duruy ordered, "Now to work, Messieurs." Sentiments of some to the contrary, his appointment and his authority were nondebatable.[8]

The council did settle down to work, most of which was done by its constituent commissions. During the next few years, in addition to fulfilling such perfunctory duties as examining textbooks for schools and reviewing requests for permission to teach or to open new schools,

6. Adeline Daumard, "Les fondements de la société bourgeois en France au XIXe siècle," in Daniel Roche, *Ordres et classes: Colloque d'histoire sociale saint-cloud 24–25 mai 1967* (Paris, 1973), 216; Duruy, *Notes et souvenirs*, II, 218–19. Albert had graduated from Saint-Cyr in 1862. Anatole was a student at the Ecole Normale and graduated in 1866.

7. Duruy, *Notes et souvenirs*, II, 230–32; Lavisse, "Victor Duruy," 246–47.

8. F(17*) 1870, AN. The most distinguished members included Amedée Thierry, Jules Baroche (superseded by Rouher), Monsignors Georges Darboy (Paris), Pierre-Louis Parisis (Arras), Nicholas Sergent (Quimper), and Jean-Baptiste Landriot (La Rochelle), Raymond Théodore Troplong, Paul de Royer, Saint-Marc Girardin, Desiré Nisard, Jean-Baptiste Dumas, Urbain Le Verrier, and Félix Ravaisson.

it reacted to bills and programs prepared by the ministry. Even though it had been stripped of any real power during Fortoul's ministry, the council provided Duruy with lively and fruitful sessions.[9]

Meetings with the council were somewhat difficult for Duruy at the beginning, when reforms were likely to be opposed by one or more of its conservative members. But in October, 1863, Duruy's archenemy, Rouher, left to become minister of state, and in 1865, Duruy engineered the dismissal of Monsignor Nicholas Sergent of Quimper on charges that the bishop slept during council meetings. Thereafter, Monsignor Pierre-Louis Parisis of Arras was the only conservative in the council. When he died in May, 1866, he was replaced by the liberal Bishop Charles Lavigerie of Nancy, and at last Duruy had an entirely congenial group with which to work.[10]

Duruy had excellent rapport with the corps of state school inspectors, perhaps because he had been one of them himself and he knew their professional needs firsthand. They gave him no disciplinary problems even though many were overtaxed by the number of schools they had to inspect (as many as five hundred schools for some primary inspectors).[11] But their situation was made easier by certain changes Duruy implemented. He used other sources of state inspection—the academic, departmental, and municipal education councils, the rectors, prefects, and subprefects—more widely than had his predecessors. He reduced the number of reports the regular inspection corps had to file annually by one-half, and he rather ostentatiously looked after the welfare of inspectors, giving them an increased sense of importance and professional dignity.[12]

9. Gerbod, *La condition universitaire en France au XIXe siècle*, 309–11. Its most interesting sessions were discussions of contemporary history in the *lycées* (November 25, 1863), the Greek curriculum (December 2, 1863), professional secondary education (November 28, 1864), anticlericalism at Liège (December 26, 1865), public secondary education for women (December 9, 1867), and programs for the Ecole Pratique des Hautes Etudes (July 4, 1868). The minutes for these sessions can be found in registers F(17*) 1870–71, AN.

10. Victor Glachant, "Monseigneur Parisis et la ministère de l'instruction publique: D'après des documents inédits," *Quinzaine*, LXVI (1905), 231; Maurain, *La politique ecclésiastique du Second Empire*, 758. Chapter I, article 3, of the Falloux Law provided that archbishops were elected by their colleagues for six-year terms on the council, renewable indefinitely. There was no provision for revocation.

11. On the role of general inspectors, see Paul Gerbod, "Les inspecteurs généraux et l'inspection générale de l'instruction publique de 1802 à 1882," *Revue historique*, XXIII (July–September, 1966), 79–106; Report on primary instruction for the department of Savoy, academy of Chambéry, F(17) 4361, AN.

12. Circular of May 26, 1866, Ministère de l'instruction Publique, *Bulletin admin-*

Duruy also had good relations with the savants in the University. He cultivated friendships with them as much out of personal intellectual interest as out of administrative concern. He lunched and dined with them on a regular basis, attended their lectures, and consulted with several of them on educational reform. Of course, the serious attention he gave to reforms in higher education, a decided improvement over the behavior of previous ministers, ingratiated him with them further. Dumas, Pasteur, Henri Milne-Edwards, Antoine Balard, and Jules Jamin became close friends. Indeed, Dumas, alienated initially by Duruy's appointment, had become one of Duruy's staunchest supporters by early fall 1863. He would continue to support Duruy unequivocably throughout his term of office.[13]

Among the savants, only Le Verrier was a problem. This great mathematician and astronomer, who had discovered the planet Neptune and who was director of the Imperial Observatory, was an autocrat who had summarily dismissed more than sixty of his colleagues and relegated others to minor tasks. Duruy bluntly described this and other grievances, writing that Le Verrier "is a teacher but he does not teach; a general inspector, but [he] does not inspect; a director, but [he] directs too much. Le Verrier does not recognize the minister. He refuses to obey orders." Later Le Verrier would neglect preparations for viewing the solar eclipse of August 18, 1868, and would publicly oppose Duruy's bill for the creation of the Ecole Pratique des Hautes Etudes. To circumvent Le Verrier's contrariety and to help deal with what became known as the "*querelle Le Verrier*," Duruy organized an oversight commission of nine scientists for the Observatory. This commission began meeting regularly and managed shortly thereafter to reverse some of Le Verrier's most objectionable abuses. Le Verrier, however, retained his post—and continued to retain it until Emile Segris became minister of public instruction in 1870.[14]

Duruy had more trouble with political figures. He was considered a parvenu and intruder at the Council of Ministers and Council of State because he was a democratic *universitaire*, and he thought and spoke differently than his colleagues.[15] Rouher, who had not forgiven him for

---

istratif de l'instruction publique (hereinafter cited as *BAIP*), V (1866), 555–57; circular of August 7, 1868, *BAIP*, X (1868), 129–30.

13. Duruy, *Notes et souvenirs*, II, 238.

14. *Ibid.*, 243; excerpt from the *Journal de Paris*, *JGIP*, 1868, p. 242.

15. These differences are clear from the contemporary newspaper accounts of Du-

the 1860 brochure on the papal states, was his chief opponent from the very beginning.[16] According to Prosper Merimée, a writer and court intimate, Rouher was often responsible for some of the compromises Duruy's programs and ideas suffered in high government circles; Rouher frequently used the pretext of insufficient monies for various projects, and he was sustained by other ministers. Rouher liked to call the reform-oriented Duruy "a bull in a china shop," a label that bemused other conservatives at court. Duruy for his part never minced words. An evildoer was an evildoer; a fool, a fool. When his first reform went before the Council of State and former education minister Esquirou de Parieu attacked it vociferously, Duruy answered in kind: "I have known you for a long time, Monsieur; it was you who brought the White Terror down on us." Duruy had little optimism about the political foresight of his colleagues. He would write to the emperor in 1867 that he had discovered a disposition among his ministerial colleagues to wish that the legislature was filled solely with government lackeys or enemies, "as though the people were not a collection of individuals and interests, who renew themselves constantly, and always have new needs which the government, vital organ of society, is supposed . . . to satisfy."[17]

Duruy's relationships with the clergy were also delicate, although only the conservatives and intransigents in the hierarchy posed difficulties. Bishop Parisis of Arras and Bishop Paul Dupont des Loges of Metz, for example, were suspicious of Duruy from the beginning, and they rarely hesitated to protest against decisions they judged harmful to the Church. The liberals in the Church, unfortunately fewer in number, were, however, a different matter. With such men as Archbishop Georges Darboy of Paris, who administered first communion and confirmation to Duruy's daughter Gabrielle in 1865,[18] Monsignor Henri Maret of the faculty of theology at the Sorbonne, and Monsignor Lavigerie of Nancy, Duruy was able to establish very agreeable friendships. The liberals in the hierarchy were often invited to join the cote-

ruy's negotiations with his political colleagues, but the point is verified in Lavisse, "Victor Duruy," 245.

16. *Centenaire de Victor Duruy*, 89 (comment by Paul Painlevé).

17. Juliette Adam, *Mes sentiments et nos idées avant 1870* (Paris, 1905), 16; Lavisse, in *Femmes diplômes*, 17.

18. Georges Darboy, *Cahiers* (11 vols.; copies in the Holley-Darboy Collection, Mount Saint Mary's College, Emmitsburg, Md.), XI, 44.

rie of savants who dined frequently at the ministry. And on one occasion, Duruy, enthusiastic about Archbishop Darboy's public expression of liberal political statements, wrote to the prelate suggesting that the rest of the hierarchy had only to follow his lead if they wished to regain wide respect in France.[19]

As might be guessed, the press had much influence on public perception of Duruy, his administration, and his reforms, and Duruy was sensitive to the importance of newspaper coverage. As minister, he had at his disposal an official publication, the weekly *Bulletin administratif de l'instruction publique*, each issue of which was divided into two parts: one official for the texts of laws, decrees, *arrêtés*, and circulars, the other unofficial for any items Duruy wished to include—speeches on education, brief notices on educational developments at home and abroad, and so forth. Duruy used the unofficial section consciously during his ministry, more than previous ministers had done. He filled its columns with a medley of moralistic sayings, such as: "In France, honor is the first reward." "A society is like an immense pyramid: the greater and more solid its base, the more its middle level will be raised and strengthened, the more its uppermost ranks will glory in intellectual enlightenment." "The modern society shines its light into its most obscure corners searching for the great man and useful citizen whose intelligence is unproven."[20] He also used the unofficial section to acknowledge the efforts of his subordinates when he had no more concrete rewards to distribute to them and to develop a sense of enthusiasm for reform within the University. Thus the unofficial section was filled with excerpts from newspapers, official reports, teachers' letters, and stories of the enormous sacrifices that were being made for education in cities and towns across France. All of these were intended to serve as models for emulation; and all made fine propaganda. "Success is for naught if it is isolated [from public knowledge]," Duruy told his rectors in a revealing confidential circular on January 7, 1866.[21]

Some of the press chastised Duruy for including in the official section a plethora of "information of little significance" and for leaving the impression that nothing had been accomplished in education be-

19. E. Ambroise-Darboy, "Notes sur Mgr Darboy" (copy of a pamphlet, H 26, in the Holley-Darboy Collection, Mount Saint Mary's College, Emmitsburg, Md.).
20. Zévort, "Victor Duruy," 489.
21. F(17) 1475, AN.

fore he became minister. But Duruy was hardly troubled by these accusations because the first was untrue for the most part and the second was not worth debating since he usually acknowledged the achievements of his predecessors in all official documents. Indeed, he ordered the creation of departmental versions of the *Bulletin* in 1865, which were to be directed specifically to primary schoolteachers, directresses of nursery schools (*salles d'asile*), primary inspectors, and cantonal delegates. In a "very" confidential circular of July 28, 1866, Duruy asked the prefects to pressure their departmental councils to vote funds for the publication and distribution of the bulletins. By 1869, sixty-six departments had established such bulletins.[22]

In addition to the bulletins, there were three other major contemporary journals of education, the *Journal des instituteurs*, the *Journal général de l'instruction publique*, and the *Revue de l'instruction publique*. The first two were published by Paul Dupont; the third by Hachette. Because they carried reviews of books on education, reports on education abroad, and discussions of ministerial programs and problems in French education, and because the latter two also sampled newspaper opinion on education, Duruy read all three. Duruy was generally on good terms with the *RIP*, which often supported his administration. But he alienated the editor of the other two journals, Paul Dupont, when he abolished the regular subsidies the journals were receiving from the ministry on January 1, 1864, and transferred the allocations to the needy area of teachers' salaries. Thereafter, the *JGIP* tended to be one of Duruy's sternest critics. Although at times the *JGIP* defended and applauded Duruy's reforms, usually it was on the opposing side, and often it engaged in lively polemical debate with the *RIP*, which was ready to do battle for Duruy.[23] The positive result of this rivalry was that the press served to awaken public opinion on matters of education. France had seen nothing similar since the lively press debates over freedom of secondary education in the 1840s.[24]

22. *JGIP*, 1866, pp. 681–82; *JGIP*, 1868, p. 50; circular, September 14, 1865, and "Very Confidential" circular, July 28, 1866, in F(17) 9395, AN; draft notes on primary instruction for the *Exposé de la situation de l'empire, 1869*, p. 16, in F(17) 2677, AN. These departmental bulletins contain some information on education at the local level which is unobtainable elsewhere (*JGIP*, 1867, p. 184).

23. For example, *JGIP*, 1864, pp. 38, 86–87.

24. Although there are substantial gaps in the treatment of the press during Duruy's

One of the several administ_ative areas in which the press became involved was that of educational budgets. Although the press was concerned about the paucity of funds available at the local level, its major target was the historically meager national budget, an area French governments had traditionally been miserly about. In the more liberal atmosphere of the 1860s the press began to attack Napoleon III's regime for spending so much on the military and so little on education. The issue was ignited after General Arthur Morin, a member of the Imperial Council of Public Instruction, presented a report to the Académie Française in September, 1864, comparing expenditures in both areas, for some of the Germanic states as well as France. France's record was the worst (see Table 1). Even the English spent more money per student than the French, the equivalent of 25 francs per pupil versus 38 sous in France. The *RIP*, the *JGIP*, and liberal and republican papers such as the *Journal des débats*, *L'Opinion nationale*, and *Le Siécle* campaigned for months during 1864, 1865, and 1866 against the insufficiencies of the educational budget, particularly in the area of primary instruction. *L'Independence belge* declared that the primary schools in France were "in the most deplorable state." The liberal republican *Le Temps* claimed it could not think of the insufficiency of funds for public education "without dying of shame." And Victor Chauvin of the *RIP* threw up the flag: "La patrie en danger."[25]

Duruy was criticized by both the press and the republican opposition for his failure to be more aggressive in demanding funds. Jules Simon and his colleagues in the Corps législatif attempted to embarrass the government at the March, 1864, budget session by proposing an amendment that would have granted an additional two million francs for the construction of *écoles communales* and an additional six million francs for the construction of primary schools for girls.[26] At

ministry, Charles Dejob's "Le réveil de l'opinion dans l'Université sous le Second Empire: *La revue de l'instruction publique* et Victor Duruy," *L'enseignement secondaire*, March 15–May 1, 1914), 65–68, 82–85, 107–10, 120–24, is still the best published source.

25. *RIP*, 1864, pp. 434, 481, 545–46, 626; *JGIP*, 1864, esp. p. 760; *RIP*, 1864, p. 626.

26. *RIP*, 1864, p. 857. At the same time, the republicans proposed a credit of 50,000 francs to study a bill for free and compulsory education (p. 858). The legislature, however, approved only 200,000 francs extra for the construction of *écoles de filles* (*RIP*, 1864, p. 14). (Pagination for the *RIP* changes with the first issue in April each year,

Table 1. Expenditures by France and Various German States on War and Instruction (francs)

States	War	Instruction
France	295	11
Austria	270	19
Prussia	276	14
Wurtemburg	218	47
Baden	182	34
Hanover	128	12

Source: RIP, 1864, p. 578.

the same time, A. Lesieur in the *RIP* accused Duruy of contenting himself with the tradition established by previous ministers "that the University should humble itself . . . that it should cost the state as little as possible, and that one could modify it, transform it, revolutionize it indefinitely, provided one did not ask anything from the [state] budget." Later, however, when Duruy was under fiercer attack on the budget by the republicans, the *RIP* and the *L'Opinion nationale* attempted to protect him by pointing out that he was handicapped by the opposition of his colleagues, especially the various ministers of finance.[27]

Duruy was hardly insensitive to the need for more money. He spoke frequently of the "shabbiness" ["*la gueuserie*"] of his budget "crushed by that of [the Ministry of] War," and he asked the Ministry of Finance incessantly for additional support.[28] He also took his case to the emperor, borrowing Pasteur's famous indictment: "France spends twenty-five million [francs] for a prefecture, fifty or sixty million for an opera, and can manage only seven or eight million for the primary education of her people."[29] But despite his modest requests, he had less than desirable immediate success. Whether he was overly timid in the face of ministerial and legislative resistance is debatable. But the legislatures of the 1860s were tightfisted, and Duruy feared compromising

when numbering begins with one again. Thus p. 857 in this citation is from the March 30, 1864, issue of the *RIP*, whereas p. 14 is from the April 14, 1864, issue.)

27. *RIP*, 1864, pp. 434–36, 804; *RIP*, 1868, p. 273; *JGIP*, 1865, p. 11.
28. Rambaud, "Victor Duruy," 489.
29. Duruy, *Notes et souvenirs*, I, 214.

proposed reforms. He often argued that the most important task was to win approval for education principles and reforms; once new programs had proved their worth, they would more easily get the necessary financial support.

All this is not to imply that the budget for public instruction remained frozen during his ministry. If the local expenditures required by the law of 1867 on primary education are added to the total increment in the national budget, the net result was a 45 percent increase. Expenses for personnel and matériel at the ministry were reduced, while modest gains were made at all levels of education. The Museum of Natural History and the Ecole des Chartes saw their allocations increased most among higher institutions. And although some additional money was pumped into the *lycées* and municipal *collèges*, the primary schools benefited most.[30]

Duruy took great pride in the manipulation of funds at his disposal. In his memoirs, he confided: "Each time a vacancy occurred in an office [at the ministry], either on account of the retirement or death of a functionary, I would interview the men who had worked with him. 'So and so,' I would tell them, 'leaves a salary of three thousand francs disposable; if you would be willing to do his work [besides your own], I will give you [in addition to your present salary] one-half of his. The rest I will keep for the increases at the end of the year . . . according to merit and amount of work.' Nobody ever refused." By 1867 some thirty jobs in the central administration were liquidated by this formula and 100,000 francs used to augment salaries. When the *Journal des instituteurs* ceased to be an official publication on January 1, 1864, Duruy used its appropriation to raise the salaries of *instituteurs*. When four million francs were needed for the reconstruction of the *lycée* Louis-le-Grand, he drew money from an account designated to rehabilitate the Sorbonne, Collège de France, and Ecole de Médecine. And in 1866 he diverted some 200,000 francs destined for the scientific expedition to Mexico into the ministry's budget for the construction of school buildings.[31]

30. Zévort, "Victor Duruy," 488; Lavisse, "Victor Duruy," 53. The annual budgets for public instruction can be found in the various volumes of [Ministère de l'Instruction Publique], *Annuaire de l'instruction publique* (Paris, various dates).
31. Duruy, *Notes et souvenirs*, II, 234; F(17) 13673, AN (letter dated December 22, 1867), as quoted in George David Weisz, "The Academic Elite and the Movement to Reform French Higher Education, 1850–1885" (Ph.D. dissertation, State University of

   The lack of sufficient money continued to plague Duruy throughout the whole of his ministry. Yet surprisingly, he remained an optimist. Thinking as much of the small budgetary gains being made as of the principles or reforms getting approved, he once shared with Camille Pelletan at the Corps législatif his basic philosophy: "À chaque jour suffit sa peine." [32]

   But each day had its rewards, especially when a minister worked sedulously. And that Victor Duruy did. This "beast of burden," as he was still fond of calling himself, continued to follow a rigorous schedule as minister. [33] His normal work day was seventeen hours long. Typically he arrived early each day at the ministry and worked all morning with his secretary general, his principal private secretary, and a regular secretary. Lavisse, who had responsibility for the increasing amount of daily mail, sorted it and brought it to Duruy without saying a word. [34] At noon, Duruy frequently had lunch with various savants. In the afternoon he returned to his office to confer with his division chiefs and to receive visitors. Appointments were kept short, on Duruy's orders. If a visitor stayed beyond a certain prearranged time, a member of Duruy's staff would intercede with an appropriate excuse. Lavisse recounts that his own frequent ploy was to announce that the archbishop of Paris was waiting for Duruy in an adjacent parlor because few people would chance being rude to Monsignor Darboy. [35] On occasion during the winter, Duruy would dine with men of letters and artists such as Gustave Flaubert, Gustave Doré, and Charles Gounod. Otherwise he remained at the office until late in the evening, working with the stoicism and passion for detail that had become a hallmark in his lifestyle and a source of his success as minister. Duruy was so conscientious as minister that he would get up in the middle of the night to

---

New York at Stony Brook, 1976), 97; Rohr, *Victor Duruy, ministre de Napoléon III*, 41–42; *JGIP*, 1864, p. 77. Obviously, those from whom the funds were taken were hardly pleased. See, for example, Dejob, "Le réveil de l'opinion dans l'Université sous le Second Empire," 123.

   32. Lavisse, "Victor Duruy," 252.

   33. R. Thamin, "Victor Duruy," *Revue pédagogique*, XLII (1903), 462, called Duruy "one of the most diligent workers [*opiniâtres travailleurs*] of his generation."

   34. Lavisse notes that because of his controversial reforms Duruy received a considerable number of highly critical letters or hate mail during the closing years of his ministry. On one occasion Lavisse opened a small, neatly wrapped box and discovered an ugly black spider inside (*Centenaire de Victor Duruy*, 105).

   35. *Ibid.*, 103.

jot down ideas as they came to him. Jules Simon complained that Duruy never took any "recreations"; he was at work incessantly.[36]

But not all of Duruy's days were spent at the ministry, reading and annotating in red pencil the manifold reports that came to his desk.[37] He also continued visiting schools as he had done as a general inspector.[38] Such visits, he claimed, gave him the right to a personal opinion and the ability to foresee the future educational needs of France. Duruy delighted in traveling incognito. He always arrived in towns unannounced so that he could see conditions as they really existed. Often he toured several towns at once, visiting all the public schools and even some of the religious institutions. This was extraordinary activity for a minister of public instruction, the *Journal des débats* observed in its July, 1864, issue. And Duruy gained much goodwill in the towns he visited. Only his ministerial colleagues had a different opinion; they were amused by the visits, and they began to call Duruy the "circuit minister." Provoked by their pun, Duruy complained to the emperor, "Make them travel around the country, Sire. With all the dossiers piled on their desks, they are barricaded behind a veritable Great Wall of China. They have lost sight of reality."[39]

"Methodical" is probably the best adjective to use in describing Duruy's handling of the ministry. He thoroughly enjoyed giving personal attention to *universitaires*, the schools, and all of the reports that came to the ministry. But standard sources of information were not sufficient for him so he adopted the practice of commissioning additional reports and statistical compilations when they seemed indicated. As a result, some of the richest sources of information on French education in the nineteenth century emanate from his ministry.[40]

36. Simon, "Notice historique sur la vie et les travaux de Victor Duruy."
37. Comments in Duruy's hand on many reports and letters that arrived at the ministry, located now in the cartons at the National Archives, attest to his extensive reading.
38. The press reported thoroughly on these visits; for example, the excerpts from *L'ami de l'ordre* in *JGIP*, 1865, p. 328, and from the *Journal de Paris*, in *JGIP*, 1868, p. 610.
39. Excerpts from the *Journal des débats* in *JGIP*, 1864, p. 450; Duruy, *Notes et souvenirs*, II, 229.
40. A fairly common complaint from Duruy's detractors was that of Gustave Huriot that Duruy's feverish activity was threatening "to submerge *la France enseignant* under a wave of writings and words. . . . Decrees, regulations, circulars, apologetic speeches, new orders, distributions of crosses and medals . . . nothing is lacking." (Excerpt from the *Courrier français* in *JGIP*, 1866, p. 239.)

Soon after he had become minister, Duruy ordered a thorough investigation of the status of all levels of French education. Although such of his predecessors as Guizot and Salvandy had commissioned studies of primary and secondary education, no one had demanded a massive study of the entire system. Largely quantitative, these reports were published subsequently as *Statistique de l'enseignement primaire*, *Statistique de l'enseignement secondaire*, and *Statistique de l'enseignement supérieur*. Later, they were supplemented by the reports on French education and achievements which Duruy commissioned for the Universal Exposition in 1867.

To provide himself with a broader perspective on French education and to keep himself abreast of developments abroad, Duruy requested reports on foreign education. Sometimes he contacted the Quai d'Orsay or foreign embassies for information. On other occasions he wrote to friends in foreign lands.[41] Frequently, he sent *universitaires* to the German states or England to study a particular program or to observe meetings of educators.[42]

All of these requests for additional information, of course, added to the paperwork that had to be done by the functionaries in the University. Duruy worked earnestly to correct this problem. He polled rectors on the reports that could be eliminated or reduced in length,[43] he consulted with his immediate subordinates at the ministry on possible reforms, and he established a special commission at the ministry to study the matter further. Ultimately, with the *arrêté* of April 17, 1866, he reduced the number of required reports by almost half.[44] But de-

41. See the communication with Dr. Rosen of Cleves in F(17) 2338, AN, for example.

42. The titles of these reports are instructive: *Rapport sur l'état de l'enseignement spécial et de l'enseignement primaire en Belgique, Allemagne et Suisse* (Paris, 1865); Jacques Demogeot, *Mission en Angleterre: Note sur l'organization des classes et la promotion des élèves* (1866); Jacques Demogeot and Henry Montucci, *De l'enseignement secondaire en Angleterre et en Écosse* (1868). See material in F(17) 9097, AN. R. D. Anderson, *Education in France, 1848–1870* (Oxford, 1975), 251, offers the titles of five other "officially inspired" reports for Duruy's ministry. All or portions of them were reproduced in the *JGIP*.

43. See *Analyse des rapports de MM. les recteurs sur les réformes à introduire dans le service de l'instruction publique spécialement en ce qui concern les attributions qui doivent leur être rendues*, F(17) 2625, AN. Since there was a centralized system of education, many of the changes represented a significant modification in the grip of Paris on the rest of the country.

44. *BAIP*, V (1866), 554–57.

spite his good intentions and his arrêté, the problem was never satis-factorily resolved.

As the nature and amount of his ministerial activity suggests, Duruy exercised enormous personal control over all that transpired in public education. Much of this owed to the character of ministerial appoint-ments during the Second Empire and the relative smallness of the bu-reaucracy. Fortoul and Rouland had enjoyed the same situation. But Duruy spent more time on programs and administrative detail and thus could exert greater influence. During the closing years of the em-pire, with trends toward liberalization and democracy gaining mo-mentum, Duruy became particularly vulnerable to charges of authori-tarianism in the press. Here was a minister supposedly sympathetic to liberty and democracy who was governing his own bureaucracy as if he were a despot. Edmond Goumy complained in *L'Opinion national* that although Duruy's despotism was enlightened, it was far removed from the hopes of those who wished to see the University move toward greater self-government. J.-J. Weiss criticized Duruy for maintaining his absolute and discretionary powers over all teaching personnel, a condition he believed contributed to low morale, especially among professors. But as interested as he was in liberal reform and the morale of the *corps enseignant* and as receptive as he generally was to an air-ing of grievances, Duruy was displeased with both attacks, which he viewed as dangerous to basic discipline within the University. Conse-quently, Duruy, or rather the ministry, answered both critics firmly with a summary of all laws relating to the nomination and revocation of personnel at every level, a list of all the legal restraints on Duruy's power, and an indication of the areas in which advisory bodies and teachers had influence over operations of the University. J.-J. Weiss and the two newspapers that supported his allegations, *L'Époque* and *L'Union*, received communiqués disclaiming that Duruy was "all-powerful." [45]

But Duruy, as even his most virulent critics were willing to admit, was hardly a Fortoul. And Duruy's administration was certainly more liberal than Rouland's. Indeed, as the *JGIP* reminded its readers in 1865, Duruy had announced formally at the opening session of the

45. *JGIP*, 1865, pp. 188–89, 315, 731, 761; *JGIP*, 1866, p. 313.

Imperial Council in 1863 that his administration would seek to undo the unsavory measures of the Fortoul years, and men of goodwill could see that he was doing so through his reforms and his more general plans, such as his effort to begin decentralizing the University by granting increased responsibilities to rectors, by giving various educational programs latitude for responding to local needs, and by moving toward the establishment of more autonomous institutions of higher education in the provinces.[46]

Historians today seeking to understand Duruy's general intentions and directions as administrator have the advantage of access to the confidential circulars Duruy issued as minister.[47] If Duruy had any recondite objectives in regard to either the University or the competitive Catholic system of education, one would expect to find evidence in the confidential circulars.

Forty-five "confidential" or "very confidential" circulars were issued during Duruy's ministry. Five relate to the clergy or Catholic education. In a confidential circular dated June 30, 1864, Duruy inquired if the royal feast of Saint Henry was observed in any of the schools.[48] On February 21, 1866, he reasserted the University's legal right to survey primary schools for girls against the opposition of certain clergymen. In November, 1866, he asked rectors for information on the use of patois in teaching in the more remote regions of France, a question that related to the clergy because some of them were especial advocates of the patois. The fourth circular, dated November 23, 1868, reminded rectors that full-time vicars were forbidden to hold regular teaching assignments. And the fifth, which appeared on the following day, asked rectors to supervise examining commissions for the *brevet simple* certificate introduced by the law of April 10, 1867, to guarantee that candidates were being carefully tested on their "objective" knowledge of French history.[49] None of these circulars displays anti-

46. *JGIP*, 1865, pp. 125–26.
47. There are three confidential circulars (one each) in F(17) 2754, 8753, and 9143, AN. The remainder are filed inconspicuously with draft and original copies of circulars in F(17) 1474 and 1475, AN. Historians in the past, apparently, have not discovered the complete set of confidential circulars because they have relied on the *BAIP* for the texts of Duruy's circulars.
48. Confidential circular, June 30, 1864, F(17) 9143, AN. The feast of Saint Henry was celebrated on July 15 by legitimists, especially those in Jesuit institutions. Rectors reported only a few such celebrations.
49. Confidential circulars, February 21, November 9, 1866, November 23, 24, 1868, F(17) 1475, AN.

clericalism, but they do indicate Duruy's intention to force the clergy to adhere to national laws and regulations.

Five more confidential circulars, three of them asking for information on the number of auditors attending courses offered by the faculties, were issued to survey higher education in cases when general inspectors were not fulfilling their legal responsibilities.[50] The purpose of these five seems to have been to avoid embarrassment in the University. Likewise, several confidential circulars were employed to protect the University from scandal or criticism.[51]

Some of the remaining confidential circulars speak to the need for ingratiating the University with local notables.[52] Others deal with questions of curriculum.[53] Finally, an assorted group of confidential circulars treats a variety of more perfunctory issues such as nominations for the rectorate of Nancy when it became vacant in 1868, or protective measures to be taken against the cholera epidemic in 1865.[54] The only design that can be perceived in the confidential circulars is Duruy's determined effort to strengthen the University.

Duruy was not one to have covert objectives, but he did have an agenda for the University, and he shared it with the emperor in a letter he wrote forty-five days after he became minister. Paraphrased, his agenda is as follows:

Primary education
(1) Ensure that all Frenchmen have at least an elementary school education. The creation of universal suffrage in France demands a literate citizenry.

50. Confidential circulars October 24, 1863, April 21, 22, December 13, 1864, F(17) 1474; confidential circular, March 28, 1866, F(17) 1475, AN.
51. Confidential circulars, July 23, 1863, F(17) 1474, concerning the dismissal of a *lycée* professor on a morals violation; February 13, 1864, January 15, 1866, F(17) 1474 and 1475, on discipline in the faculties and *lycées*; January 19, 1868, January 28, 1867, F(17) 1475, on the laxity of standards in *lycées* and faculties; and June 22, 1866, F(17) 1475, AN, on the financial liabilities primary schoolteachers would incur temporarily from the extension of gratuity.
52. Confidential circulars, October 20, 1865, F(17) 1474, January 12, July 25, 1867, May 15, 1869, F(17) 1475, AN. The circular of July 25, 1867, for example, requested that *instituteurs* present themselves, for "political" reasons, at ceremonies of the Legion of Honor, and the circular of May 15, 1869, instructed rectors to give mayors—so important for the financial welfare of the schools—a place of honor at all academic ceremonies.
53. Confidential circulars, March 18, 24, October 28, 1864, on forthcoming baccalaureate examinations; October 4, 1864, requesting suggestions for the reform of the baccalaureate; and October 22, 1864, requesting a candid opinion from rectors, *proviseurs*, and *principals* on the *bifurcation* program, all in F(17) 1474, AN.
54. Confidential circulars, September 1, 1864, October 14, 1865, F(17) 1474; January 30, 1866, F(17) 1475; September 17, 1868, F(17) 2754, AN.

(2) Encourage Frenchmen to continue education into their adult years so they will not forget the skills and knowledge they acquired as children in elementary schools.

(3) Eliminate abuses in the payment of teachers' salaries by requiring regular payments; require that all female teachers receive a minimum of 400 francs a year.

Secondary education

(4) Establish a true secondary and technical education in France, not to teach specific skills but to provide modern agriculture and industry with future workers who will have had general advanced study in science and the nonclassical humanities.

(5) Strengthen traditional secondary education in the classics, science, philosophy, and history for the sons of the well-to-do classes, particularly the bourgeoisie.

Higher education

(6) Cure the "somnolent laxity" in higher education.

Female education

(7) Organize and expand public education for women, which heretofore has been left "in the hands of people who are neither of their time nor of their country."[55]

Duruy hoped for nothing less than a broad renovation of the French education system to make it truly competitive with the best educational systems in Europe and equal to the promises of his nation's energies and resources.

Duruy's plan for his ministry, then, was ambitious, but Duruy was an ambitious man, not for himself but for the principles in which he believed. This ambition was obvious in Duruy's selfless dedication to work and long hours at the ministry, his insistence on unimpeachable standards of behavior for *universitaires* and bureaucrats, and his conviction that the University had to be given firm direction. (See Appendix B for the structure of the University in the 1860s.) Duruy went to work immediately after receiving his appointment, and he moved quickly to ensure that his immediate entourage at the ministry and the Imperial Council contained men on whom he could depend. Pillet,

55. Duruy, *Notes et souvenirs*, I, 196–98. Duruy states in his memoirs that he had the tacit consent or specific approval (from private audiences) of the emperor for his basic ideas and reforms (*ibid.*, 196, n. 1).

du Mesnil, Glachant, Robert, and Lavisse became his chief associates. The Imperial Council's membership was revised to make it more useful to the task of liberal reform. Duruy was aware that good relations with all segments of the University and the larger community were essential, and he cultivated contacts with Frenchmen in certain key areas. But he refused to dissimulate or compromise his objectives for the sake of wooing conservatives, which he felt would leave him without a meaningful program of reform. Duruy spent enormous amounts of time studying reports and generating major surveys of French education[56]—all for the purpose of being able to argue more forcefully for changes in the system and for additional funding. Finally, Duruy gave full notice of the direction in which he wished to take the University. At the first meeting of the Imperial Council he formally announced that his administration would reverse the damage of the Fortoul years. And in a letter to the emperor he set out his seven major objectives for the University. Ambition and firmness of purpose thus describe Duruy's approach to the ministry. As he said to the staff in his office on the first day: "I arrive knowing my *métier*, or at least what needs to be accomplished here."

56. Statistics Duruy gathered on the social origins and career aspirations of secondary school pupils in 1864, for example, have provided the basis for an extremely useful study by Patrick J. Harrigan, *Mobility, Elites and Education in French Society of the Second Empire* (Waterloo, Ontario, 1980).

IV · The "Crusade Against Ignorance" Primary and Popular Education

All questions relative to popular education are now the order of the day.
—Charles Robert, *Plaintes et Voeux* (1864)

The second half of the Second Empire [is] one of the most important periods in the history of popular and worker education.
—Benigno Cacérès, *Histoire de l'éducation* (1964)

By the third quarter of the nineteenth century in France, most if not all members of the governing classes had become persuaded of the need to educate the popular classes. The political and social upheavals of 1848 had convinced them that the workers must be inoculated against the luring promises of utopian reformers and inculcated more solidly with the ideals of religion, respect for authority, and patience with socioeconomic change. Furthermore, by midcentury the growing complexity of industrial and agricultural life and the mounting sophistication of weaponry in Europe were persuading significant portions of the governing classes that popular education was an economic and strategic imperative. Only widespread primary education could provide a nation with intelligent and skilled workers and competent soldiers.

Duruy's thoughts echoed these views. As a liberal, however, he was also convinced that universal suffrage, created in 1848, necessitated a literate and enlightened electorate and that education was the key to improving the quality of life for the working and agricultural classes.

When Duruy studied the needs of primary education closely shortly after taking office, he found much need for fundamental reform. Two publications prepared by Charles Robert gave him a detailed picture of conditions that generally obtained in the rural areas of France. The first work, *Plaintes et voeux preséntés par les instituteurs publics en*

1861, was a summary of the essays prepared by teachers for Rouland in 1861. It showed that although roughly four-fifths of all school-aged children (defined as those between the ages of seven and thirteen) in rural areas were setting foot inside classrooms, their attendance seldom surpassed more than a few months and absenteeism was rampant. Also, in many areas "schools" were little more than small, narrow, and insalubrious basements or abandoned hovels; they lacked basic school furniture, blackboards, books, and other supplies. The second work, Robert's *De l'ignorance des populations ouvrières et rurales de la France*, a companion piece based on the same sources, sketched the unrelieved misery of rural areas, where superstition, gross habits, blind prejudices, and tenacious resistance to change (such as Honoré de Balzac portrayed in *The Peasants*) reigned supreme. It disclosed that there was little if any real appreciation for education among the overwhelming majority of peasants, rural workers, and rural officials, who generally viewed education and the schools with suspicion. Some parents argued that educating rural and working-class children would benefit only the upper classes, who had an unquenchable thirst for profits. Others confided that teachers and officials used the schools to propagate the metric system (which was still largely unknown in departments such as Orne) so that peasants could be cheated on weights and measurements. For many rural inhabitants, school was, at best, a *garderie*; at worst, it was a correctional institution that forced peasant children to learn a language (French) that was alien to the local patois. Indeed, the words "prison schools" appeared frequently in the memoirs.[1]

In urban areas, fortunately, primary education for boys was flourishing, having made especially rapid gains since the Guizot Law of 1833. And primary education for girls was making steady progress, thanks particularly to the growth of women's religious orders after 1850. The large towns of France did not have masses of poor children who were without instruction, as existed in cities like Glasgow.[2]

1. Robert, *Plaintes et voeux présentés par les instituteurs publics en 1861*, 8–21; Robert, *De l'ignorance des populations ouvrières et rurales de la France*, 2–11, 13–24. Desert found some of the same conditions obtaining as late as the eve of the Ferry Laws ("Alphabétisation et scolarisation dans le Grand-Ouest," 165–67).

2. Arnold, *Popular Education of France*, 101.

The difference between towns and cities and rural areas was caused by differentials in not only resources (the more richly endowed urban communities versus the poorer rural communities) but also appreciation for education or social demand. The urban popular classes were much more affected by "written culture." By the mid-1850s they had begun to view illiteracy as a disgrace and were more likely to try to defend themselves against their employers and to advance their socioeconomic status through education. In 1863 in Paris, eighty-seven out of every hundred workers and eighty-nine out of every hundred boys could read and write. Lack of time was cited as the greatest obstacle to worker education.[3]

Duruy, however, had to be concerned with the nation as a whole, and, especially given that it was entering a modern, industrialized age, he found too many unacceptable problems or deficiencies in primary education. Duruy considered illiteracy and nonattendance at schools to be major problems. He was also troubled that 832 communes still lacked primary schools, even though these represented only 2 percent of the total number of communes. He also was displeased that 61 percent of the communes had no separate facilities for girls (although 18,147 communes had the less desirable mixed schools [écoles mixtes], which accepted children of both sexes). Nor was he comfortable that more than 900,000 (or 33 percent of all) children between the ages of seven and thirteen (more girls than boys) received no schooling at all (see Table 2). To be sure, the majority of school-age children (4,018,427) were attending school.[4] And yet, as Duruy pointed out time after time in his speeches (he was the first minister to do so), attendance at school was no guarantee of education because an estimated 40 percent of the children who left school in 1863 were, as Duruy labeled them, non-valeurs.[5] These children learned nothing either because they had not attended school long enough to profit from the instruction or because the instruction was faulty. Duruy was also concerned that libraries and classes for adults were primitive and that

3. Augustin Cochin, Paris: Sa population, son industrie (Paris, 1864), 54–56; Furet and Ozouf, Lire et écrire, I, 149.

4. F(17*) 3160, AN.

5. Furet and Ozouf, Lire et écrire, I, 174; transcript of Duruy's Rapport de S. Exc. M. le Ministre à S. M. l'empereur, précédant la statistique de l'enseignement primaire for 1863, in JGIP, 1865, p. 141.

the teaching profession at the primary level was one of the most unattractive forms of employment in all of France. Not only were salaries low (some 5,000 *institutrices*, for example, were forced to live on less than 400 francs a year—or roughly the subsistence level for a single person in France in the 1860s), but pensions were outrageously meager: after thirty or forty years of service in public education, an *instituteur* could expect to retire on 90 sous a day.[6]

The illiteracy problem was complex.[7] In the first place, there were many degrees of literacy and semiliteracy. There were people who could read and write, people who could read but not write, people who, as Jean Hébrard points out, could "read" only those works they knew pretty much by memory, people who could write but not read, and finally, some people who could sign their names even though they could not read or write.[8] In the second place, there were a variety of factors—social, economic, professional, demographic, and cultural—that affected literacy. The introduction of modern industry into a town, for example, often led to a decline in literacy for several years, and considerable emigration from the countryside to urban areas frequently led to overcrowding in schools followed by a decline in literacy. Finally, the statistics were not always reliable, as a journalist perusing the list of illiterate conscripts in 1865 for the *JGIP* discovered. The list included the names of students at an *école normale*, two students enrolled in the professional faculties, an *instituteur*, and a *maître d'étude* at a *collège*. The anomaly is in part explained by carelessness on the part of conscription authorities, in part by the fact that some young men feigned illiteracy in order to escape conscription.[9]

Literacy or illiteracy rates were thus only crude measures of reality,

6. Lavisse, "Victor Duruy," 246; F(17*) 3158, AN.
7. Harvey Graff reminds us that "literacy studies are perhaps closer to a beginning than an end. Research is far from complete" (Graff [ed.], *Literacy and Social Development in the West: A Reader* [Cambridge, 1981], 6).
8. Jean Hébrard, "École et alphabétisation au XIX⁰ siècle (Approche psycho-pédagogique de documents historiques)," *Annales: Economies, sociétés et civilisations,* XXXV (1980), 71–73; Furet and Ozouf, *Lire et écrire,* I, 227–28. Charles Robert alleged in an 1865 speech that many young people at twelve years of age could read and write but could not sign their names (*JGIP*, 1865, p. 572).
9. Furet and Ozouf, *Lire et écrire,* I, 12, 19, 96, 131, 176, and *passim*; Georges Duveau, *Les instituteurs* (Paris, 1957), 102; Raymond Oberlé, "Etude sur l'analphabétisme à Mulhouse au siècle de l'industrialisation," *Bulletin du Musée Historique de Mulhouse,* LXVII (1959), 109; Matthew Arnold, *Matthew Arnold on Education,* ed. Gillian Sutherland (Baltimore, 1973), 84; *JGIP*, 1865, p. 651.

Table 2. Percentage of Children Aged 7–13
Not Attending School in 1863

Department	Percent	Department	Percent
Ain	10	Garonne (Haute)	36
Aisne	12	Gers	20
Allier	42	Gironde	16
Alpes (Basses-)	12	Hérault	12
Alpes (Hautes-)	21	Ille-et-Vilaine	22
Alpes-Maritimes	40	Indre	58
Ardèche	38	Indre-et-Loire	28
Ardennes	5	Isère	24
Ariège	51	Jura	1
Aube	2	Landes	35
Aude	33	Loir-et-Cher	16
Aveyron	22	Loire	20
Bouches-du-Rhône	29	Loire (Haute-)	48
Calvados	7	Loire-Inférieure	34
Cantal	18	Loiret	13
Charente	31	Lot	36
Charente-Inférieure	32	Lot-et-Garonne	22
Cher	42	Lozère	5
Corrèze	53	Maine-et-Loire	12
Corse	62	Manche	9
Côte-d'Or	2	Marne	5
Côtes-du-Nord	55	Marne (Haute-)	0
Creuse	23	Mayenne	10
Dordogne	40	Meurthe	7
Doubs	3	Meuse	1
Drôme	27	Morbihan	57
Eure	19	Moselle	5
Eure-et-Loir	6	Nièvre	30
Finistère	53	Nord	13
Gard	18	Oise	25

Table 2 (continued)

Department	Percent	Department	Percent
Orne	12	Seine-Inférieure	13
Pas-de-Calais	13	Seine-et-Marne	8
Puy-de-Dôme	46	Seine-et-Oise	4
Pyrénées (Basses-)	33	Sèvres (Deux)	23
Pyrénées (Hautes-)	2	Somme	11
Pyrénées-Orientales	43	Tarn	40
Rhin (Bas-)	10	Tarn-et-Garonne	30
Rhin (Haut-)	24	Var	30
Rhône	6	Vaucluse	21
Saône (Haute-)	0	Vendée	30
Saône-et-Loire	19	Vienne	33
Sarthe	24	Vienne (Haute-)	56
Savoie	17	Vosges	0
Savoie (Haute-)	9	Yonne	3
Seine	32		

Source: Computed from statistics in F(17*) 3160, AN, published later as *Statistique de l'enseignement primaire, 1863*.

as Duruy was well aware, but they were, nevertheless, convenient in-dications of the extent of the need for more popular education. When Duruy entered office, the national illiteracy rates as measured by the most reliable single criterion—the inability to sign one's name on his or her marriage license—were 28 percent for men and 42 percent for women.[10] As a rule, illiteracy rates for urban areas were much lower than the national averages, and for rural areas they were higher. Illit-eracy rates were generally lower in the north and northeastern por-tions of France (above the famous St. Malo to Geneva or Maggiolo line) than they were in the south and southwest. France had made steady progress toward the eradication of illiteracy since the Reforma-tion, but for Duruy France had not yet gone far enough. In light of the

10. Cipolla, *Literacy and Development*, 119, 124.

exigencies of universal suffrage, the growing needs of commerce, industry, and technology, and the increasing sophistication of European society, the illiteracy rates everywhere had to be brought as close to zero as possible. Thus as his first major reform in primary education, Duruy attempted to have the legislature pass a law instituting free and compulsory primary education.

Neither the concept of gratuity nor that of compulsion was new in France. Advocates of both appeared during the Old Regime and the Revolution. But efforts over the years to write the principles into law failed because of the continuing domination of conservative attitudes toward popular education. Of the two principles, gratuity was certainly the less objectionable, especially because it was usually only partial and because many in the upper classes thought of it as a form of charity. But absolute gratuity for all of France was another matter, as Carnot discovered in 1848, when his bill for free and compulsory education was roundly defeated by a coalition of conservatives. His bill, which carried a fine of twenty to five hundred francs plus a suspension of voting rights for five years, was condemned as a "menace to religion and society," a revolutionary threat to the social order, and a dangerous utopian scheme.[11] In article 24 of the Falloux Law, legislators returned to the old formula of granting free education only to those families who could not afford to pay for it.

Unfortunately, the Falloux provision for gratuity never had the effect that legislators and educators in 1850 intended. Gratuity did not solve the problem of school attendance and obviate the need for compulsion. Newspaper after newspaper in the 1860s pointed to the fact that the students that were eligible for gratuity never attended school, and they could cite cases of declining school attendance rates after schools were made tuition-free.[12] Thus pessimists or opponents of free education concluded that the extension of gratuity would further devaluate primary education. They typically argued that people respected only what they paid for. More important, however, was the fact that gratuity was never given a full chance to operate. Just three years after the passage of the Falloux Law, Fortoul limited gratuity to the two eldest school-aged children in any indigent family, the very

11. Gontard, *Les écoles primaires de la France bourgeois*, 131.
12. Furet and Ozouf, *Lire et écrire*, I, 290.

children who were most likely to be sent off to work. In addition, the extension of gratuity to the poor was limited by the machinations of local authorities, who sometimes inflated the number of eligible children so they could use the gratuity privilege for political favors. At other times, they simply deleted the names of truant children or children of parents who were considered a public nuisance and substituted the names of their friends' children.[13]

The issue of free education came to a head in January, 1864, before Duruy actually had a chance to act. During discussions on the budget in the legislature, sixty deputies led by the Saint-Simonian Adolphe Guéroult and the republican Léonor Havin signed a petition demanding the creation of absolute gratuity. Deputies of all political persuasions rose to debate the issue. Even the duc de Morny intervened to speak on behalf of the petition. Conservatives led by de Parieu and the future minister of public instruction, Segris, however, got the upper hand and argued convincingly that absolute gratuity would place an unfair tax burden on the wealthy. The liberal press attempted to influence the legislators and turn back the tide. La Presse, for example, pointedly asked where these conservatives were when credits were voted for the wars in Cochin China and Mexico. The only legitimate and necessary war, it professed, was the guerre à l'ignorance. But the conservative opposition managed to hold sway, and ultimately the petition was defeated 225 to 16.[14]

Undaunted by the defeat of the republican proposal, Duruy had faith that opponents would soon be converted by the mounting tide of public opinion in favor of gratuity. Already his ministry had been petitioned by the general councils of Jura, Allier, Côte-d'Or, Loiret, Vosges, Creuse, Saône-et-Loire, Corrèze, Basses-Pyrénées, and Hautes-Alpes for absolute gratuity and by the councils of Corrèze, Loiret, and Basses-Pyrénées for obligation. The literature favoring gratuity and obligation was growing annually, and after the January, 1864, legislative debates, the liberal and republican press gave continuous support to the cause. Additionally, Charles Robert had published his De la necessité de rendre l'instruction primaire obligatoire en France (1861) and other brochures arguing that the 1860 Treaty of Commerce with

13. Pillet's report in F(17) 9115, AN.
14. RIP, 1864, pp. 713, 697.

England made gratuitous and compulsory education imperative. Even students at the Sorbonne rallied to the cause in their newspaper *La Rive Gauche*.[15]

But the task of converting opponents was still a difficult and complex one. The gratuity issue, already complicated by its relation to volatile social and cultural issues, was endangered somewhat by its link to obligation but more so by its association with a movement to secularize the schools (*laicité*). Duruy would have preferred to have omitted the latter, but some of his most enthusiastic supporters in the liberal and anticlerical press saw gratuity, obligation, and laicization as all of one piece. As a consequence, the principle of gratuity was attacked by a broader spectrum of opposition than it would have had otherwise. Most of the criticism came from classical liberals, whose prevalence in nineteenth-century France Dennis Sherman has demonstrated, and from conservatives. The classical liberals, respectful of education on its own terms, were nevertheless appalled that Frenchmen might be coerced into sending their children to school. Thus the liberal *Le Temps*, for example, protested that obligation was despotic. Even the conservative press borrowed this argument, which explains the otherwise surprising protest of the monarchist *L'Union* that the measures were a travesty of liberalism. But most of the conservative protest was fueled either by concerns over the costs of gratuity or over the damage that would be done to the Church and religion. The religious schools, outside of those run by certain orders such as the Christian Brothers, would be forced to close their doors because they would not be able to compete with the free state schools, and French youth would be channeled into Godless public schools, which would "*scientifier*" everybody. Arguments against gratuity went on and on; some critics protested that given the deplorable conditions of schools in the countryside, gratuity and obligation were a material and physical impossibility; others argued that discipline in the schools would be destroyed by the addition of unruly children from the lowest socioeconomic echelons of society. But Félix Dupanloup of Orleans was the critic who threw up the red flag by asserting at the Congress of Malines in August, 1864, that gratuity was socialistic. In sum, many of

15. Seignobos, *Le déclin de l'empire et l'établissement de la Troisième République*, 42.

the old controversies over education which had been prevalent in the
debates of the 1840s were revived in 1864 with the same spirit of
party.[16]

What is perhaps most surprising is that Duruy could not count on
the full support of public school officials and teachers. Few *universitaires* still believed that education should be confined to the governing classes, but though most favored the extension of popular education, they were divided on how to achieve that object. One group
favored a gradual approach, allowing popular education to extend itself naturally as larger portions of the masses came to appreciate it.
Anticipating the argument of François Furet and Jacques Ozouf that
the spread of literacy was a function of social demand, they believed
that people could not be forced to become literate and educated even if
the law said they must be. After all, they pointed out, Prussia still had
a hard core of 600,000 uneducated children. The other group favored
state intervention, arguing cogently that the modern state could ill afford to wait for the natural evolution of attitudes and values among
the illiterate. Holders of both opinions, for the most part, had no particular quarrel with the principle of gratuity, but the first group objected strenuously to the measures that would be attached to the implementation of gratuity, and it was on these grounds that many
universitaires departed from the wishes of their minister. Aristide Beslais has estimated that only 2 rectors (out of 17), 4 inspectors of academy out of every 100, 26 primary inspectors out of every 196, and 19
out of every 100 of the *instituteurs* supported absolute gratuity. How
many favored obligation is unclear. Of the 1,116 *instituteurs* who
wrote to Rouland in 1861, 457 were in favor of obligation (302 of
these demanded penal sanctions), and 216 (including 114 from the
group of 457 favoring obligation) were in favor of absolute gratuity.
Sixty-six were against absolute gratuity, but a sizable number favored
some form of demigratuity.[17] Only two conclusions can be drawn with

16. Dennis Sherman, "The Meaning of Economic Liberalism in Mid-Nineteenth
Century France," *History of Political Economy*, VI (1974), 171–99; *JGIP*, 1864, pp.
804, 78; excerpt from the Catholic *Le monde* in *RIP*, 1865, p. 673; Rohr, *Victor Duruy, ministre de Napoléon III*, 137–38.
17. Furet and Ozouf, *Lire et écrire*, I, 57 and *passim*; Aristide Beslais, "Obligation,
gratuité, laicité," *La revue socialiste*, no. 160 (February, 1963), 176–77; Robert, *De
l'ignorance des populations ouvrières et rurales de France*, 35–36, 44, 46, 50, 53.

certainty from these figures and the archival reports. First, it is clear that there were as many divergent opinions on gratuity and obligation among educators as there were among the educated public at large. Educators were not simply accepting the best judgment of their minister. And second, schoolteachers who opposed absolute gratuity did so largely because they knew that the loss of tuition money would diminish their already meager salaries, at least until the traditionally penurious deputies were willing to guarantee them a living wage.

The staff in the primary education division at the ministry and especially Charles Robert had been working since October, 1864, on the details of an omnibus primary education bill that included provisions for free and compulsory education. In January, 1865, the draft of the bill was sent to the Council of State for approval. Meanwhile, it was also under discussion at a joint session of the Private Council (Conseil privé) and the Council of Ministers. Although the emperor and empress were anxious to associate the regime with educational reform and lent Duruy strong moral support during the joint session meetings, the provisions for gratuity and obligation ran into heavy opposition. The majority of imperial advisers protested that absolute gratuity was "too radical."[18] The duc de Morny and Prince Napoleon were alone in supporting it enthusiastically. In the wake of this conflict, Napoleon decided to establish a special commission comprised of Persigny, Marshal Jean-Baptiste Vaillant, Duruy, and Prince Napoleon to study alternatives.

Disappointed but undeterred by the formidable opposition, Duruy decided to make a strong written appeal to the emperor. In a letter of February 6, he pointed out the political and economic advantages of the new measure and discussed how gratuity might be implemented. Gratuity and obligation would benefit the regime both abroad in its rivalry with England and Germany and at home in combating the growing opposition from political factions on the left. Elaborating on the latter, Duruy advised the emperor:

> From a political point of view, it is urgent to act: against the Orleanists, by offering a law of 1865 as an answer to that of 1833 of which they never

18. Harold Kurtz, *The Empress Eugénie, 1826–1920* (Cambridge, Mass., 1964), 196–97. Kurtz, who has read the empress's letters in the Alba Archives, claims that Eugénie collaborated more effectively with Duruy than with any other minister during the Second Empire. *JGIP*, 1865, p. 82.

cease to boast; against the clericals, who live in darkness, by creating light; against the republicans, by stealing their ammunition. The Baron de Seebach, minister of Saxony, heard the son of Arago say: "Gratuity and obligation, the emperor will never implement them; he is not liberal enough; but if he does implement them, he will register a coup against us from which it will be very difficult to recover." [19]

Although gratuity would necessitate the imposition of new taxes, there were three possible courses of action: the *grand projet*, the *moyen projet*, and the *petit projet*. The *grand projet* would place the full responsibility for absolute gratuity on the state. Over a period of three years the legislature would have to augment the budget for primary education by 7 million francs annually until the requisite 27 million francs was attained. The *moyen projet* would distribute the financial responsibility among the state, the departments, and the communes. Each commune would be required to add three additional centimes of each tax franc and the departments, two additional centimes; the state would contribute the remaining money. The third plan, the *petit projet*, would assign the total financial responsibility to the communes, although only on a voluntary basis. To elect the *petit projet*, however, was to elect the status quo because communes already had the option of creating free schools. Clearly, this option would result in little improvement in the immediate future. Duruy argued that it was "no crime" to impose new taxes for primary education on the wealthy because they could afford them and because they did not represent the numerical majority of the nation. "With universal suffrage," he counseled the emperor in a poignant statement, "the government has only being unpopular with the masses to fear." [20]

Napoleon seemed persuaded by Duruy's letter. In his speech from the throne on February 15, 1865, he proclaimed that "in a land of universal suffrage every citizen should know how to read and write." He announced that a bill on primary education would be submitted shortly to the legislature. But by this time the Council of State had already eliminated the principle of obligation from the draft bill and was diminishing the provision on gratuity. Furthermore, opposition to the two principles had fully crystallized among the ministers. On February 27, a distraught Duruy complained to the emperor: "M. Boudet

19. Duruy, *Notes et souvenirs*, I, 211.
20. *Ibid.*, 213.

[the minister of the interior] told Robert, my secretary-general, this morning, 'We are all against the project of your minister; it should suffice to put a little money into this business and then finish with it. Then there will be no problems.'"[21]

Traditionally, ministerial consensus was unnecessary in this authoritarian regime, but the overwhelming opposition of his colleagues was beginning to be a decided problem, particularly because the magistrates in the Council of State shared similar views. Yet Duruy realized that the emperor could intervene in his behalf and that favorable public opinion could also exert important pressures. It must have been this intellection, as well as knowledge that Napoleon essentially supported his principles, that prompted Duruy to publish a lengthy report on free and compulsory education in the *Moniteur*. The report was nothing less than an undisguised bid for public support against Duruy's unsympathetic colleagues, and it drew public attention to the schism that existed in the Council of Ministers, a novelty for the Second Empire.[22]

The report, which appeared on March 6, 1865, began with a statement on the weaknesses of primary education in France and then gave a long discussion of the principles of gratuity and obligation. In the introduction, Duruy noted that the illiteracy rate in France had been declining over the years but that the recent conscript figures (see the map below) proved that it was still too high, especially compared with the Prussian average of only 4 percent illiteracy among conscripts. The French illiteracy rate, which was undeniably higher for the nation as a whole than it was for conscripts, was an obstacle to political, social, and economic development. Furthermore, it seemed to Duruy that illiteracy was related to immorality, incivility, and (as Baron Charles Dupin's famous statistics suggested) crime—and crime was on the ascendancy in the Second Empire.[23]

Faulty pedagogical methodology certainly was responsible for some

21. Victor Duruy to Napoleon III, February 27, 1865, copy of a letter in possession of Mme Albert Duruy.

22. *JGIP*, 1865, p. 163; *RIP*, 1865, p. 785.

23. Howard Zehr, "The Modernization of Crime in Germany and France, 1830–1913," *Journal of Social History*, VIII (Summer, 1975), 128. Duruy's judgment was fairly typical for Victorians, as, for example, the reports in F(17) 4358–63, AN, demonstrate. But not all educated Frenchmen shared this opinion, particularly not those who knew of studies in the 1830s which revealed the absence of a correlation between education and low rates of criminality. See Françoise André Isambert, "Religion et développe-

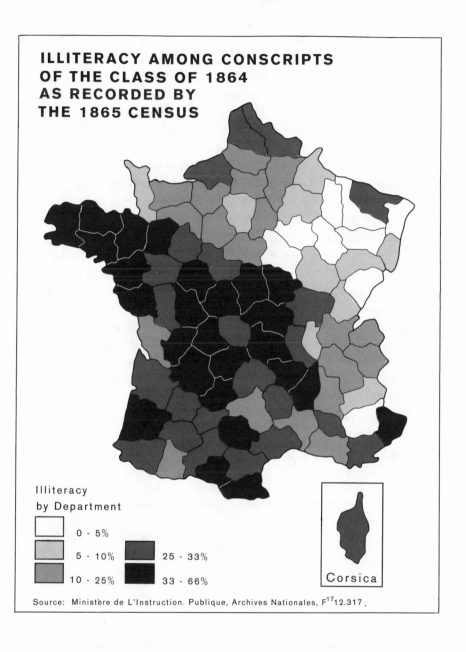

ILLITERACY AMONG CONSCRIPTS OF THE CLASS OF 1864 AS RECORDED BY THE 1865 CENSUS

Illiteracy by Department

0 - 5%
5 - 10%
10 - 25%
25 - 33%
33 - 66%

Corsica

Source: Ministère de L'Instruction. Publique, Archives Nationales, F^{17}12.317 .

of this illiteracy, but Duruy attributed the greater part of it to poor school attendance. Of the roughly 4 million children who attended school in 1863, only 2.5 million attended with some regularity, according to Charles Robert's computations. A ministerial survey of the most common reasons for nonattendance showed that seven excuses were most typically offered by parents to functionaries: lack of schools, distance of the school from the child's home, difficulties of communication, physical infirmities, idiotism, the expense of schooling, and the uselessness of education. In any event, few students attended school for more than four or five months a year, and only 40 percent remained in school after taking first communion at the age of twelve. The latter, Duruy observed, was not a problem in Protestant countries, where first communion was postponed until a child was sixteen.[24]

A forceful if not total solution to these problems and to the problem of getting unschooled children schooled seemed to lie in the creation of free and compulsory education. Beginning first with the concept of obligation, Duruy traced its history and all of the attempts that had been made to introduce it in France. Then he sketched the arguments that were being used against compulsory education and offered rejoinders to each. A paraphrased summary of these arguments with Duruy's rebuttals is as follows:

Major Arguments Against Compulsion in 1865	Duruy's Rejoinders
1. It is an unjust limitation of parental freedom by the state, a violation of the *droit de famille*.	1. Parents have certain rights, but as participants in society they have to bend to the will of the state when the common good of all is at issue.

---

ment dans la France du XIXe siècle," *Archives de Sociologie des Religions*, VIII (January–June, 1963), 64. Curiously, in 1866, the ministry commissioned its own study of the issue (*BAIP*, V [1866], 186), and thereafter Duruy no longer spoke of illiteracy and criminality in the same breath. Baron Charles Dupin's *Conclusion des recherches statistiques sur les rapports de l'instruction populaire avec la moralité des diverses parties de la France* (Paris, 1827), argued that a substantial proportion of the criminal population was illiterate and argued that schooling could divert many young people from a life of crime.

24. Charles Robert, *Instruction primaire* (Strasbourg, 1863), 17; F(17*) 3160, AN. Duruy obviously did not know that the percentage of children leaving school at about twelve years of age was high in England also (Johnson, "Educational Policy and Social Control in Early Victorian England," 109).

2. An already authoritarian state would gain an unnecessary accretion in its powers.

2. There is nothing political about obligation. The state would not dictate which school a child should attend, only that children should know how to read, write, and count. Obligation is no violation of liberalism.

3. Parents will lose the economic benefits of children.

3. The notion that the child is the property of the father is "pagan and false." Fathers who subject themselves to short-term sacrifices will profit in the long run from filial respect. Further, these sacrifices *contribute to the moral life of the family* because fathers will be forced to plan family life more carefully.

4. Obligation is financially and materially impractical in this epoch.

4. Nonsense. If Paris can be rebuilt and 50 to 60 million francs spent on an opera alone, then this objection is unfounded.

5. Someone will have to pay for obligation.

5. True, but the new tax burden will fall on those who can most afford it.

6. Discipline in the schools will be destroyed by the influx of so many poor children.

6. Unruly and uncooperative children can be handled just as the state handles unruly citizens.

7. In communes where there are no religious schools, parents will be forced to send their children to public schools.

7. True, but there is nothing to fear in public schools. "What is taught there is what children of all religions should know. . . . The explanation of [particular] dogma belongs to the ministers of the different religions and belongs elsewhere."

Duruy's rejoinder to the last argument embodied his concept of secular morality for the schools. It was not atheistic; it was neutral. Duruy claimed in his memoirs that he had had no desire to create religious war over the issue of obligation such as the legislators of the Third Republic did.[25]

25. Ministère de l'Instruction Publique, *L'administration de l'instruction publique de 1863 à 1869* (Paris, 1870), 180 (hereafter *AIP*); Duruy, *Notes et souvenirs*, I, 201.

Gratuity was treated in Duruy's report just as obligation was, first with an exposition of its history, then with an exploration of the objections to it. Duruy reported that with certain exceptions (for example, in the Landes), the rich generally opposed gratuity because they realized that they would have to pay for it.[26] Many religious orders, especially those that charged tuition and would suffer new competition from free public schools, were opposed. And several communes, for example those in Haute-Vienne, opposed gratuity, fearing that increased school enrollment would saddle municipalities with the expense of hiring more teachers and building new schools.[27] Duruy hoped to overcome the opposition by exposing it.

Such was the report that appeared in the *Moniteur* on March 6. Ominously, the *Moniteur* did not include at the bottom of the report the usual notation "Lu et apprové" (by the emperor), which had in fact appeared on the final copy Duruy submitted. Furthermore, on the next day, apparently on Rouher's instigation, the *Moniteur* announced that the views contained in the report were the "personal" views of the minister, not those of the government.[28] The report had been released to the public, it explained, "because of the importance of the information it contained." When Duruy learned how the *Moniteur* had treated his report, he contacted the emperor and asked him to force the paper to correct itself. But the emperor took no action. The outraged Duruy then decided to tender his resignation. The emperor, however, refused to accept it and prevailed upon Duruy to stay and continue his fight.[29]

The press now speculated rather freely on the *Moniteur* incident. The *Courrier du dimanche* told its readers that Duruy had displayed extraordinary mettle in not resigning after such a "slap in the face." *L'Epoque*, taking up Rouher's defense, and the *RIP*, taking Duruy's, battled over the issues both in their succeeding numbers and, after lawsuits for slander were brought, in court. Joseph Perrin, writing in *L'Epoque* stated proudly that *L'Epoque* was the only nonreligious paper to take a courageous stand against the minister; all of the other nonreligious journals either sympathized with Duruy or remained si-

26. Report for the Landes, April 2, 1866, F(17) 9375, AN.
27. Fourth report, 1865, for Haute-Vienne, *ibid*.
28. *JGIP*, 1865, p. 358.
29. Adam, *Mes sentiments et nos idées avant 1870*, 17. Her father was privy to the information through Prosper Merimée.

lent. The truly curious reaction, Perrin noted, was that of *Le Constitutionnel*, which had an unbroken tradition of praising the government and its ministers. Caught in an uncommon dilemma, *Le Constitutionnel* "has held itself strangely silent." Perrin conjectured, "Are there" then two governments, the one public, represented by the *Moniteur* and the councils which reject the absurd principle of free and compulsory education; the other, intimate and hidden, which prepares in secret a renewed offensive for these principles?"[30] Certainly Perrin's suggestion seemed to explain the otherwise strange exchange between the emperor and Duruy.

During March and April the Council of State was still working on the draft bill from the ministry, and Duruy continued to speak publicly in its behalf. Gratuity already existed in Paris and in many French towns; it was now needed in the impoverished countryside. Lifting the educational level of the whole of France was a matter of national pride; France no longer was the leader of the civilized world. Then, for the first time publicly, Duruy argued, through a statistical comparison, that gratuity and obligation were the only means by which the state might check the progress of the religious congregations. In 1843, the religious orders had taught only 22 percent of the elementary school population. But in twenty years they had more than doubled their number of schools and students. They had "conquered" nearly one million (903,757) students, and by 1863 they taught 37 percent of the elementary school population.[31]

The legislature also discussed the issues. Several republicans, especially Havin and Carnot, spoke in favor of the ministry's bill; the opponents, however, continued to speak of the "violence and brutality" of coercion, and de Parieu strenuously objected that the state could not afford gratuity. Joseph Perrin, writing in *L'Epoque*, noted also that several deputies, already irritated by the increase in expenses for public works, were flatly opposed to spending money on any new causes, no matter what they were. These same men became enraged later when several members of the opposition, notably Jules Simon, Havin, Guéroult, and Oscar Planat, proposed a loan of 140 million francs for primary instruction. When the debates were finished, a vote was taken

30. *JGIP*, 1865, pp. 205, 357–58, 259.
31. *AIP*, 206–207.

on an earlier amendment that the republicans and especially Jules Simon had presented, which simply favored the institution of absolute gratuity, and it was defeated 240 to 17. That vote, Joseph Perrin told his readers, had great significance. Even though the Corps législatif had not voted directly on a government bill, it had registered a direct vote against a minister of the government.[32]

Perrin's observation was most perspicacious. By voting against the Simon amendment and indirectly against Duruy, or at least against one of the major principles he espoused, the legislature came close to exercising in 1865 a privilege that it would be granted in the reforms of January 19, 1867—the right of directly interpellating ministers. The republicans, wittingly or not, had contrived this singular turn of events. Additionally, the vote against the Simon amendment meant that on the issue of gratuity Duruy was now rejected by both the legislature and the government. Had Duruy not chosen to call attention so publicly to the difference between his intentions and the government's, he would not have found himself in such an extraordinary situation. On the other hand, his decision to take a stand usefully revealed at the time and reveals for us today how complicated the constitutional balance of the authoritarian regime had become as the result of both the liberal concessions the emperor had made since 1860 and the freedom he gave to Duruy in his position as minister.

The Council of State continued to debate Duruy's bill through March, April, and May. In March, Joseph Perrin observed that Duruy, hoping to retain some of his original objectives, was placed in the anomalous situation of having to support before the Council of State half-measures that were not his own but those of his ministerial colleagues. This behavior was typical of a cabinet, not a council of ministers. Perrin claimed that Duruy had unwittingly played a key role in this momentary and delicate transformation of the constitution of 1852.[33] Eventually, the Council of State approved a modified version of Duruy's bill, which stated that the government could offer financial assistance to any commune that wished to transfer some of its tax revenues to the school budget to create free primary education. Thus Duruy's original plan was compromised considerably, but Duruy took

32. *RIP*, 1865, pp. 783, 17; *JGIP*, 1865, pp. 314, 258.
33. *JGIP*, 1865, p. 181.

momentary consolation in having at least won support for the principle of gratuity at the national level. Unfortunately, however, the bill arrived at the legislature too late for debate. Duruy was forced to wait for a new legislative session the following year.

In the interim, the official *Bulletin administratif de l'instruction publique* (*BAIP*) continued to encourage the establishment of absolute gratuity. It carefully announced every instance in which a municipal council decided to vote gratuity. In December, 1865, it launched an even more vigorous campaign in favor of absolute gratuity, and the press responded proportionately. Indeed, gratuity and compulsion continued to be burning issues throughout the rest of 1865 and 1866. The *JGIP* maintained its opposition to both principles with the editor, Charles Louandre, contending that once the two precepts were established for primary education, it would be only a matter of time before they would be demanded for secondary education.[34] The clerical and anticlerical press battled over the religious significance of gratuity and obligation, the former charging that the supporters of absolute gratuity were, for the most part, adversaries of Christian education; the latter taunting the clergy by claiming that young children would be freed from the yoke of the Church.[35] Books and pamphlets covered the argument in detail. Jules Simon's *L'Ecole* (1865), which studied the political and social ramifications of free and compulsory education, was read widely. And anonymous brochures such as *De l'instruction obligatoire comme remède aux maux sociaux* (1866) abounded.

The debate over gratuity and obligation became so lively that it began to irritate Duruy's ministerial colleagues. In August, 1865, they asked him to refrain from speaking about gratuity and obligation. Duruy refused, politely and firmly.[36] He hoped to increase support for his principles by keeping the issue before the public and continuing to demonstrate their logic.

Articles on popular education continued to appear in the press, stimulated further by the "new crusade" that was launched in its favor by the *BAIP* in December, 1865.[37] The one noticeable change in the

34. *Ibid.*, p. 474.
35. See *JGIP*, 1866, p. 93. The article by Louis Jourdan in *Le Siècle* for the second week of March, 1867, is a good example.
36. Excerpt from *L'Opinion nationale*, *JGIP*, 1865, p. 499.
37. *JGIP*, 1865, p. 766, and 1866, p. 158.

campaign was the virtual disappearance, in both the *BAIP* and the liberal press, of references to obligation, although *L'Opinion nationale* denied that the ministry had dropped its desire for compulsion.[38] A probable explanation for the change in official publications is that a significant political shift occurred at this time. Two of the staunchest supporters of gratuity and obligation, the duc de Morny and Prince Napoleon, had disappeared from the scene. Morny had died in early March, 1865, and Prince Napoleon, "Plon-Plon," had resigned as vice-president of the Private Council in May, 1865, after he was reprimanded by the emperor for his liberal and anticlerical speech at Ajaccio. The conservative and dedicated authoritarian Rouher, Duruy's archenemy at court, then became the dominant political power next to the throne. When the *Moniteur* of September 13, 1865, announced the end of liberal concessions, Duruy must have quickly decided to limit his public campaign to the less controversial issue of gratuity.

While waiting for the new legislative session to begin, Duruy used his administrative powers to make certain lesser changes concerning problems that had troubled him ever since he took office. In March, 1866, convinced that the limitation placed on gratuity by Fortoul was a violation of the law of 1850, he abrogated the ceiling on the number of indigent children who could be admitted gratuitously to the schools and promoted the abrogation as evidence of the emperor's "constant solicitude for the laboring classes." This act made more than 100,000 children eligible for gratuity. In June, to help teachers who suffered financial losses as a result of the extension of gratuity, he established a special fund for subventioning salaries. Finally, irritated that many communes that were legally obligated to establish schools had not yet done so, Duruy instructed prefects to apply new pressure on the negligent municipal councillors. To stimulate education by other means, he established prizes for the fifteen-year-old and eighteen-year-old currently doing agricultural or manual work who best remembered what they had learned in school, and he commissioned the publication of statistical tables showing illiteracy rates for the various departments and arrondissements. From these tables, maps were developed and published (apparently by independent groups such as the Ligue de

38. See *JGIP*, 1866, pp. 170–72, 281; also see the excerpt from Charles Sauvestre's article in *L'Opinion nationale* in *JGIP*, 1866, p. 313.

l'enseignement), and Duruy urged local officials and teachers to display them in all schoolrooms and public facilities. He was no doubt hoping to stimulate a sense of competition among localities.[39]

The bill on primary education, which had arrived at the Corps législatif too late for discussion in 1865, was resubmitted. It was sent first to a committee for preliminary review, where it became entangled in lengthy discussions. Both Duruy and Jules Simon complained publicly about the delay, but the bill was reported out of committee only at the end of the legislative session, too late for serious action. The legislature voted to save it for 1867.[40]

On January 17, 1867, the emperor announced that as his "New Year's gift to the people," he intended to grant a number of new political concessions. The law on meetings would be made more liberal, the press would no longer be responsible to prefects, and the legislature would gain the right to interpellate ministers on government policies. On the same day Napoleon convened his ministers and demanded their resignations, explaining that he wished to form a more liberal cabinet. But when he had constructed his new cabinet, there were few changes. Marshal Adolphe Niel replaced Randon at the Ministry of War, and two political neutrals were given the ministries of Marine and Public Works. Everyone else stayed in place, including Duruy. On Count Walewski's advice, Napoleon had secretly offered the Ministry of Public Instruction to Emile Ollivier in a bold effort to neutralize some of the republican opposition, but Ollivier refused this "most enviable of ministries" until the government made additional liberal concessions.[41]

Thus Duruy remained in office to superintend the parliamentary de-

39. *BAIP*, V (1866), 87–89; *JGIP*, 1866, pp. 73–74; confidential circular, June 22, 1866, F(17) 1475, AN; *BAIP*, II (1864), 150–52 (circular, August 13, 1864); Committee of the Groupe Havrais of the Ligue de l'enseignement to Victor Duruy, August 20, 1868, and Victor Duruy to the inspector of academy of the Seine-Inférieure, August 31, 1868, F(17) 2681, AN. According to Ernest Legouvé, Duruy also had a large map of France on the wall of his office that gave the status of literacy in the various parts of France. The white areas stood for those places where Frenchmen could read "very well"; the gray areas for those where Frenchmen could "scarcely read"; and the black areas for those where Frenchmen were "totally illiterate." Duruy once told Legouvé: "I stand before this map just like a conqueror before the country that he wishes to invade" (Legouvé, *Dernier travail, derniers souvenirs* [Paris, 1898], 260–71).

40. Duruy, *Notes et souvenirs*, I, 221; Rohr, *Victor Duruy, ministre de Napoléon III*, 144.

41. Excerpts from Ollivier's *Le 19 janvier*, chap. XIV, in *JGIP*, 1869, 146–49.

bates on his bill. It was resubmitted on February 15, 1867, the day after the emperor, in his speech from the throne, had urged the legislature to support it. The bill was now given a full hearing. It was reported out of committee quickly and was discussed in the midst of great excitement over the new right of interpellation. During six meetings all of the old issues concerning state education were revived. Charles Kolb-Bernard, one of the leaders of the Catholic opposition, for example, denounced the continuing state monopoly over education, calling it part of the "political pantheism" of the regime. Jules Simon argued that the bill did not extend educational reform sufficiently. If the state really wished to express its liberalism and true concern for educational reform, it would terminate the *lettre d'obédience* privilege of the female teaching orders and depoliticize the nomination and revocation of teachers by transferring this authority from the prefects to the municipal councils. It would implement absolute gratuity and create *lycées* for women. Spurred by Simon's comments, the republicans proposed two amendments to the bill, one to create absolute gratuity, the other to transfer the power of appointing teachers from prefects to inspectors of academy. Neither amendment passed; indeed, the first was defeated 211 to 32. Deputy Stiévenard-Bethune avowed that he would never vote for absolute gratuity until the state had enough money to repair all of the miserable hovels that posed as schools in the empire. Deputy François Malézieux resurrected the traditional fear of *déclassement* and argued that the expansion of primary education among the working classes would only make them malcontent and ungovernable; workers were better left in their "blissful ignorance." Such was the opposition with which Duruy had to contend. He agreed with the liberals that the bill was a compromise, but after all, he told them, the ministry was forced to work within the realm of the possible ("À chaque jour sa peine!"). And realm of the possible it was, because at the end of the sixth session a direct vote was taken on the bill, and it passed unanimously.[42]

Duruy was thus the first minister of the Second Empire to have successfully defended his "own" bill before the legislature. This political accomplishment was specifically noted by Edmond Goumy in the

42. *JGIP*, 1867, pp. 205, 231, 238, 159, 144; extracts of the deliberations of the Corps législatif in the *Moniteur universel* beginning March 2, 1867.

RIP: "It is to M. Duruy that this signal honor of inaugurating the modest renaissance of the parliamentary regime has fallen."[43]

On March 15, the bill was sent to the Senate. Debate was so lively that the *RIP* predicted that the Senate would exercise its new suspensive veto and return the bill to the legislature. But Duruy dissuaded the senators, and the bill was passed on April 3, 99 to 1.

Promulgated on April 10, 1867, the law quickly became known as the *loi Duruy* or Duruy Law. Article 1, which was modeled somewhat after a bill Rouland had developed earlier, required all communes of five hundred or more inhabitants to establish an *école de filles*.[44] It thus effectively granted to female education what the Guizot Law had given to male education thirty-four years earlier. Additionally, it required all mixed schools to hire sewing teachers. The first provision anticipated the establishment of eight thousand new girls' schools, the second, the establishment of sixteen thousand new sewing teacher positions. A jubilant Duruy later wrote to the emperor, "Imagine the number of women who are blessing you; their appreciation is an electoral victory [of sorts] which should be respected."[45]

Article 8 provided for the establishment of absolute gratuity in all communes that were willing to allocate four additional centimes per tax franc for the purpose; if the additional allocation was not sufficient for absolute gratuity, the department, and if necessary, the state, would have to provide a subsidy. In essence, this provision represented Duruy's *moyen projet* as described in the February 6, 1865, letter to the emperor. Duruy, of course, would have much preferred the enactment of the *grand projet*, giving responsibility for the financing of absolute gratuity solely to the state, but he had at least won the government's oblique support for the principle of absolute gratuity, and he counted that as an accomplishment.[46]

As a corollary to the gratuity provision, the law provided in article 15 for the creation of incentive funds (*caisses des écoles*), which would be used to recompense assiduous students, buy clothing, food, furni-

43. *RIP*, 1867, p. 769.
44. Prefects were instructed not to press for the creation of girls' schools too quickly lest they excite opposition that would compromise the establishment of these schools for a longer period of time (F(17) 9115, AN).
45. Victor Duruy to Napoleon III, undated copy of a letter in possession of Mme Albert Duruy.
46. *Ibid.*

ture, and textbooks for indigent children, encourage the establishment of adult education classes, and purchase additional books for school libraries. Approved without debate by the legislature because it necessitated no state expenditure, article 15 called upon the generosity of municipal councils and philanthropists.[47]

Only one change—but an important one and the first since 1834—was made in the primary school curriculum: article 16 elevated history and geography from the list of optional subjects. Article 16 enjoyed overwhelming support from the legislature, its sole opponent having been the bishop of Amiens, who feared, as he later wrote to Jules Baroche, that Catholic children would be taught to respect Protestants as equal members of the Christian family. Although Duruy was no doubt the article's most vigorous champion, he later issued a confidential circular to rectors asking them to guard carefully against the teaching of disloyal historical interpretations.[48]

Article 2 of the law of April 10, 1867, was a victory for rural education in that the village schools (*écoles de hameau*) were accorded legal recognition. Like the mixed schools, these village schools were a financial and educational expedient, as poignantly described by the primary inspector of Haute-Savoie: "In winter when the roads are covered with snow, the regular school in the main village of the commune is often too distant for the young child. It is either these [rural] schools or nothing."[49] The village schools were attractive to the small communities because a *brevet de capacité* was not obligatory for village schoolteachers so they could be run by anyone who wished to teach. Therefore, the communities could pay village teachers (known as adjuncts) whatever they wished. Not surprisingly, the quality of education in these schools was poor, but their creation was a step in the right direction. After the passage of the Duruy Law, two thousand new village schools appeared in the countryside.

Finally, the law of April 10, 1867, contained several articles that regulated the income of teachers. Articles 4 and 5 set minimum annual

---

47. *BAIP*, VIII (1867), 6–7; X (1868), 494–95.
48. Furet and Ozouf, *Lire et écrire*, I, 165; Bishop of Amiens to Jules Baroche, January 21, 1868, F(19) 3972, AN; confidential circular to rectors, November 24, 1868, F(17) 1475, AN.
49. Report on primary instruction for Haute-Savoie, academy of Chambéry, November, 1865, F(17) 4360, AN.

salaries in regular schools (boys', girls', and mixed schools) at 400 and 500 francs for *institutrices* and in village schools at 350, 400, and 500 francs for adjunct teachers (*instituteurs* and *institutrices*), depending on their rank. Eight other articles provided compensation for teachers who either had accepted the additional burdens of adult education or had suffered a loss in salary as a result of the creation of absolute gratuity in their municipality.[50] The indemnity offered to teachers of adult education courses should be seen as a canny means of raising elementary schoolteachers' salaries.[51]

Duruy, the first minister of the Second Empire to have successfully defended a bill of his own before the Corps législatif and the Senate, emerged with a greatly strengthened ministry. Most of the press and most *universitaires* hailed the passage of the *loi Duruy*. Only a few criticized it as not going far enough. The *RIP* had hoped that the law would also establish secondary education for girls, *La Presse* wanted an article improving retirement benefits, and certain liberal papers made their usual plea for an end to the *lettre d'obédience* practice and the depoliticization of teaching appointments by giving the power of appointment and dismissal back to the municipal councils. But Jules Simon, acting as a spokesman for liberals and moderate republicans, wrote to Duruy assuring him that it was absurd to expect so many major changes in one law. Simon congratulated Duruy on achieving so much.[52]

Not all of the press was as sober as the *RIP* and *La Presse* had been. The satirical *Le Charivari* had a bit of fun with some of the hyperbolic statements Duruy had made at the Corps législatif. One of its cartoons showed Frenchmen leaving a cabaret to march to a school across the street. Another depicted a prison bearing a sign that announced that it was closed for lack of prisoners (*cause d'inutilité publique*). Next to the prison was a glowing street light with the words *Instruction Primaire* painted on its glass encasing. Choosing to join in the fun and to

50. The full text of the law is in *BAIP*, VII (1867), 341–45. Details on the implementation of the law are in F(17) 9116–18, AN.

51. Carter Jefferson, "Worker Education in England and France, 1800–1914," *Comparative Studies in Society and History* VI (1964), 355; Duruy, *Notes et souvenirs*, I, 230–31.

52. *RIP*, 1867, p. 770; *JGIP*, 1865, p. 355, and 1867, pp. 165–66; Jules Simon to Victor Duruy, undated, Duruy letters, 114 AP-1-XXII, AN.

redirect the satire, Duruy wrote to the editors of *Le Charivari*, thanking them for their support.[53]

Lest it be implied that the press forgot the principle of obligation, it should be noted that the editors and contributors to the *JGIP*, the *RIP*, and *Le Charivari* all continued to puzzle over the ministry's silence on the subject.[54] Duruy had spoken at the legislative session of March 2, 1867, of the moral obligation that gratuity implied, but he said nothing about obligation per se. And thereafter the *BAIP* made no mention of it. That Duruy had decided to eliminate obligation from the goals of his administration is obvious in a reply he sent to petitioners of obligation in Haute-Vienne in January, 1869. "The institution of obligation," Duruy wrote, "does not coincide with the principles of the regime at the moment."[55] Had he been writing to a confidant, he probably would have admitted that he had gained all that was politically possible at the time.

The remaining two years of Duruy's administration brought a slow but steady increase in the number of communes that voted for the less controversial issue of gratuity. In 1867, just over 10 percent (3,433) of the communes in France enjoyed absolute gratuity; by 1869 some 2,814 additional communes had voted for it. In the short run this showing was a failure for Duruy, who had hoped for much more, but in the long run the law was responsible for turning aside "one of the principal obstacles to frequentation—monthly tuition." By 1876–1877, 58 percent of the children in public schools were attending free of charge.[56]

The law of April 10, 1867, was certainly the climax of Duruy's reforms in primary education in that it was a comprehensive national law, but it was far from representing the totality of Duruy's efforts at this level. Other reforms, some substantial, others small, were promoted to deal with the various problems of primary education.

Duruy made several attempts to improve and diversify primary education. He authorized fifteen-minute recesses in the three-hour classes of the elementary schools and added music, agricultural education,

---

53. *Le Charivari*, March 24, April 8, 16, 1867.
54. *JGIP*, 1867, pp. 119, 174; *RIP*, 1868, p. 706; *Le Charivari*, February 15, 1868.
55. F(17) 2511, AN.
56. Draft for the *Exposé de la situation de l'Empire*, 1869, p. 20, in F(17) 2677, AN; Furet and Ozouf, *Lire et écrire*, I, 173.

and gymnastics to the curriculum. The program in agricultural education was a response not only to the widespread economic misery of
many rural areas of France but also to the desertion of the countryside, which had become an issue of national concern. Indeed, Duruy even attempted to give hope to those who were complaining that it
was difficult for young men to find suitably educated young women to
marry in rural areas by devising, with his subordinates, a special syllabus of agricultural education for girls (see Appendix C). The program of gymnastic education, which grew out of Duruy's knowledge
of the development of sports and gymnastics in England and the German states, and his novel (for that time) conviction that exercise and
physical fitness were essential to the well-being of students prompted
an amusing set of cartoons in Le Charivari showing young children
hanging from poles in classrooms like monkeys swinging on trapezes.
Duruy also tried to make the schools more attractive by creating annual contests in the cantons (concours cantonal) between both young
and adult students in elementary classes and by promoting certificates
of primary education (certificats d'études primaires). These various
measures won Duruy many accolades from educators and the press.[57]

Duruy also continued the impetus given by Rouland for the establishment of school libraries. He regularly reminded educators of the
importance of an ample supply of good reading materials for students,
and in April, 1864, he established the Commission for School Libraries to suggest appropriate books and to alert teachers and other
authorities about books that might be dangerous to public morals and
beliefs. Lists of books approved by this commission were then printed
in departmental bulletins. Duruy urged the commission to give particular attention to books of regional and local value, including publications on local economy and industry. In 1865, Duruy sent E. A. de
l'Etang to England to research ideas that the French might borrow
from the popular library movement there. Exploiting interest in adult
education courses, he advised the directors of night school classes to

57. Decrees of July 2, 1866, February 3, 1869, and arrêté of December 21, 1867, in
AIP, 325, 749, 533; H. Forestier, "L'enquête de 1856 sur la désertion des campagnes,"
Bulletin de la Société des Sciences historiques et naturelles de l'Yonne (Auxerre), XCVII
(1959), 271–73; BAIP, V (1866), 538–47, and VIII (1867), 932–40; Le Charivari,
March 15, 1868; circular, July 11, 1865, BAIP, IV (1865), 35–37; Marcel Spivak, "Le
développement de l'éducation physique et du sport français de 1852 à 1914," Revue
d'histoire moderne et contemporaine, XXIV (1977), 34.

establish subscription drives for library books among adult students who might donate a franc or two to the cause. He encouraged private benefactors and publishers to donate useful books, especially those that taught "by examples and accounts, respect for law, love of country, [and] the sentiment for work." Hachette donated 100,000 books in 1868 alone. During the six years Duruy was in office, the number of school libraries more than doubled from about 5,000 in 1863 to more than 12,000 by 1869.[58]

To be sure, the introduction of school libraries was a slow and difficult process. Lack of sufficient money for libraries and rural apathy were probably the most important obstacles to their creation. The academic inspector in the Morbihan, for example, related that although industrial workers were greatly attracted to the idea, farmers ridiculed reading. And the inspector of Tarn-et-Garonne disclosed that the only people who read books from the school libraries were the teachers. Yet Duruy was frequently told that local authorities were the chief problem—they thought that they, not the teachers, should have control over the school libraries.[59]

This controversy over the control of the libraries was really a debate over which books were good and which were bad or dangerous, and Duruy was forced to arbitrate several disputes. The most serious one involved the library in the city of Saint-Etienne. The irony of the case was that it did much to cast suspicion on school libraries although it involved not a school library but a popular library in the city.

Several citizens of Saint-Etienne sent a petition to the Senate protesting that certain dangerous books, including Ernest Renan's *La vie de Jésus* and Pierre Proudhon's *Révolution sociale*, were available in the library. The incident probably would have been resolved routinely had Saint-Beuve not spoken so eloquently against the petition and had Baroche not chosen to submit the case to Duruy. *L'Avenir national* inflamed the dispute by publishing a letter from the students at the Ecole Normale Supérieure congratulating Saint-Beuve on his speech. Such public excitement arose that soon the empress intervened and at-

58. Anderson, *Education in France*, 147; circular, November 2, 1865, in *AIP*, 249–57; F(17) 10736; *BAIP*, IV (1865), 797; *AIP*, 256; *BAIP*, X (1868), 199; *AIP*, 859; F(17) 10736, AN.

59. See especially the reports for Lot and Tarn-et-Garonne in F(17) 10736 and the reports for Morbihan, Caen, Eure, and Côtes-du-Nord in F(17) 9376, AN.

tempted to close the Ecole Normale. Duruy acted quickly. By summoning to the fore his finest diplomatic skills, he managed to assuage the empress and spare the school, although he was forced, subsequently, to remove both the director of the school (Nisard) and the head of the scientific section (Pasteur) and to place the school under the legal restraint of a license.[60] Ultimately, the prefect of Lyons issued an *arrêté* to retire the offensive books at Saint-Etienne, and the clamor abated.

Still, the issue of good books versus bad books continued to be a problem. Frenchmen were worried not only about books that challenged accepted religious and social or political doctrines but also about books that were a threat to cultural values. As the prefect of the Ille-et-Vilaine wrote to Duruy, "People are generally suspicious of the moral standards presented by novels, and since there are so many novels in the concessions, the reputation of the school libraries is being compromised. It would be wise to reduce their numbers substantially in the future so the clergy cannot claim that the public school libraries contain too many dangerous books."[61] There is no concrete evidence that Duruy followed the advice of the prefect, but there are grounds for suspecting that he did because Duruy typically bowed to local wishes so long as he did not have to compromise one of his major principles.

One good example of Duruy's willingness to concede to local preferences is the way he handled debates over whether a school should be religious or lay. In every case that arose during his ministry, Duruy sided with the wishes of the majority of the students' fathers.[62] An-

60. Nisard remained an *inspecteur général,* and Pasteur was transferred to the Sorbonne. Duruy also managed to obtain a seat for Nisard in the Senate. These were the most favorable terms he could hope for, given the desire of the emperor and empress to close the school (Duruy, *Notes et souvenirs,* II, 241–42).
Anderson, *Education in France,* 230, has argued, "It is typical of the favourable treatment of Duruy by historians that the dismissal of Pasteur has never been held against him." But Anderson fails to take into account that most historians as well as most contemporaries of Duruy knew of his abiding friendship with Pasteur. Duruy always attended Pasteur's lectures, and he was generous in granting Pasteur leaves of absence, especially when the latter was engaged in studying the silkworm disease. See, for example, Williams, *World of Napoleon III,* 160–62.
61. Report of July 14, 1866, F(17) 9375, AN.
62. See, for example, Ministère de l'Instruction Publique, *Réponse de Son Excellence le Ministre de l'Instruction Publique à la petition des habitants de Maisons-Alfort pourtant demande d'une école laique de filles dans la dite commune* (Paris, 1865).

other good example of Duruy's open-mindedness is the way he ultimately dealt with the issue of local patois.

In *Peasants into Frenchmen*, Eugen Weber has called the patois issue
"the worst problem plaguing schoolteachers through the whole of the
nineteenth century."[63] Although it would be difficult to envision a satisfactory ranking of the importance of educational problems in the
nineteenth century, such as Weber's assertion demands, the patois
problem, an issue of sizable political and educational dimensions, was
certainly important. According to the official statistics for 1863, out
of 37,510 communes, there were 8,321 (more than half the communes
in twenty-four departments) where no French was spoken. Out of
4,018,427 children between the ages of seven and thirteen, 44,328
(about 11 percent) spoke no French, and another 1,490,269 (about 37
percent) spoke or understood French but could not write it.[64] And subjective assertions, the memoirs of the schoolteachers in 1861 for example, suggest that the problem of the patois might have been even
greater and more pervasive than the official statistics betray.

The problem with the patois was that either as a language, "a dialect that has made good," or as a full-fledged patois, "a debased dialect" (to borrow Auguste Brun's distinctions), it was a matter of cultural survival and local pride in most remote areas of France.[65] In
regions such as Provence the patois were particularly lyrical, and whole
treasuries of local folklore, superstitions, and songs were at stake.
French-speaking residents in such areas were viewed as outsiders. In
the Vaucluse, French-speaking residents were called *Franciot*, in Al-
sace, *Welch*, and in hundreds of other areas a variety of other names,
none of them complimentary. Immigrating teachers and priests alike
were forced, willingly or unwillingly, to adopt the local patois. But
once the priests had established themselves and had succeeded in kin-
dling or rekindling the faith in an area, they were often reluctant to
disturb the faith by taking a stand against the patois. Nonetheless, Duruy found that most of the priests in the southern and western portions of France were well disposed to assist him in promoting French.[66]

63. Eugen Weber, *Peasants into Frenchmen* (Stanford, 1976), 73.
64. F(17) 3160, AN.
65. Weber, *Peasants into Frenchmen*, 80.
66. Report of January 4, 1867, F(17) 9147, AN.

Only those in the northern and eastern departments, where there were strong separatist movements, refused to cooperate.

Between 1864 and 1868, there were four disputes over patois, two in the Moselle (at Créhange and Malling) and two in the Nord (at Steenvoorde and in the arrondissements of Hazebrouck and Dunkirk) in which Duruy was forced to intervene. In each case, Duruy had received complaints from families or functionaries that the clergy were forcing even French-speaking children to speak the local patois. At Créhange, Duruy refused to involve himself in the teaching of catechism in the patois, but he declared that the schools were *écoles françaises* and therefore French alone should be used. At Steenvoorde, he instructed officials to mediate the dispute without either accepting at face value the view of the clergy that French would harm the faith or "doing any direct damage to local customs." At Malling and in the arrondissements of Hazebrouck and Dunkirk he prevailed on the local bishops to intercede with their clergy, arguing in a form letter that was ultimately sent to several bishops that the acquisition of French would be particularly beneficial to the young men of the area when they sought promotions later in the army and industry. But neither Dupont des Loges (Metz) nor René Regnier (Cambrai) cooperated.[67]

Prompted by the disputes that arose and genuinely interested in the dissemination of French in the countryside, Duruy commissioned in May, 1864, a highly detailed survey of the extent of regional language and dialect usage—the only report of its kind for modern France.[68] (Table 3 gives the percentage of communes in each department where French was not spoken in 1863. As Eugen Weber has pointed out, the areas using the patois were not exclusively frontier regions.) Duruy also asked prefects for additional information on the patois and for suggestions on how French might be promoted without (now using his standard formula) "doing injury to the customs, habits and local pre-

67. The prefect of Moselle to Victor Duruy, January 10, 1865, F(17) 9147, AN; Duruy's annotation on Fleury's letter of October 27, 1866, *ibid.*; F(17) 14295; F(19) 1949, AN; Maurain, *La politique ecclésiastique du Second Empire*, 869–70; Duruy, *Notes et souvenirs*, I, 329.
68. Philippe Vigier, "Diffusion d'une langue nationale et résistance des patois en France au XIXe siècle," *Romanticisme*, XXV–XXVI (1979), 201. The report appears in F(17*) 3160, AN. I have not replicated it here because it is in Weber, *Peasants into Frenchmen*, 498–501.

Table 3. Percentage of Communes in Each Department Where French Was Not Spoken in 1863

Department	Percent	Department	Percent
Ain	.01	Garonne (Haute)	.95
Aisne	.00	Gers	1.00
Allier	.00	Gironde	.00
Alpes (Basses-)	.96	Hérault	.98
Alpes (Hautes-)	.00	Ille-et-Vilaine	.00
Alpes-Maritimes	.60	Indre	.00
Ardèche	.53	Indre-et-Loire	.00
Ardennes	.00	Isère	.58
Ariège	.99	Jura	.00
Aube	.00	Landes	.93
Aude	.99	Loir-et-Cher	.00
Aveyron	1.00	Loire	.00
Bouches-du-Rhône	.00	Loire (Haute-)	.90
Calvados	.00	Loire-Inférieure	.00
Cantal	.00	Loiret	.00
Charente	.24	Lot	.92
Charente-Inférieure	.00	Lot-et-Garonne	.39
Cher	.00	Lozère	.00
Corrèze	.74	Maine-et-Loire	.00
Corse	1.00	Manche	.00
Côte-d'Or	.00	Marne	.00
Côtes-du-Nord	.47	Marne (Haute-)	.00
Creuse	.00	Mayenne	.00
Dordogne	.00	Meurthe	.11
Doubs	.00	Meuse	.00
Drôme	.57	Morbihan	.46
Eure	.00	Moselle	.39
Eure-et-Loir	.00	Nièvre	.00
Finistère	.96	Nord	.13
Gard	.00	Oise	.00

Table 3 (continued)

Department	Percent	Department	Percent
Orne	.00	Seine-Inférieure	.00
Pas-de-Calais	.00	Seine-et-Marne	.00
Puy-de-Dôme	.95	Seine-et-Oise	.00
Pyrénées (Basses-)	.52	Sèvres (Deux-)	.00
Pyrénées (Hautes-)	.96	Somme	.00
Pyrénées-Orientales	.00	Tarn	.97
Rhin (Bas-)	.81	Tarn-et-Garonne	.00
Rhin (Haut-)	.41	Var	1.00
Rhône	.00	Vaucluse	.00
Saône (Haute)	.00	Vendée	.00
Saône-et-Loire	.00	Vienne	.00
Sarthe	.00	Vienne (Haute-)	.53
Savoie	.00	Vosges	.00
Savoie (Haute-)	.00	Yonne	.00
Seine	.00		

Source: F(17*) 3160, AN.
Total Population of France: 37,382,225.
Percentage of the population that did not know French: 20 (.19865).
Percentage of communes in France where French was not spoken: 22.3.
Percentage of school-age children (7–13 years) who did not know French: 11.

dilections."[69] In February, 1867, Duruy established a special commission to examine the prefects' suggestions.

Furet and Ozouf devote a full chapter to the possible relationship between patois and illiteracy, thereby raising the question why Duruy never, in any of his letters or ministerial directives, joined teachers and inspectors in attributing illiteracy to the presence of the patois.[70] Du-

---

69. Eugen Weber, "Who Sang the Marseillaise?" in Jacques Beauroy, Marc Bertrand, and Edward Gargan, *The Wolf and the Lamb: Popular Culture in France from the Old Regime to the Twentieth Century* (Saratoga, Calif., 1977), 165; confidential circular, November 9, 1866, F(17) 1475, AN.
70. Furet and Ozouf, *Lire et écrire*, I, 324–49.

ruy probably realized, as Furet, Ozouf, and their associates ultimately discovered, that the existence of the patois by itself was no obstacle to literacy (or to economic development). Certainly he had the stunning examples of Dunkirk and Hazebrouck, both Flemish-speaking arrondissements, where the literacy rates topped those of some Francophone arrondissements.

In all events, Duruy, ever the student of history, had a deep and sincere appreciation for cultural diversity. Indeed, the ministry strongly promoted the learning of foreign languages in secondary schools; it would have been almost contradictory for the ministry to make a bold attack on local languages per se.[71] But the patriotic Duruy was also convinced that all who lived under the French flag should know French. French was as necessary for good citizenship as it was for advancement in the world.

Duruy's perspicacity probably told him that local languages and dialects would die out as urbanization and industrialization affected the more remote parts of the country. For him, therefore, it was sufficient to encourage Frenchmen who did not know French to become bilingual—which he did indirectly by way of the letters he sent to bishops and prefects—and to rely on schoolteachers, libraries, and adult education courses to encourage the learning of French.[72]

Duruy concerned himself also with *salles d'asile* (preschools), which had first appeared in France in the middle of the eighteenth century. As charitable institutions, they were created for working mothers with children between the ages of two and six. They did not become popular, however, until after the second decade of the nineteenth century, when the demand increased and they came to be appreciated for their educational benefits (they offered a little reading, writing, and counting, in addition to the regular program of games, singing, and recreation).[73] The state gave them official recognition in 1833, and Mme Marie Pape-Carpentier, a French pioneer of the preschool movement, founded the first normal school for preschool teachers in 1848.

By 1863 the preschools were still funded solely through private do-

71. Duruy's statement to the Corps législatif, March 9, 1867, F(19) 1949, AN.
72. Duruy penciled a note to himself on a report on patois, dated 1866 or 1867: "necessity for adult education" (F[17] 9147, AN).
73. See Marie Matrat and Pauline Kergomard, *Les écoles maternelles* (Paris, 1889), and Rousselot, *Histoire de l'éducation des femmes en France*, II, 366.

nations, although the state increasingly imposed its supervision over them. When Duruy came into office he discovered that the demand for these schools had outstripped the supply and that there were not enough teachers to fill available positions in them. Sympathetic to the needs of working mothers and interested in the pedagogical benefits of the preschools, Duruy lowered the minimum age for directresses and assistant directresses in preschools, created a model preschool in each department for the training of teachers, and ordered that hot food be served to children in the schools. In the law of April 10, 1867 (article 21), he established a more precise distinction between the preschools and the regular primary schools by forbidding parents from placing children in primary schools before they were six years old. This clarification of jurisdictions helped in the development of preschools, and by 1868 there were 3,669 of them with 432,000 children of both sexes.[74]

Adult education enjoyed an even greater boost from Duruy's efforts. Relatively newer than the preschools in that it dated only from the period of the Revolution (decree 22 frimaire, Year I), adult education also did not experience its true beginnings until the 1830s, when industrialists, private societies (notably the Association Polytechnique formed in 1830), and religious orders began to establish night schools and Sunday schools for the industrial classes. Commonly known as *cours du soir, cours d'adultes,* or *cours populaires,* the adult education classes were recognized by the state as institutions of primary education and were regulated by provisions of the laws of 1836, 1847, 1848, and 1850. In 1850, Baron Boulay de la Meurthe considered them so essential to the economic progress of the nation that he urged in a letter printed in the *Moniteur* that they be made obligatory for the estimated 14 million illiterate adults.[75]

Archival documents reveal that, like the classes of the mechanics institutes in England, the adult courses in France were actually a mix of primary and secondary level courses. Owing to the students they at-

74. Articles 57–59 in the Falloux Law; Rohr, *Victor Duruy, ministre de Napoléon III*, 65; Lavisse, "Victor Duruy," 48; Charles Robert, *Les ameliorations sociales du Second Empire* (Paris, 1868), 26.

75. Ponteil, *Histoire de l'enseignement en France,* 216–19; Gréard, *Education et instruction,* I, 100–102; see also Raymond Labourie, "Les oeuvres de jeunesse et l'éducation populaire, 1830–1870," in Baker and Harrigan, *Making of Frenchmen,* 521–42.

tracted and the faculty that taught them (mainly *instituteurs* and *institutrices*), most were elementary classes; reading, writing, arithmetic, land surveying, geography, history, and economics were the most common subjects.[76] But there were also a significant number of courses that offered training in vocational skills or an introduction to literature, history, or geography such as was usually offered to students of the *lycées* and *collèges*. The higher-level adult classes became even more popular during Duruy's ministry, especially because he was able to attract more professors of *lycées* and faculties and *regents* of *collèges* to the cause of popular education. The curriculum of these higher-level courses would be regulated, eventually, by article 9 of the law of June 21, 1865, which specified ornamental design, drafting, modern foreign languages, bookkeeping, and the elements of geometry. Many of the lectures given in the courses, especially those that were favorable to the government, were published and sold to the public for 25 centimes.

Attendance at the courses was limited by the Falloux Law to apprentices over twelve and to adults (defined as anyone over eighteen). Although David I. Kulstein found in his study on economics instruction for workers that some adult courses in Paris actually attracted more industrialists and *patrons* than workers, the reports of rectors show that the major source of clientele for the courses in the provinces was the working class.[77] The absence of tuition in most areas facilitated the attendance of this group.

Until 1848, the number of courses grew modestly each year, aided by small ministerial subsidies. But in the aftermath of the June Days, the courses vegetated as a result of a decrease in ministerial subventions and a drying up of philanthropic contributions. In 1850 there were 4,037 adult courses with 78,356 students; ten years later there were 4,394 courses with 125,647 students. Neither Fortoul nor Rouland was sympathetic. Matthew Arnold and others explained away the overall decline in the number of courses since the July Monarchy

76. Edward Royle, "Mechanics Institutes and the Working Classes, 1840–1860," *Historical Journal*, XIV (1971), 309, 314. Additional information on the economics courses is in David I. Kulstein, "Economics Instruction for Workers During the Second Empire," *French Historical Studies*, I (1959), 225–34.
77. Kulstein, "Economics Instruction," 233. Most of the rectors' reports are in F(17) 4360–64, AN.

(there had been 6,434 courses in 1845) by arguing that it was the result of the natural improvement in national literacy.[78] Duruy, however,
refused to believe that adult education was no longer necessary.

To a large extent, Duruy was propelled into reviving adult education
by his concern for the economic and intellectual liberation of the
working classes. Before both the Council of Ministers and the emperor
he had been a vigorous supporter of a variety of reforms intended to
improve the lot of the workers: the right to strike (granted in 1864);
the abrogation of article 1781 of the Civil Code, which accorded more
weight to the employers' opinions than to workers' demands; industrial accident insurance (instituted by the law of 1868); safety measures for working children and women; and profit-sharing. He regularly urged the emperor not to leave the plight of the workers to the
adversaries of the government, who were to be found both on the
right, where the Count de Chambord was attempting to woo workers
to Legitimacy, and on the left, where Jules Simon and the International
were active.[79]

Beyond supporting political and economic reforms for workers, Duruy also championed their intellectual liberation, which he told the
mayor of Dijon in a statement that expressed deeply held convictions,
was a question of "morality, dignity, and well-being for individuals
[and a question of] force and greatness for the country." An uneducated man is only half a man. The worker who does not possess any
transcending understanding of his role in the industrial and agricultural processes becomes frustrated by the superior economic forces
that dominate his life. Education is the only protection against socialism and communism.[80]

Adult education was thus an important solution to many of the
problems of the working classes. It was also an answer to the economic and political needs of the country. Duruy hoped it could help
reclaim older Frenchmen for industry, compensate for the deficiencies
in education among the young, acquaint more Frenchmen who spoke

78. Rohr, *Victor Duruy, ministre de Napoleon III*, 149, n. 373; Arnold, *Matthew
Arnold on Education*, 82.
79. Charles Robert, "Victor Duruy," *Bulletin de la Société de participation aux bénéfices* (Paris), XVI (1894), 173–78; Victor Duruy to Napoleon III, September 16,
1865, copy of a letter in possession of Mme Albert Duruy.
80. *Centenaire de Victor Duruy*, 46.

only a patois with the French language, and reduce illiteracy (although only 13.1 percent of its entering students were totally illiterate by Duruy's calculation, so successes in this area would be modest).[81] Adult education was also Duruy's answer to the difficulty of keeping children in school beyond first communion.[82] Finally, adult education had immediate military implications at a time when a new bill on the army was under consideration by the government.

Military considerations, in fact, may have been the immediate stimulus for the campaign Duruy launched in favor of adult education in the winter of 1865–1866 (Instruction of November 2, 1865). J. Larocque in the *JGIP* asserted that the campaign was directed especially to the conscripts who would be part of the class of 1865, and he spoke of mayors and *instituteurs* going directly to the homes of these young men and leading them to class so they would not be illiterate when they appeared before the military recruiting boards.[83] At any rate, in 1865 there were only 7,828 adult courses with 186,787 students (a significant increase over the Rouland years nonetheless), but by the end of the following year, there were a phenomenal 24,686 courses with 595,506 students.

Duruy campaigned for adult education in many ways. He urged rectors and municipalities to establish the courses, and he encouraged municipalities to offer them free of charge. He urged teachers interested in teaching the courses to use the schoolrooms and furniture in place for elementary schoolchildren. He gave the adult education courses a more precise structure, created contests and award assemblies for the best students, extended the primary school certificate to the courses, supported the preparation of books on regional economy and development for the courses, and encouraged the creation of libraries for them. To reward teachers who volunteered to teach the courses, he praised them lavishly in his speeches, calling them true missionaries, and he established a system of medals; later, by virtue of the law of April 10, 1867, he would be able to offer them a cash indemnity for their troubles. To protect the courses from political dis-

81. Furet and Ozouf, *Lire et écrire*, I, 300–301; penciled note in Duruy's hand on an 1866 or 1867 report on patois in F(17) 9147, AN.

82. Circular, July 4, 1866, in *BAIP*, VI (1866), 31–33.

83. Instruction of November 2, 1865, *AIP*, 249–56; Laroque's article, "Le campagne des classes d'adultes, 1865–1866," *JGIP*, 1866, pp. 636–37.

pute, Duruy charged rectors and prefects with surveillance of them so that they would not be used to promote political doctrines hostile to the state or interpretations of history that blackened the work of the Enlightenment or Revolution. "The simultaneous employ of these diverse means, modest in appearance but powerful because of the cooperation of so many good people," Duruy told the rectors in a statement he would have applied to many of his other programs, "will lead to something great."[84]

Many proponents of popular education were overjoyed by the administration's efforts. Louis Michel in the ever-loyal *RIP* effused: "The adult courses are, in our opinion, the true schools of education of the people. By reason of the age of the students, the education is broader than in the classes of the young children, and the words of the teacher are more attentively received by the minds which are aware of the costs involved." Many industrialists praised Duruy. The general director of tobacco manufacturing, for example, told him that the majority of personnel for the tobacco industry came from the adult courses. And workers acknowledged Duruy's efforts on their behalf handsomely in the reports they prepared for the Universal Exposition of 1867. There was some criticism that teacher-volunteers were being overworked by their new responsibilities and that they were being pressured into volunteering for the courses. To check for possible abuses, Duruy regularly visited the courses in Paris, and on two occasions he reduced the daytime teaching load of teachers who also taught night classes (30,222 teachers in 1866).[85]

Duruy was perturbed about the resistance to adult education that he

84. AIP, 249–56; JGIP, 1865, pp. 54, 458 (on the circular of August 13, 1864, which specified that students would compete at the cantonal, arrondissement, and departmental levels; that prizes at the two lower levels should be books or savings passbooks and at the departmental level should be scholarships to model farms or to the *écoles des arts et métiers*; and that all responsibility for the awards was left to the rectors); BAIP, IV (1865), 35–37 (circular, July 11, 1865); BAIP, VI (1866), 184–86, 762; Duruy, *Notes et souvenirs*, I, 238 (decree, March 20, 1869); AIP, 256; BAIP, V (1866), 25 (on the establishment of gold medals worth, first, 200 francs, then 250 francs, for the most deserving teacher in each department); *ibid.*, 137–38 (on additional prizes established, especially in the name of the imperial prince and by Hachette); F(17) 1475, AN (confidential circular, September 30, 1865); F(17) 10362, AN (confidential circular, January 12, 1867); and AIP, 256.
85. JGIP, 1865, p. 191; BAIP, IX (1868), 90–91; Georges Duveau, *La vie ouvrière en France sous le Second Empire* (Paris, 1946), 436–62; JGIP, 1865, pp. 160–61; 1866, pp. 153, 219; AIP, 251–52; and BAIP, V (1866), 87.

encountered. Surely he was accustomed to the well-known ambiva-
lence of industrialists to worker education, but he was apparently un-
prepared for the reservations of his ministerial colleagues and some
functionaries. The former offered him no support but accused him of
attempting to flatter the masses. Some functionaries, like the unnamed
prefect Duruy cites in *Notes et souvenirs*, were opposed to the extra
responsibilities surveillance of night schools entailed. At Nièvre and elsewhere, municipal councils, backed by large landowners, who feared
the loss of their labor supply to the cities, opposed financial allocations for adult classes. Duruy's "municipalization" of the courses had
proved to be one of the weaker aspects of the program.[86]

The press constantly criticized him for failing to fund adult education sufficiently. State subsidies for the courses averaged only four
francs per course, which did not stretch far in courses destined to last
four months. In places where adults paid a token tuition (10 percent of
the adults attending night school in 1867 paid an average of three
francs for their courses) or municipal councils were sympathetic,
teachers did not have to pay for heating and lighting out of their own
pockets. But in other places, apparently, teachers were obliged to contribute their money as well as their time and energy. Enthusiasm
among teachers for adult education under these conditions would not
endure, as *Le Siècle* and *L'Etendard* pointed out, unless the ministry
could offer something more than medals. Members of the various societies for popular education and philanthropists donated funds to
adult education courses. And Duruy, urging municipalities to assume
the costs of the courses for their own benefit, won increases in departmental subsidies to adult education. In article 7 of the law of April 10,
1867, Duruy ultimately secured full indemnification of all teachers of
adult education.[87]

Despite the criticism and problems Duruy faced, the courses began
to flourish soon after he launched his campaign in late 1865. In 1866
there was an extraordinary increase in the number of courses and

86. Jefferson, "Worker Education in England and France," 363; Duruy, *Notes et souvenirs*, I, 231–32, 235–36; *BAIP*, IV (1865), 767–85.
87. *Centenaire de Victor Duruy*, 100; *Le siècle* (January 14, 1868); *JGIP*, 1866,
p. 797; *AIP*, 250; F(17) 4360–64, AN: *BAIP*, VI (1866), 31–33 (circular, July 4,
1866).

Table 4. Adult Education Courses in France, 1848–1869

To April of Academic Year	Number of Courses			Number of Students		
	Total	For Men	For Women	Total	Male	Female
1848 (Jan.)	7,000	–	–	117,000 +	–	–
1850	4,037	–	–	78,356	–	–
1860	4,394	–	–	125,647	–	–
1865	7,828	7,418	400	186,787	173,250	13,537
1866	24,686	22,980	1,706	595,506	552,939	42,567
1869	33,638	28,172	5,466	793,136	678,753	114,393

Source: Compiled from statistics in Gontard, *Les écoles primaires de la France bourgeois*, 189–90. Figures for 1848 from *JGIP*, 1865, p. 572.

number of students enrolled. Increases continued through the end of Duruy's ministry (see Table 4), and the courses flourished into the 1870s, carried along on the momentum that Duruy created.

Many of the adult education courses were established by private societies of popular education, which were active in various independent education programs. Most, like the Société de l'enseignement populaire at Versailles, which was dedicated to adult education for workers, or the larger Société d'instruction élémentaire, to which Duruy belonged, were composed of republicans and anticlericals. Some, however, were associated with various religious groups.

The only society with which Duruy had problems was the Ligue de l'enseignement. Developed from Jean Macé's Société des bibliothèques communales, which was founded in 1862 in the department of Haut-Rhin as a "Landwehr de l'enseignement," and inspired by the Belgian Ligue de l'enseignement of 1865, the French league became active as an arm of the Masonic lodges after 1866. Immediately, it began to attract anticlericals and republicans, including such nationally prominent figures as Jules Ferry and Jules Favre. By January, 1870, it would boast 59 departmental affiliates and 17,856 members.[88]

88. *L'Opinion nationale*, October 25, November 15, 1866; Mona Ozouf, *L'école, L'église et la république, 1871–1914* (Paris, 1963).

The Catholic hierarchy repudiated the league as soon as it had become cognizant of the league's affiliation with the Masons. Dupanloup in his *Alarmes de l'épiscopat* condemned it as an egregious effort to convert all schoolteachers (and consequently all schoolchildren) into Freemasons. And the prelate of Metz, Bishop Dupont des Loges, waged an especially fierce campaign against the league *cercles* that were particularly strong in the eastern departments.[89]

When in December, 1866, Duruy was called to render an opinion on the league, his first reaction was one of circumspection. He replied to the rector of Strasbourg, who had written to inquire of the official attitude of the administration toward Macé, that no position had been formulated. "The true instruments in the crusade against ignorance [however] are you and me . . . the whole University. . . . In a country such as ours, there is no room for these leagues [to become entrenched] between the University and the religious orders." He noted that the societies could become absorbed in the many opportunities provided by the administration, but if the league intended to establish a "parallel government" (of education), it could not be tolerated. Duruy thus advised waiting to see which direction the league would take.[90]

By late spring, however, two developments prompted Duruy to become more favorable to the league. The first was an interview with Jean Macé, which led Duruy to believe that the league posed no real threat to the work of the ministry. The second was Duruy's discovery that a Catholic society had been formed "to combat the laic schools." This society, the great growth in the religious school system, and the concomitant decision of the Catholic Ultras to unseat him (as will be discussed in chapters VI and VII) convinced Duruy that the league could be of some service to the University. But he never gave the league (an extralegal organization that could not be officially approved by a minister of the still authoritarian empire) his public blessing, as Louis Bourgain has claimed. And his reservations about the league kept many teachers from joining it.[91]

89. Henri Edouard Dutoit, *Dupanloup: Choisir les meilleurs textes* (Paris, 1933), 521–25; F(19) 2537, AN.

90. Victor Duruy to the rector of Strasbourg, December 7, 1866, copy of a letter, F(17) 2681, AN.

91. F(19) 2681, AN; Louis Bourgain, *L'église de France et l'état au dix-neuvième siècle (1802–1900)* (2 vols.; Paris, 1901), 177; Labourie, "Les oeuvres de jeunesse et d'éducation populaire," 539.

A high point in Duruy's career was the Universal Exposition of 1867, which allowed him to place on display, before the eyes of Europe and the world, France's great educational achievements. Under Duruy's guidance the ministry developed for presentation at the exposition a great variety of reports on the mathematical, physical, and natural sciences, on the moral and political sciences, and on the role of French letters in general education. His subordinates prepared booths containing samples of students' work, textbooks, pictures of schoolrooms, and other items for this "intellectual exposition." Duruy took advantage of the exposition to promote and demonstrate his concern for teacher education. He made special arrangements to facilitate the visits of schoolteachers to the exposition (reduced round-trip fares by railroad and free lodging in Parisian boarding schools that were closed for the summer), and he provided the schoolteachers with a wide variety of educational experiences, including lectures on pedagogy at the Sorbonne and visits to model farms in the environs of Paris. Duruy also used the occasion to stimulate concern for popular education on an international level, both by placing the achievements of France on view to all foreign visitors and by inviting all foreign nations to participate in the educational exposition. Only Italy, Switzerland, and the state of Massachusetts accepted (the education commissioners of Massachusetts sent a complete classroom, including its teacher and students, to demonstrate American pedagogy), but this was an accomplishment in the history of international expositions.[92]

Duruy was the first minister of public instruction since Guizot to give major attention to popular education. But whereas Guizot was motivated by a conviction that the savage masses had to be taught to control their passions,[93] Duruy was motivated by the belief that the masses had a right to an education that was suitable to their station in life and that would prepare them for the world of modern technology and industry. Duruy, as we have seen, spoke of "reclaiming" adults for industry through night school courses.

92. Ministère de l'Instruction Publique, *Rapports adressés à S. Exc. M. le ministre de l'instruction publique par les membres de la commission chargées d'examiner les travaux d'élèves et les moyens d'enseignement exposés au ministre et au Champs-de-Mars* (Paris, 1867); *JGIP*, 1865, pp. 713–14, 778, 1866, pp. 92, 777, 1867, p. 150.
93. Furet and Ozouf, *Lire et écrire*, I, 142.

Duruy's most encompassing achievement was the omnibus law of April 10, 1867, fittingly dubbed the Duruy Law. The Duruy Law gave girls' schools legal parity with boys' schools (making it actually the "first organic law of primary education for girls").[94] It also improved working and living conditions for public schoolteachers, added two important courses—history and geography—to the primary school curriculum, and committed the state to supporting absolute gratuity at the local level (Duruy's *moyen projet*).

Duruy first adopted but then abandoned the principle of compulsory education. The political opposition to compulsion was too great and the emperor too halfhearted in his support. Duruy decided not to compromise what momentum there was for gratuity by pushing simultaneously for compulsion. The winning of optional gratuity at the national level was victory enough; even Bishop Dupanloup, one of Duruy's fiercest opponents, thought that Duruy's accomplishment was major.[95] Compulsion, of course, was only one means, albeit the most radical, of expanding popular education. There were many more ways to employ state action, and Duruy used a variety. Most appreciated by sympathetic contemporaries was his encouragement of adult education courses.

Several of Duruy's reforms helped to improve the quality of popular education. The addition of history and geography to the required curriculum of the primary schools and gymnastics, music, and agricultural education to the optional curriculum are only the more prominent examples. Duruy also made important advances by encouraging the development of school libraries and the teaching of French in all schools.

The opposition to Duruy and the criticism he received for his many initiatives were lively and loud, and indeed they often overshadowed or seemed to overshadow the praise and support he received. But such is not surprising given the political nature of education in nineteenth-century France. The important point is that the opposition or criticism forced Duruy to back down fully on only one reform—that of compulsion; they did not prevent him from winning partial or substantial victories in any of the other areas in which he was active.

94. Charles Fourrier, *L'enseignement français de 1789 à 1945: Précis d'histoire des institutions scolaires* (Paris, 1965), 145–46.
95. XIXAB523, Félix Dupanloup Papers, AN.

V · The Modernization of Secondary Education

Since the second half of the nineteenth century secondary education has been going through a very grave crisis which has not yet reached its end. Everyone recognizes that it cannot remain what it was in the past [exclusively humanistic], but we do not see with the same clarity what it is to become.
—Emile Durkheim, Sorbonne lectures (1902–1903)

In the middle of the nineteenth century, public education in France, like that in most countries, was sharply divided along class lines. The primary schools with more than four million students in 1863 were popular institutions serving the lower classes. The secondary schools with just over 140,000 students were relatively more elite institutions serving the upper classes, from the petit bourgeois to the aristocracy.[1] So rigid were the class implications of the two systems that affluent parents typically sent their youngest sons not to the regular *écoles de garçons* but to the elementary classes of the secondary schools. In an era of advancing wealth and popular education, the possession of a secondary education was still one of the most widely accepted means of distinguishing the bourgeoisie from the lower classes.[2]

To possess a secondary education was to possess a classical and humanistic education. At its base were Latin and Greek, which a student took during the full eight to ten years he attended a *lycée* or *collège*. In combination with the other subjects in the secondary curriculum— French literature, history, geography, philosophy, mathematics, and

1. Patrick J. Harrigan, "Historians and Compilers Joined: The Historiography of the 1970s and French Enquêtes of the Nineteenth Century," in Baker and Harrigan, *Making of Frenchmen*, 15; Harrigan, *Mobility, Elites and Education in French Society of the Second Empire*, 13. There is a useful discussion throughout the latter publication, beginning on page 9, about the meaning and extent of elitism in French secondary education.

2. For the most recent statement on class and education, see Harrigan, "Historians and Compilers Joined," 15.

some modern languages and science—this Latin and Greek base was designed to develop moral and humanistic values, mental excellence, the ability to think critically, and a facility for lucid and eloquent expression. Classical education so conceived was believed to be the only solid basis for real thought; without it one was considered "merely a parvenu in intelligence."[3] Classical education was the hallmark of the educated Frenchman and the foundation upon which French genius was built.

In the last decades of the eighteenth century but especially after the first quarter of the nineteenth century, critics of this rigid class system of education began to demand a measure of democratization to provide the lower levels of the middle classes and the upper levels of the lower classes with advanced education suitable to jobs in commerce, industry, and agriculture. As Baron Hippolyte Chauchard, a deputy in the legislature, would argue in 1864: "In the present state of Europe, the creation of railroads, the ease of transportation and communication, the increasing multiplicity of international relations, the infinite development of commercial and credit transactions, and the innumerable practical applications of science have impressed on industry and commerce an unprecedented activity. We must prepare men who are capable of dealing with the characteristic evolution of modern society."[4]

Reform-oriented Frenchmen, especially those of the bourgeoisie, were also concerned about the growing demand for secondary education. Large numbers of the lower middle class who could finally afford the tuition of municipal *collèges*, which were less expensive than the private *collèges* or *lycées*, were sending their sons to school for a classical education. Many of these young men, however, became frustrated by the rigors of the classical curriculum for which they had little taste and left after two or three years. Others stayed to complete their studies and compete for the difficult baccalaureate degree, only to discover that its possession did not automatically lead to a comfortable career. Not only were the hurdles into the *grandes écoles* formidable but opportunities for finding a suitable career thereafter were not especially

3. Louis Trénard, *Salvandy en son temps: 1795–1856* (Lille, 1968), 421.
4. Chauchard's speech to the legislature, reproduced in *JGIP*, 1865, pp. 333–42.

plentiful.[5] Consequently, many young men from the intermediate classes found that they had to accept positions that were more mediocre than they anticipated.[6] Reformers feared that a large pool of frustrated young males (*déclassés*) was being produced.

There were no easy solutions to the problem because a large number of Frenchmen still considered the classical secondary curriculum sacrosanct. But there was growing support for the idea that young men from families in the intermediate socioeconomic range should be provided with a vocationally oriented secondary education.

Sharing the traditional views on the value and purposes of French classical education yet convinced that the secondary curriculum must respond to the needs of the new industrial and commercial classes, Duruy took up the problems of secondary education as soon as he became minister. As the result of his many years of teaching at the secondary level and his more recent experience as inspector, he determined that three reforms were imperative. First, the state would have to make a new commitment to classical studies because these alone produced the "aristocracy of intellect" that was the backbone of the French nation. As he wrote eloquently in his memoirs: "Since France is the true moral center of the world, let us assure to the children of the well-to-do classes, to those who will fill the liberal careers, to those who, by their natural qualities, their birth, or their wealth, are called to the highest ranks of society, let us assure to them with letters and sciences, philosophy and history, the largest and most fertile cultivation of the mind, in order to fortify the aristocracy of intelligence. . . . and give legitimate balance to this democracy which overflows its banks." Second, the classical program would have to be revised and strengthened to eliminate boredom, routine, and sterile exercises. State schools would have to be made competitive with the Catholic secondary schools and able to set good pedagogical examples for the new Catholic schools. And third, Fortoul's program of vocational education would have to be replaced by a comparable but improved program that would make secondary education truly national through its

5. Lenore O'Boyle, "The Problem of an Excess of Educated Men in Western Europe, 1800–1850," *Journal of Modern History*, XLII (1970), 471–95.
6. Patrick J. Harrigan, "The Social Origins, Ambitions and Occupations of Secondary Students in France During the Second Empire," in Lawrence Stone (ed.), *Schooling and Society: Studies in the History of Education* (Baltimore, 1976), 216.

accessibility to the lower classes. As Duruy put it on one occasion, "The time has come when the first duty of the state is to give to democracy . . . the intellectual and moral virility which is essential to it if it is to fulfill peacefully its political and social destiny." [7]

Duruy began with an assault on the deficiencies in classical education. He first restored the philosophy course in the terminal years of the curriculum to its "full rights and honor" by reintroducing the metaphysics and psychology of Victor Cousin. Cousin's eclectic program of philosophical speculation, which had been the philosophic program of the July Monarchy, had been terminated in 1852 by political conservatives who held it responsible for some of the pernicious doctrines that culminated in the revolution of 1848. Fortoul had been forced in 1852 to rename the terminal class "logic" and to reduce the previous philosophy program to a series of "safe" syllogisms, which students were required to memorize and regurgitate on the baccalaureate examination. To Duruy the logic course was too similar to the scholasticism of the Middle Ages. It prepared young men for examinations, but it did not teach them to think independently or offer them sufficient opportunities to understand the sterility of positivism and materialism. Duruy's new syllabus was designed to reverse this approach and to give students exercises in fundamental moral truths such as respect for neighbors and love of public good and peace on earth, which coincided with the teachings of all religious denominations. [8]

The new syllabus for philosophy was studied by a special Imperial Council committee presided over by Bishop Darboy and then submitted to the entire council, all of whose members except the bishop of Langres approved it. "What do I wish to do, Monsignor?" Duruy re-

7. Duruy, *Notes et souvenirs*, I, 197–98, 255 (italics added); *AIP*, 492. Patrick Harrigan has pointed out that Catholic secondary schools educated one-third of the secondary population between 1851 and 1882 and that the percentage steadily increased during those years so that between 1854 and 1867 the Catholic schools almost doubled their enrollment. By the mid-1860s, they began to compete seriously with state schools (Harrigan, "Catholic Secondary Education in France, 1851–1882 [Ph.D. dissertation, University of Michigan, 1970], 1, 15; Harrigan, "Social and Political Implications of Catholic Secondary Education During the Second French Empire," 48).

8. Duruy, *Notes et souvenirs*, I, 279; Doris S. Goldstein, "'Official Philosophies' in Modern France: The Example of Victor Cousin," *Journal of Social History*, I (1968), 259–79; R. Jacquin, "Hippolyte Fortoul a-t-il banni la philosophie?" *Revue des sciences religieuses* (Strasbourg), a. 31, n. 4 (1957), 383–87; and excerpt of Duruy's speech before the Imperial Council in *RIP*, 1863, p. 257.

sponded to his critic in a famous exchange. "The contrary of what you have done. Where do I wish to go? Toward the light."[9] The new syllabus became law by the decree of June 29, 1863, and was complemented by an *agrégation* for philosophy which Duruy established on July 9.

Universitaires and liberals alike were delighted with the reform. Catholics generally remained suspicious of or hostile to it, convinced that it was further proof of Duruy's desire to secularize French education. Yet Duruy continued to defend it, and Montalembert sent a letter of congratulations, confessing that he had never understood how the University could have submitted itself to the inferior settlement of 1852. Duruy's reform corrected Fortoul's "mutilation" of philosophy and restored psychology, theodicy, and ethics, the latter an especially large feature in the new program.[10]

In July, 1863, Duruy submitted a proposal to the Imperial Council for the introduction of contemporary history into the classical curriculum. Arguing that young Frenchmen who would be controlling their country in several years knew nothing of the milieu in which they lived because history courses in *lycées* and *collèges* took historical developments only to 1815, Duruy suggested a comprehensive syllabus of political, intellectual, and economic history for the period since 1815. He argued that teaching of economic and political history would help prevent a repetition of the miseries of 1848 by demonstrating "that nothing durable is improvised." And intellectual history would help young men understand the *zeitgeist* of their time. Overall, he hoped that the contemporary history course would help to mellow factions in France and draw the country closer together.[11]

Duruy's proposal was truly innovative. History was a fairly new subject in the secondary curriculum, dating from the Restoration, and it had weathered difficult times, especially because conservatives feared that dangerous ideas might be taught in history classes. Under the July Monarchy, history gained acceptance as a discipline, but the

9. Darboy's presiding over the committee and a comment in his diary, *Cahiers*, XI, 8, indicate that he saw no threat to Catholicism in the new program. The bishop of Langres is quoted in Lavisse, *Un ministre*, 55–56.

10. F(17) 4360–61, AN; *RIP*, 1864, p. 643; Duruy, *Notes et souvenirs*, I, 199–200; Jacquin, "Hippolyte Fortoul a-t-il banni la philosophie?" 385; Anderson, *Education in France*, 176.

11. *AIP*, 17–21.

reaction of 1852 put an end to its early flowering in the secondary schools, ironically just as writings by professional historians were becoming more scientific or objective. The *agrégation* in history created in 1830 was abolished, and history teachers were "invited" to use history to teach ideas and moral lessons that were approved by the regime. Historians were relieved when Rouland became minister of public instruction in 1856, but he only reestablished the history *agrégation* and counseled history teachers against spending too much time on wars and battles.[12]

Duruy took the important step forward. He created a course of contemporary French history, which focused on the period from 1815 to the Second Empire, and he put the course in the class (or year) of philosophy. Duruy placed emphasis on political, intellectual, and economic history, which meant that the course departed radically from the old method of teaching history that was concerned only with great men, great ideas, and what Duruy called "battle history." The purpose of the new course, as Duruy explained it at the *concours général* of August, 1863, was to teach young men who would soon be governing France how their society was organized and what its needs and desires were.[13]

The Imperial Council approved the syllabus almost unanimously, although it revised the text to eliminate certain of Duruy's highly interpretative and liberal statements.[14] The course in contemporary history for the secondary schools of France was then made law by the decree of August 3, 1863.

The emperor was one of the first public supporters of the new program, praising it in his speech at the opening of the legislative session late that fall. Such liberal papers as *Le Siècle*, the *Journal des débats*, *L'Economiste français*, and the *Journal des économists* followed in turn.[15] But not surprisingly, some liberals were dissatisfied. The liberal democratic *Courrier de dimanche* was opposed to the introduction of economic history in the new curriculum, and *L'Epoque* feared that

12. Paul Gerbod, "La place de l'histoire dans l'enseignement secondaire de 1820 à 1880," *Information historique*, XXVII (1965), 123–29.
13. *AIP*, 10–11.
14. *JGIP*, 1865, p. 463.
15. *Ibid.*, 1863, pp. 854–56, and 1864, p. 328; *RIP*, 1863, p. 449; *JGIP*, 1863, pp. 838–40.

pressure would be placed on students to articulate the establishment's view of history. Republicans such as Eugène Pelletan, who carried the republican argument to the Corps législatif in 1865, echoed the fear that students would be converted into adulators of the empire and that the program provided too many opportunities for the dissemination of official propaganda. *L'Epoque* cited the recent question for the *concours général* as an example. Would the sons or grandsons of men such as Guizot, Cavaignac, Falloux, Montalembert, Persigny, and Raymond-Théodore Troplong all be expected to give the same answer in their essay on the events that had occurred in Europe from 1846 to 1865? Lenossier in *Salut public* of Lyons found the whole affair amusing: since students henceforth would have a greater knowledge of international developments, the prize-winning essay in the annual *concours général* could be sent as an information circular to all French diplomatic agents abroad.[16] The press discussed the new program passionately. Perhaps the most outraged were the religious and legitimist press, among which only the *Journal des villes et campagnes* viewed the program with objectivity.[17] *Le Monde* and the *Gazette de France* waged a crusade against the new program for over a year.

Duruy and his functionaries were aware that the contemporary history course could be used as much to spread propaganda against the regime as to support the regime. Thus they surveyed the teaching of the course closely. The rector of Besançon on his own initiative collected copies of corrected written assignments from the history classes on a weekly basis, and other rectors made similar checks.[18] Duruy, in his capacity as rector of the academy of Paris, convened all of the professors of history in the *lycées* of Paris and Versailles on October 8, 1863, and warned them against "an indiscreet zeal . . . [for] the present" and "an unjust condemnation of the past." In his July 16, 1864, questionnaire he again asked functionaries all over France to certify that the teaching of both philosophy and contemporary history was morally and politically irreproachable.[19] Although professors of con-

16. *RIP*, 1863, p. 435; *JGIP*, 1865, p. 462, 477, and 1864, p. 329.

17. *RIP*, 1863, p. 435.

18. Third trimester report, 1863, for the academy of Besançon, F(17) 2650, AN; reports in F(17), 4359, AN.

19. Duruy quoted in *RIP*, 1863, p. 450. Questions 3 and 8 in Chapter III of the questionnaire of July 16, 1864, F(17) 6843, AN.

temporary history probably had some difficulty teaching their subject objectively, serious indiscretions must have been rare because the press reported no problems and the archival cartoons for this period reveal that only one accusation was ever leveled against a professor.[20] Apparently the threat of dismissal, which Duruy reminded his subordinates he was ready to employ, was sufficient to keep professors in line.

Duruy continued to reform the classical program in late 1863 and 1864. By the circular of September 29, 1863, he triggered a minor revolution in French language instruction by ordering modern language professors to group their students by ability and not by the number of years they had studied a foreign language. An accompanying order directed professors to rely on the natural method of teaching languages. Contemporary methods, Duruy believed, were ineffective because few students learned to speak foreign languages fluently. He specified that in the future great attention should be given to oral and written exercises in class. Professors should not attempt to teach too much formal grammar, and above all they should religiously avoid philological and grammatical curiosities. Their mission was pragmatic, not scholarly. Furthermore, professors were to confine themselves both to one-hour classes so that students would not tire of languages so quickly and to the foreign language most logical for the region of France they inhabited: German in the northeast, English in the northwest, Italian in the southeast, and Spanish in the southwest. Italian and Spanish had never before been taught in the French secondary curriculum. Duruy preferred that students master one language instead of dissipating their energies and learning two poorly. To strengthen the teaching of foreign languages, Duruy reestablished the modern foreign language *concours* for the *lycées* of Paris and Versailles and reinstituted the special *agrégation* for modern languages. To complement these improvements he attempted to create a special section of modern languages at the Ecole Normale, which would send its best students abroad for one year to perfect their language abilities, but he failed to get the necessary budgetary allocation.[21]

20. F(19) 3972, AN. Bishop Angebault of Angers accused Zévort at the *lycée* of Angers of systematically attacking Catholic education in his history courses. The inspector of academy, when consulted by Duruy, claimed that Zévort was innocent. But too many sensitive issues had been raised by the incident, and Zévort was ultimately replaced.

21. The instruction of September 29, 1863, is reproduced in *AIP*, pp. 22–32. The report and the decree for the special section of the Ecole Normale begin on page 30.

Attention was also given to the baccalaureate, which was by mid-century one of the most important educational institutions in France. Established by Napoleon Bonaparte as a sanction for secondary studies, it eventually became a requirement for entrance into the higher government schools and liberal careers. As education ministers during the first half of the century tightened requirements for the baccalaureate, the degree became more and more, as one historian has put it, a kind of *croix d'honneur* for distinguished secondary studies. It became the crown of a general education and the badge of a bourgeois elite.[22]

The checkered evolution of the baccalaureate in the first part of the century produced an examination for the degree that had many undesirable features. In the early 1850s, Fortoul significantly improved the examination by simplifying and reducing the material covered and by giving the scientific baccalaureate equal standing with the literary baccalaureate, but major problems still remained to be resolved when Duruy took office. Among the most important was that preparation for the examination was sterile and mechanical—largely a matter of memorization and cramming—because of the existence of the study manual and the practice of drawing questions from the manual by lot for the examination. The examination was as much a matter of chance as memorization. The study manual and the method of selecting questions had been inaugurated by Victor Cousin to guarantee high intellectual standards and the probity of professors giving the examination. With the passage of time, however, a wide gap developed between the subject matter taught in the upper grades of the *lycées* and that tested in the baccalaureate examination, and students typically neglected their studies in the last years of school. Duruy reported on one of his inspection tours that professors complained that they no longer had attentive students in their classes but only candidates preoccupied with preparing for the baccalaureate.[23]

A few educators agreed with Antoine Cournot that the best solution was to abolish the baccalaureate altogether.[24] But the majority of men

Duruy's plan for dividing the countryside into four language areas was first presented to Rouland in a report dated June 17, 1862, F(17) 7563, AN.

22. J. B. Piobetta, *Le baccalauréat* (Paris, 1937), 1, 316; Ponteil, *Histoire de l'enseignement en France,* 391.

23. Piobetta, *Le baccalauréat,* 24, 107, and passim; Ponteil, *Histoire de l'enseignement en France,* 180–84, 266–67.

24. Piobetta, *Le baccalauréat,* 119.

who expressed themselves on the subject called instead for serious reforms—an expansion of the written tests at the expense of the less reliable oral ones that predominated; a reduction in the variety of baccalaureates (there were five types of science baccalaureates); further
reductions in the subject matter treated (the examination had become
encyclopedic in nature after the *certificat d'études* had been suppressed in 1849); and an end to various irregularities and opportunities for cheating.

His experience as a *lycée* professor and his years as an inspector had
given Duruy strong views on the baccalaureate. Ideally, he believed
that the baccalaureate had two functions. First, it was supposed to
prove that students graduating from secondary schools had learned
how to think, write, and speak; it was not supposed to be a prize for
students with the best memories. This was the distinction he had in
mind when he emphasized at the July 7, 1863, meeting of the Imperial
Council that secondary schools were supposed to "produce men," not
just *bacheliers*. And second, the baccalaureate was intended to protect
the *grandes écoles* from accepting incapable students. But Duruy believed that neither of these functions was being adequately fulfilled.[25]

Before proposing reforms in the baccalaureate, Duruy decided to
test for another problem he suspected. In October, 1863, he informed
rectors that there would be only one topic nationwide for the forthcoming examination.[26] Essays written by the candidates would be corrected as usual by faculty professors, but then they would be sent to
the ministry for comparison. After the examinations were held and the
results tabulated, Duruy discovered, as he had suspected, that there
were great discrepancies in the grading of examinations, many of them
the result of carelessness or excessive leniency on the part of faculty
professors.

In confidential circulars on March 18 and October 4 and 28, 1864,
Duruy reproached erring professors for their carelessness or excessive
leniency and urged them to give future examinations more serious attention. Then, in the decree of November 27, 1864, he abolished the
study manual and, of course, the practice of drawing test questions by
lot from it. Thereafter, as one *universitaire* put it, the baccalaureate

25. F(17*) 1870, AN (session, July 7, 1863); *BAIP*, II (1864), 543–45.
26. *BAIP*, XIV (1863), 377–78.

examination ceased to resemble a lottery. It became instead a serious examination, which Duruy specified would henceforth test the subjects taught in the classes of rhetoric, philosophy, and elementary mathematics, the final three years of the secondary schools. In subsequent directives, Duruy increased the written portion of the examination, giving it greater weight in the final evaluation; made a French composition in philosophy mandatory; abolished the alternative scientific baccalaureates except for one (the *baccalauréat-ès-sciences restreint*) that was specifically designed for medical students; ended the exceptions allowed previously on the age of candidates taking the baccalaureate examination; terminated the practice of voting by *boules* on the achievement of the candidates in favor of subjective designations (from "failed" to "very good") of their performance; and exempted students who had won prizes in the literary or scientific competitions (*concours généraux*) from relevant portions of the baccalaureate examination. The latter measure reflected Duruy's desire to underscore the radically changed nature of the baccalaureate under his administration—it was restructured to be a test of, as he put it, secondary studies "well done."[27]

Duruy's reform of the baccalaureate was accused by a few opposition newspapers of "consolidating and universalizing the University monopoly" and of striking "a fatal blow to private education." Victor Laprade, a classicist, judged in a sensational book entitled *L'éducation homicide* (1867) that Duruy had not reduced the amount of material covered by the baccalaureate. Laprade's main complaint seems to have been that Duruy extended the scientific portion of the examination. But otherwise the reform was universally praised. The *Journal des débats* concluded in 1864: "This suppression [of the study manual] was . . . [beneficial and] a natural consequence of the return to the teaching of philosophy." Classical studies had been restored to their prominence of twelve years earlier, it proclaimed, and that meant progress because it reversed the decadence that had set in after 1852 with the confusion in the baccalaureate programs. Most educators were soon concurring that the burdens on students had eased. And by 1867, the

27. F(17) 1474, AN; BAIP, II (1864), 545; report of E. Taillefert for the Commission on Secondary Education at Toulouse, F(17) 4360, AN; *BAIP*, II (1864), 546–55 (regulation of November 28, 1864), and III (1865), 387–97 (regulation of March 25, 1865).

deans of the faculties all noted major improvement in the quality of the examinations, which they believed reflected stronger classical studies in the secondary schools as well.[28]

Attached to the baccalaureate reform was Duruy's creation of a *concours général* by the decree of May 28, 1864, for all of the students in secondary schools across France. The decree generalized a program that had existed in the academy of Paris for some time and had appeared to be one of the major reasons for the strength of classical studies in the capital. By extending the *concours* to the rest of the nation, Duruy hoped he could stimulate the provincial *lycées* and *collèges* to improve their programs in the classics. If all worked according to plan, the provincial institutions would become much more attractive to parents, and the Parisian institutions would drain fewer students from the countryside. Likewise, the Parisian *lycées* and *collèges* would be stimulated by competition from the best students of the provinces. Duruy explained the reform retrospectively in *Notes et souvenirs*: "The somnolence of the old schools where teachers and students languished was fortunately shaken when one could see the student of an obscure *collège* challenge the victors of Paris. It was an academic decentralization which harmed no one and profited everyone."[29]

These reforms—the restoration of philosophy, the introduction of contemporary history, the reform of modern language instruction, the revision of the baccalaureate examination, and the creation of the *concours général*—were the only revisions Duruy wished to effect in the classical program for the moment. Believing he needed additional and precise details on certain problems in the curriculum before proceeding further, he prepared and submitted a lengthy questionnaire to all academic rectors on July 16, 1864. Then, leaving the rectors to gather their data, he turned to review the difficulties in Fortoul's vocational education program, which was known as *bifurcation*.

Bifurcation, created by Fortoul in 1852, had a substantial history that included both private and state efforts to develop appropriate forms of technical education for young men.[30] It is not necessary to

28. Excerpts in *JGIP*, 1864, pp. 781–83; *RIP*, 1864, p. 497; excerpt in *JGIP*, 1864, p. 792; Piobetta, *Le baccalauréat*, 129–30.

29. *BAIP*, I (1864), 383–86; Duruy, *Notes et souvenirs*, I, 284.

30. See Frederick B. Artz, *The Development of Technical Education in France*,

enter into the details of this history, but it is important to recognize that the creation of the *écoles centrales* by the Directory in 1795 was the first attempt ever made by the French state to provide technical and scientific education at the secondary level. Unfortunately, support for these modern schools was not sufficiently widespread, and when the Directory was overthrown and Napoleon was firmly ensconced in power, they were abolished and the classical secondary schools were restored. Napoleon was responsible for the abolition of the *écoles centrales*, but he was supported by conservatives in French society, who were convinced that the state need only concern itself with the training of a small cadre of professional experts to fill civilian and military jobs.

The first breach in this attitude came in 1833, when the July Monarchy decided to require the establishment of *écoles primaires supérieures*, offering some vocational courses in all communes exceeding six thousand inhabitants and all *chefs-lieux* of the departments (article 10 of the Guizot Law). But the higher primary schools failed to attract the students from the commercial and industrial classes they were created to serve. The new social classes preferred instead to send their sons to the more prestigious secondary schools. As a consequence, municipal *collèges* in the 1840s began to offer vocational courses, and Salvandy (minister of public instruction, 1845–1848) promoted the transfer of the higher primary school curriculum to certain *collèges*, which were then renamed *collèges françaises* to reflect their nonclassical orientation.

By the time the Falloux Law was being prepared, educators and legislators had concluded that creation of the higher primary schools had been a mistake. By remaining silent on these schools in the Falloux Law, they quietly released communes from the obligation of maintaining them, but some higher primary schools and *collèges français* continued to exist. The situation changed only after Fortoul, a former Saint-Simonian and an heir to the views of Salvandy and the reformers of 1848, decided to impose on the secondary institutions of the University an integrated program of science and modern subjects. Known as *bifurcation*, this program was the brainchild primarily of chemist

---

1500–1850 (Cambridge, Mass., 1966), and C. R. Day, "The Development of Higher Primary and Intermediate Technical Education in France, 1800 to 1870," *Historical Reflections/Réflexions historiques*, III (1976), 49–66.

Jean-Baptiste Dumas, although Le Verrier, Nisard, Félix Ravaisson, and others were consulted on the construction of certain parts of the curriculum. The secondary-level grades were numbered from eighth to second in ascending order. Second was followed by rhetoric and logic, each covering more than its name implies. A student typically entered a secondary school at the age of ten. *Bifurcation* reorganized the secondary curriculum into two tracks after the fourth grade, one the regular classical (literary) track, the other the scientific (technical) track. Students in the classical section took Latin, Greek, logic, and elementary geometry, physics, chemistry, and biology, while students in the scientific section took arithmetic, algebra, geometry, physics, chemistry, biology, trigonometry, mechanics, linear and commercial design, and the elements of logic. Students in both tracks also took a common core of courses—French, history, geography, and modern languages. At the end of three years, the students in the two sections were reunited for the last year of the curriculum—logic.

The novel scientific section became fairly popular with students in the years immediately following its creation, especially during 1854–1857. Seventy-two percent of the 130 *lycées* and *collèges* with *bifurcation* that submitted figures to the ministry in response to question 2 of the July 16, 1864, questionnaire reached the zenith of their enrollments in the scientific section by 1857.[31] Thereafter, its enrollments fell off precipitously.

The scientific section, especially in the municipal *collèges*, attracted large numbers of students, initially because it offered an escape from the rigors of the classical section. By 1857, however, the weaknesses of the scientific section had become apparent, and students and families began to doubt its value. The enmity of University professors, who were devoted to the classical program, did not help. Most professors viewed the scientific section as inferior, and their attitude was communicated to students and parents. Its inferiority was further confirmed by its tendency to attract the academically weaker students, but it was crippled by other problems. The scientific sections generally lacked appropriate materials and laboratories. The science taught was too

31. The data for this computation were collected from the reports in cartons F(17) 6843–48, AN. I wish to thank Denis Blum for computing the annual percentages in science and classics.

theoretical. Teachers were not adequately prepared to teach in the scientific section because their training had been primarily in the classics. And finally, parents began to feel that their sons were being forced to commit themselves to *bifurcation* too early in their studies.[32]

In 1857, Fortoul's successor, Rouland, polled teachers in the Paris region and found that none of them were satisfied with *bifurcation* as it existed. Some suggested modifying portions of it. Others urged its total abolition. But Rouland was pressured to maintain the program or some facsimile of it by scientists, economists, industrialists, and even anticlericals, who believed that scientific education gave state schools an edge over parochial schools. Caught between differing viewpoints but committed both personally and politically to continuing a technical education program, Rouland established a commission, chaired by Dumas, to review *bifurcation* and develop an alternative. This commission made its report on professional and technical education to the Imperial Council of 1862. The council was still discussing the report when Duruy became minister a year later.

By 1863, the question of technical education was receiving a great deal of attention from both the government and the press, sparked by the report of a jury at the London Exposition of 1862, concluding that France had fallen far behind other countries in technical education. Seriously concerned, Napoleon III must have asked both the Ministry of Public Instruction and the Ministry of Agriculture, Commerce, and Public Works to help resolve the question for both ministries had study commissions reviewing the problem.[33]

Duruy, a disciple of those democrats who preached the need for a French version of the German *Realschulen*, was sympathetic to the task the emperor had assigned his ministry, although he regularly pointed out that the programs of the two ministries would necessarily be different. The function of education programs sponsored by the Ministry of Agriculture, Commerce, and Public Works was "to train hands," whereas the function of education programs sponsored by the Ministry of Public Instruction was "to train minds."

32. Reports in F(17) 4359, 4361, and 6843–48, AN.
33. Charles Robert, *Considerations générales sur le Group X* (Paris, 1863), 9–10; Ministère de l'Agriculture, du Commerce et des Travaux Publics, *Enquête sur l'enseignement professionel ou recueil de dépositions faites en 1863 et 1864 devant la Commission de l'Enseignement Professionel* (Paris, 1864), v, viii.

Duruy always maintained that he became convinced of the need for technical education at the secondary level when, as an inspector, he watched the young son of a farmer at the *lycée* of Coutances struggling with Latin and Greek. Duruy claimed that this experience "haunted" him until he began to work on his own technical program, particularly because he could not help but remember also that "there were in France 18 or 20 million farmers [*agriculteurs*] and 2 million industrial workers or small employers, without speaking of 1.2 million workers [*employés*] or wage earners; the rest practiced the liberal professions or lived on its income [*rentes*]. For the latter and for the children who showed favorable dispositions, there were 80 *lycées* and 250 *collèges*; for the others, nothing, that is outside of an insufficient number of technical or commercial schools." Since society was "becoming more industrial daily," he was convinced that it "was urgent to create an order of studies which would be appropriate for the children of these 33 million men." During his speech at the annual prize ceremony for the *concours académique* in Paris in August, 1863, Duruy signaled publicly that he was ready to begin where Rouland left off.[34]

While the Ministry of Public Instruction was completing its study of the report prepared by Dumas's commission, Duruy directed inspector Jean-Magloire Baudouin to study technical education in Belgium, the German states, and Switzerland, and he began to dismantle the *bifurcation* program. On September 2, 1863, the *bifurcation* program was transferred from the end of the fourth grade to the end of the third. In October one of the baccalaureates created for *bifurcation*, the *baccalauréat-scindé*, was abolished. Then the physics and chemistry classes were strengthened. At this point Duruy paused to determine the need to proceed further. On October 5 and 22, 1864, he sent confidential circulars to *universitaires* asking whether *bifurcation* as modified by his new measures should be retained. Glachant tabulated the replies and found that the overwhelming vote was for abolition. Duruy then abolished *bifurcation* on December 4, 1864.[35]

In the fall of 1864 and the spring of 1865, the ministry's new pro-

34. Duruy, *Notes et souvenirs*, I, 167, 252–53; *AIP*, 8–11.
35. *JGIP*, 1864, p. 776; F(17) 1474 and 9099, AN; *AIP*, 126–28. Baudouin's report was published in 1865 under the title *Rapport sur l'enseignement spécial en Belgique, en Allemagne, et en Suisse.*

gram for secondary education was taken first to the Council of State, then to the Corps législatif and Senate. It emerged from the Council of State with a name that had been gaining popularity since 1847 and which Duruy much preferred: *enseignement secondaire spécial*. The *spécial* signified for Duruy that whereas "classical education is the same everywhere, special education should *vary* in [the] several localities, according to the character of the dominant industry." [36] Clearly, as can be seen in the argument of the *rapporteur* of the bill to the Council of State, the new name represented a calculated bid to gain *universitaire* acceptance of the nonclassical program: the purpose of special education was to accustom students not to a multitude of facts but to a knowledge of method, the art of observation, and experimentation, all of which would open their minds to learning through research and invention. [37] From the Council of State the bill was sent to the Corps législatif, where it was debated on May 30 and 31 and then approved unanimously. Although some deputies and senators, such as Adolphe Granière de Cassagnac, had expressed fears that the state would jeopardize its classical program by creating special education, both bodies approved the measure without much deliberation because they did not have to vote money for it. Lavisse later reported that many of Duruy's colleagues were amused; they expected special education would come to an immediate and "ridiculous" (Lavisse's word) end. [38] But special education, which became law on June 21, 1865, did not fail.

Duruy had presided over two years of "laborious discussions" on professional education, and now special education, which had a history going back to Richelieu, was enacted into law. Duruy considered this (and would for years) one of the greatest achievements of his ministry. [39]

One of the great virtues of special education, "which fits so well with the general political plan of the empire," Duruy wrote the emperor, was that it was both conservative and liberal in nature. It was conservative in that it would counter the tendency of young men to

36. Duruy, *Notes et souvenirs*, I, 256.
37. *RIP*, 1864, p. 30.
38. Lavisse, "Victor Duruy," 54.
39. Duruy, *Notes et souvenirs*, I, 258, 254.

emigrate from the countryside and would keep young men who would ultimately take jobs in the commercial and industrial sectors of the economy from overtaxing the classical curriculum. It was liberal in that it made French secondary education truly national and modern in content by providing a curriculum appropriate to the needs and future employments of the lower classes.[40] In other words, special education was a program that could promote social harmony and economic satisfaction.

Special education was neither an apprenticeship program for industry nor a preparatory program for the *grandes écoles*. By his reestablishment of *cours préparatoires* in the *lycées* (circular, March 24, 1865) Duruy provided (as Fortoul had earlier) a means by which students could elevate themselves from special education to the *grandes écoles*, a flexibility developed in the program which later caused Charles Louandre to speak of Duruy's *trifurcation*.[41] But special education by itself was to be a general education program for young men who would become foremen in factories, skilled workmen, businessmen, and the like. It offered its own form of *culture générale* to young students "who could postpone their entry into the workshop, bank or factory for two or three years."[42] Special education's *culture générale* was supposed to liberate young men, to save them from becoming, as Duruy put it, "slaves to the machine." It would give them a new sense of dignity in the pursuit of their *métier*.

The shape and content of the new program were specified by the law of June 21, 1865, and by the instruction of April 6, 1866. Special education was an abbreviated program compared with *bifurcation*. No longer, thanks considerably to Duruy, did secondary students have to take classical studies for five years before beginning their nonclassical education. Now they could begin as soon as they entered a *lycée* or *collège*, a modification that made special education much less expensive than *bifurcation*. The curriculum of special education duplicated that of the higher primary schools—religious and moral instruction; French grammar, composition and literature; history and geography;

40. Victor Duruy to Napoleon III, October 25, 1866, in *ibid.*, II, 228. The letter is misdated 1886 in the memoirs.
41. *JGIP*, 1865, p. 411.
42. See Célestin Bouglé, *The French Conception of Culture Générale and Its Influence upon Instruction* (New York, 1938); *AIP*, 126–29.

applied mathematics, physics, mechanics, chemistry, and biology and their applications to agriculture and industry; linear design, accounting, and bookkeeping—except that the history program specified the teaching in the fourth grade of contemporary history and two hours weekly of the history of inventions. Without drawing public attention to its establishment, a special preparatory year for academically weak students was added by Duruy in September, 1865. One of the innovations in the curriculum, for which Duruy was probably responsible, was its arrangement in concentric circles. That is, the full complement of courses was offered in each of the four years, but the content of each course became more advanced as a student proceeded from one year to the next. The important virtue of this new feature (which Duruy could not sufficiently stress) was that a student could leave school at any time possessing at least some degree of vocational general education. Another important innovation was that a secondary student could transfer from the classical curriculum to the special education curriculum or vice versa any time he wished as long as he compensated for his academic deficiencies. The last major innovation in the special education curriculum was the addition of a course in public and private morality in the third and fourth years, the one departure from the scheme of concentric circles. Again, Duruy's contribution to this feature of the program is clear. The course in morality was to be special education's equivalent of the classical program's philosophy. As Duruy described it, the course was "less a series of philosophical lessons than morality in action, explained by science" (precepts such as Cicero developed in *Duties*). This course in morality was secular but not atheistic for it was designed to encourage in students a "strong conviction of their moral obligations toward themselves, society, and God" and a dislike for the materialism that was a threatening product of industrial progress.[43]

To encourage students to complete all four years of the new program, Duruy instituted a *certificat d'études* for special education which became, on the initiative of two of his colleagues, a passport to

43. Text of the law of June 21, 1865, in Rohr, *Victor Duruy, ministre de Napoléon III*, 202–203; instruction, April 6, 1866, in *AIP*, 276–87; Duruy, *Notes et souvenirs*, I, 252; Gerbod, "La place de l'histoire dans l'enseignement secondaire," 130; confidential circular, September 30, 1865, F(17) 8708; AN; *AIP*, 43–44, 622–32.

jobs in the lower echelons of the Ministry of the Interior and the Ministry of Finance. To provide an element of academic competition for students, Duruy created a *concours général* for special education. And finally, to provide patronage for vocational education, Duruy attached *conseils de perfectionnement* to the special education program (article 3 of the law of June 21, 1865). Duruy viewed the *conseil de perfectionnement* as a keystone to the program: the success of special education depended on the sincere cooperation and effectiveness of the members of the councils.[44]

Schools such as the Ecole des Chartes and the Conservatoire des Arts et Métiers had had their own *conseils de perfectionnement* for some time, but *conseils de perfectionnement* had never formed a part of the *bifurcation* program. It is not entirely clear who was responsible for their inclusion in the special education program, but it is easy to suspect that it was Duruy because on August 26, 1865, he created a Conseil Supérieur de Perfectionnement to preside over the lower councils and to report to the Imperial Council. The membership of the local councils included a few functionaries: the *inspecteur d'académie*, the *proviseur* or principal of the secondary institution, and the mayor. The remainder of the members came from business, industry, engineering, farming, and so forth. The functions of the councils were outlined in Duruy's instruction of April 6, 1866. The councils were to meet at least three times a year to discuss the development and special needs of the locality. They could add courses to the special education curriculum or delete them as they wished. (The council at Lille, for example, added a course in rural economy.) They participated in examinations for special education students, supervised the technical collections of special education, assisted in student placement, and annually submitted a report to the Conseil Supérieur de Perfectionnement. The councils were especially responsible for implementing the formula Duruy pressed onto special education: "To each according to his needs and abilities."[45]

The last Second Empire resumé of the annual reports from the *con-*

---

44. *JGIP*, 1866, p. 746; decree of December 21, 1867, in *AIP*, 529–32; *ibid.*, 355.
45. Decree of August 26, 1865, in *AIP*, 245–49; *Exposé de la situation de l'empire* for 1866, as reproduced in *JGIP*, 1867, p. 169; *JGIP*, 1867, p. 1; and Duruy's inauguration speech at the special education *lycée* of Mont-de-Marsan, as reported in the *Journal des Landes*, October 21, 1866.

seils de perfectionnement, which was published in January, 1869, provides a detailed evaluation of the early success of special education under Duruy. In 324 reports special education was said to be gaining supporters throughout France except in some towns in the Midi. At Lectorne, sons of artisans and other special education students were teaching the concepts they had learned at school to their fathers. In the Nord, at Dunkirk, Quesnay, Valenciennes, Soissons, Hazebrouck, and Thionville, students learned about "the making of sugar and beer, the canals, oil works, laundries, flour mills, glassworks, iron and copper foundries, pottery works, coal mines, and workshops for the curing of bacon. Each visit is then the subject of an essay in which the students give an account of what they saw: the best copies are chosen and placed aside to be read at a meeting of the council." In agricultural regions students, often accompanied by officials of local agricultural societies, visited model farms and collected samples of plants and minerals for subsequent study in class. At Clermont, Pamiers, le Vignan, Poitiers, Figeac, and Château-Thierry distinguished barristers gave special education students lessons in common law twice a week. Many municipal councils gave subsidies to the special education teachers so they could extend their collections of scientific and industrial materials.[46]

But special education did not develop without difficulties. The reports indicated that most localities still found laboratory installation prohibitively expensive. Modern language professors continued to resist the conversational portion of language instruction. And more generally, the special education program needed extension almost everywhere. Of the 325 institutions that offered special education in 1867–1868 (with a total enrollment of 18,463 students), only some 20 had the full four-year program. The majority of schools offered three years and found it necessary to precede the special education program with the preparatory year Duruy had provided. Still, it was a new program, only one year away from its inception, when the annual reports for 1867–1868 were collated; with time, the problems could be resolved.

46. *AIP*, 890–907. Some of the agricultural societies were generous to the special education program in their areas. In Yonne, for example, the agricultural society gave the *collège* of Joigny rich collections of instruments, seedlings, and fruits.

An institution that proved invaluable to the special education program and corrected a difficulty that had plagued *bifurcation* was the normal school Duruy created for special education in the old Benedictine Abbey at Cluny. Duruy could have established a division for special education at the Ecole Normale Supérieure, but he was convinced that it would not succeed in the shadow of the strong classical program. A rural setting was much more in keeping with the nature of the new program, and spacious facilities in the countryside permitted the establishment of orchards and horticultural collections.

The abandoned abbey of Cluny, along with 100,000 francs for renovations, was donated to Duruy by the general council of Saône-et-Loire, which was presided over by the Saint-Simonian Eugène Schneider of Le Creusot. The municipal council of Cluny chipped in another 70,000 francs for the renovation of Cluny, and some fifty-three departmental councils responded to Duruy's request for the creation of two new scholarships in each department for students who wished to attend the new school. Railroad companies began to donate scholarships for individual students. And Duruy created twenty scholarships from his own funds. Special education and Cluny were so important to Duruy that he suggested to the emperor that some of the eighty-four *écoles normales primaires* might be abolished so that funds could be shifted to the new normal school, but the emperor was reluctant to make such a bold move.[47]

An *agrégation* was created for students who would graduate from Cluny, and the school opened for business on March 6, 1866. Duruy named Ferdinand Roux, a veteran of technical education, its first director and made him responsible for most of the details of organization. But Duruy intervened frequently with advice about establishing the proper atmosphere at Cluny. On November 12, 1866, for example, Duruy wrote to Roux: "It will be in good taste to do things very modestly, not for economy, but to mark the institution and to form its general atmosphere. No formal paraphernalia, few dishes, but carefully prepared and of good quality with an exquisite cleanliness; nothing of Paris, nor of Lyons." Luxury and pomp were to be shunned religiously. Clunyites were to live as simply and as dedicatedly as their predecessors had at the abbey. They were to go forth as missionaries of

47. *BAIP*, II (1864), 150–51; *RIP*, 1865, pp. 262–63; Duruy, *Notes et souvenirs*, I, 260.

the new education.[48] Duruy reveled in the analogies he could draw between the old and new inhabitants of Cluny.

After some initial hesitation, Duruy decided that a Catholic chaplain should be attached to Cluny. But he urged Roux to guard against letting the "chaplain brandish his great theological saber to kill Voltaire and Rousseau." The chaplain was supposed to confine himself strictly to parochial duties. Yet at the same time, Duruy advised Roux that Cluny should accept only *des croyants*, a policy undoubtedly geared to protect the institution from clerical attacks.[49]

The pedagogical emphasis at Cluny was to be on practice and application. When Duruy found the Latin program and the *leçons d'analyse* too difficult and involved, he reproved Roux. Latin was allowed only as a "luxury"; Cluny was not the rue d'Ulm. More important were the practical experiences students would have with the vast collections established at Cluny, which were accommodated in a special museum: raw materials, specimens of work, illustrations and designs for locomotives, saws, boats, woodwork and carpentry models, a piano that could be disassembled and reconstructed, contemporary inventions donated by inventors, and a variety of implements. Duruy's solicitations were most productive. The faculties sent duplicates of technical instruments, the minister of war sent a collection of diverse agricultural products from Algeria, Milne-Edwards gave a large and important paleontology collection, the Louvre sent a plastics collection, the Museum of Natural History organized an experimental garden at Cluny, and a variety of groups donated books for the library. In a letter to the emperor on November 15, 1866, Duruy effused: "Your Majesty will have the first technological museum of Europe at Cluny. This will be the best book and the best instruction for this school of the applied sciences."[50] To provide students and professors with an opportunity to experiment with new pedagogical methods (which were supposed to be a hallmark of Cluny), Duruy established a practice-teaching school, an *école annex*, in which professors and administrators were to oversee the young student teachers.

Cluny grew fairly rapidly while Duruy was in office. Its initial en-

48. Ferdinand Roux, *Histoire des six premiers années de l'Ecole Normale Spéciale de Cluny* (Paris, 1889), 44; Victor Duruy to Ferdinand Roux, December 7, 1866, *ibid.*, 49–50.
49. *Ibid.*, 44, 48–49.
50. *Ibid.*, 53–56; Duruy, *Notes et souvenirs*, I, 263.

rollment of 92 students in the fall of 1866 increased to 218 within a few months. Most of them, both scholarship and tuition students, stayed for two years, when they received a *brevet de capacité*. A few students remained for a third year to prepare for the new *agrégation*.

Cluny and the *école annex* must be seen as preeminent in a larger system of model schools for special education. Four were established while Duruy was in office: the *lycée* of Mont-de-Marsan to serve the southwest; the *lycée* of Mulhouse to serve the northeast; the *lycée* at Napoleonville (Pontivy) specializing in agricultural training to serve the northwest; and the *collège* of Alais, specializing in metallurgical studies, to serve the central portion of the south. But Duruy also envisioned the establishment of one or two more model schools for the southeast and the far north. The purpose of each was both to demonstrate the new methodology of special education and to serve as an example of how languishing municipal *collèges* could be revived by the new curriculum. Mont-de-Marsan was a case in point: in the spring of 1866 enrollments at the school, which was then a *collège*, were so low that its very survival was in jeopardy. In October, 1866, however, the school was transformed into a *lycée* of special education, and one month later it had so many new students that the rector of Bordeaux judged that an annex was necessary. Duruy hastened to make an example of the school. At the inauguration of Mont-de-Marsan on October 15, Duruy pointed out that the 251 classical communal *collèges* had a total budget of 11 million francs, yet they produced only 253 *bachelier-ès-letters* each year. In cold financial terms, that meant that the *collèges* expended 43,500 francs to produce each *bachelier*. Although Duruy's figures were obviously skewed because only 152 of the 251 *collèges* were in full operation and the *collèges* trained hundreds of students who did not complete their studies, his point was well made. Shortly thereafter, the idea of converting languishing *collèges* and *lycées* into institutions devoted exclusively to special education began to catch on.[51]

51. *Exposé de la situation de l'empire* for 1866, as reproduced in *JGIP*, 1867, p. 170; report from Lot-et-Garonne, June, 1866, F(17) 4361, AN; *JGIP*, 1866, pp. 676–78, 729, and *passim*. According to the *Exposé de la situation de l'empire* for 1866, the *collèges* where special education had become the predominant or the exclusive curriculum were Castres (Tarn), Lectourne (Gers), Parthenay (Deux-Sevres), Forbach (Moselle), Sainte-Marie-aux-Mines (Haut-Rhin), Bruyeres (Vosges), Tournus (Saône-et-Loire), and

Outside France, Duruy created a model institution of special education at the *lycée* of Galata-Seraï in Constantinople. Had time permitted, he probably would have realized his dream to establish others at Bucharest, Smyrna, Alexandria, Tunis, and Corfu. His complete plan for a Université de France en Orient was intended to extend French science and the French intellectual sphere of influence, which he felt were rapidly being engulfed by the Italian, Austrian, and British throughout the East. Despite support from Ferdinand de Lesseps, however, only Galata-Seraï was successful.[52]

Before Duruy's *enseignement secondaire spécial* can be evaluated, two other areas must be assessed: the clientele and the opposition to the program. Robert Anderson has studied the clientele of special education in detail in his dissertation on secondary education during the Second Empire, but a report from the inspector of Ariège for June of 1868 offers a convenient summary: "(1) Students belonging to the bourgeoisie, but judged, by experience, unintelligent and incapable of following the classics program; these are the poorest students; (2) the sons of rural proprietors, managers, farmers; (3) sons of entrepreneurs, craftsmen, drivers [conductors], engineering foremen, employees of the various [government] administrations; (4) sons of soft-drink vendors, innkeepers, small industrialists, small merchants, [and] workers." All of the other reports from functionaries confirm that special education drew students from these same classes, the very classes Duruy had hoped to attract. Only one anomaly was reported, and that was in the department of Ain, where a great number of seminarians were taking special education. Altogether, in 1868, the young men taking special education represented 25 percent of the population in public secondary schools (18,463 out of a total enrollment of 71,594). Unfortunately, no such general statistics are available on the percentage of students enrolled in *bifurcation*, but a review of the pertinent documents and literature suggests that special education recruited in

---

Montélimar (Drôme). The *conseils municipaux* of Bayonne (Basses-Pyrénées), Thiers (Puy-de-Dôme), Clermont (Oise), Cognac (Charente), Dieuze and Sarrebourg (Meurthe), Sarreguemines (Moselle), Vignan (Gard), Saint-Nazaire (Loire-Inférieure), Saint-Servan (Ille-et-Vilaine), Manosque (Basses-Alpes), and Beziers (Hérault) had also expressed their earnest desire to convert their *collèges* totally to special education.

52. Duruy, *Notes et souvenirs*, I, 272–73; Ferdinand de Lesseps to Victor Duruy, June 3, 1866, F(17) 8702, AN; the documents on Galata-Seraï, F(17) 4613, AN.

1868 about as many secondary students as *bifurcation* had as late as 1864. The noteworthy difference between the two in the realm of recruitment is that special education was offered in more schools than *bifurcation* had been, which in combination with such other factors as the improved features of special education ultimately meant that more students would be attracted to the program. Statistics for 1876 reveal that the enrollment in special education had grown to 28.6 percent.[53]

The opposition to special education arose in large part from the negative reputation bequeathed by *bifurcation* and, certainly, other previous technical education programs. Special education still looked too much like *bifurcation* to some people, and indeed some argued that it was only *bifurcation* under a new name. Thus the same classicists, the same prestige-conscious parents, and the same staunch anti-materialists who had opposed *bifurcation* became the ardent opponents of the new *enseignement des épiciers*, as some of its fiercest opponents had been calling technical education. Also, the same conservatives who had attacked *bifurcation* were now attacking special education for social and economic reasons. Cardinal Ferdinand Donnet, for example, protested in 1866 that Duruy's special education "*pushes* our young people toward administrative, industrial, commercial, literary, and artistic skills which make them disgusted with rural life." But *L'Union* feared the opposite, asserting that special education was undemocratic because it placed the rural students outside the route of liberal careers. In addition, certain manufacturers, businessmen, and technical reformers opposed the vocational program in the secondary schools because they were convinced that the Ministry of Public Instruction had no real understanding of the needs of technical education; only the Ministry of Commerce did.[54]

Special education also suffered from its own set of problems, which

53. Robert D. Anderson, "Some Developments in French Secondary Education During the Second Empire" (Ph.D. dissertation, Oxford University, 1967), 247ff.; report from the inspector of Ariège, academy of Toulouse, June, 1868, F(17) 4363, AN; report of M. Olivier in the department of Ain, academy of Lyons, June, 1869, F(17) 4364, AN; *L'instruction en France, 1851–1869*, as reproduced in *JGIP*, 1869, p. 260; and Rohr, *Victor Duruy, ministre de Napoléon III*, 130–31. The percentage for 1876 has been computed from the figures in Anderson, *Education in France*, 222.

54. Gontard, "Une réforme de l'enseignement secondaire," 7; *JGIP*, 1866, p. 665; report of the rector of Chambéry, November 23, 1864, F(17) 4359, AN; Vial, *L'enseignement secondaire et la démocratie* (Paris, 1901), 272, cited in Gérard Vincent, "Les professeurs de l'enseignement secondaire dans la société de la 'Belle Epoque,'" *Revue d'histoire moderne et contemporaine*, XIII (1966), 61; *RIP*, 1866, pp. 721 (emphasis added),

were related to the problems of *bifurcation*. Most important, there was insufficient funding. Duruy had won the principle of his new program in 1865 but not a centime of support from the state. In 1866 and 1868 the Corps législatif voted 220,000 francs as a subsidy to Cluny, but all money for special education programs around the country came either from Duruy's regular budget (in the form of subventions) or from the municipalities. Consequently, few *collèges* and *lycées* were able to purchase sufficient collections and scientific instruments for their laboratories. Also, the recruitment to Cluny was much slower than the ministry had anticipated so that special education programs could not be supplied with well-qualified teachers quickly enough. Further, special education, which was still in its infancy when Duruy left office, would suffer from lack of continuing ministerial support; Duruy's successors did not share his commitment to it. Although special education was continued for another twenty-five years, future ministers of public instruction, who were more conservative, tended to favor the creation of higher primary schools, which did not encourage "inappropriate ambitions." And despite the plethora of circulars Duruy disseminated and the speeches he made, there was still considerable misunderstanding about the nature of both special education and Cluny. So disillusioned was Duruy's son-in-law and adviser, Charles Glachant, that he suggested Cluny be closed and special education salvaged by itself. And finally, but not least in importance, it appears that industry in the late 1860s was unable to provide special education graduates with an adequate supply of jobs appropriate to their new skills.[55]

Yet despite its only moderate success, special education was a vastly improved program of technical secondary education. It had its own model schools, its *conseils de perfectionnement*, and its normal school. And under the Third Republic, as we have seen it, it would claim a

347; Day, "Development of Higher Primary and Intermediate Technical Education in France," 55, 64; and Armand Audiganne, *Les populations ouvrières et les industries de la France* (2 vols.; Paris, 1860), II, 270.

55. See Rohr, *Victor Duruy, ministre de Napoléon III*, 130 (but the archival reports which Rohr did not touch [p. 8] also verify the lack of monies for laboratory collections and equipment); Robert Anderson, "Secondary Education in Mid-Nineteenth Century France: Some Social Aspects," *Past and Present*, no. 53 (November, 1971), 146; Ringer, *Education and Society in Modern Europe*, 120; note from Charles Glachant to Duruy, undated, F(17) 8708, AN; F(17) 4361–63, AN; Duruy, *Notes et souvenirs*, I, 253; F(17) 4361–62, AN.

larger percentage of students—in spite of the preference of successive ministers of education for higher primary schools.

Returning his attention once more to the classical program in the closing years of his administration, Duruy made a minor but logical modification in baccalaureate procedures with the *arrêté* of July 28, 1867. Students already possessing the *baccalauréat-ès-sciences* but going on to take the *baccalauréat-ès-lettres* were excused from its scientific section. Then, by a circular in March, 1867, he generalized a practice common in some secondary schools—the creation of alumni societies that provided the schools with financial support, especially in the form of scholarships and placement assistance for their graduates. To the obligatory portion of the curriculum he added art and two subjects—plain-song (which had been optional before) and gymnastics— which Salvandy had attempted to introduce earlier.[56]

But Duruy was moving toward more major reform by late 1867 and early 1868. Indeed, he had in mind a complete modernization of the classical curriculum. And he had three basic reasons for such a change. First, he was disturbed by the routine, tedium, and pedantry of classical studies. The curriculum needed to be brought to life by new methods and a reduction in the number of scholastic exercises. Second, he wished to improve the position of the *lycées* in the face of Jesuit competition in the preparation of students for the *grandes écoles* of the state.[57] He was concerned mainly that so many students from Jesuit schools were being admitted to Saint-Cyr (69 out of 301), particularly because they were sons of legitimists. And finally, he wished to strengthen the classical program so that special education could never be blamed for its weakness. Throughout many of his speeches, but particularly in the one at the *concours général* of August, 1865, and in the one before the Corps législatif on July 17, 1868, Duruy spoke of the decadence that had pervaded classical studies in the 1850s as a result of the "invasion of politics." This charge seemed to locate him more with the opposition than the government, but he received no rebuke from the emperor for his criticisms.[58]

56. *BAIP*, X (1868), 63; *JGIP*, 1867, p. 181; Lavisse, "Victor Duruy," 49; *RIP*, 1865, p. 705; *AIP*, 749; Trénard, *Salvandy en son temps*, 911.
57. Duruy, *Notes et souvenirs*, I, 289–90.
58. *JGIP*, 1868, p. 467.

Politics aside, the general reforms of the classical curriculum that Duruy wished to implement universally were the same ones he had been implementing quietly at the experimental *lycée* of Versailles. The "Versailles Program," as it was known, consisted of nine reforms: shorter classes (one to one and a half hours in length), with recreations in between; longer and more frequent recreations with gymnastics; students in Greek separated according to their competencies; Latin optional in the second grade (the weaker students were excused); history essays graded for literary style and grammar as well as content; grammar classes divested of philological and pedantic exercises; grammar taught pragmatically; dictated corrections in class suppressed; and modern languages begun earlier in the curriculum. Of all of these reforms, Duruy considered the first the most important.

Duruy attempted to provide adequate time for functionaries and professors to acclimate themselves to the new reforms. He had recommended most of the reforms to the rectors when they met with him as a group for the first time in 1863 in Paris. In the following year in his lengthy questionnaire of July 16, 1864, he included several questions that related to these reforms. And in the reforms he implemented in modern language instruction in 1864 he gave professors experience with some of the modifications he wished to extend to the rest of the curriculum. Believing, perhaps naively, that he had broken down some of the resistance to change by 1868, he sent a final questionnaire to *proviseurs* and principals of *lycées* and *collèges* in April of that year to test the readiness of the University for the new reforms. Table 5 indicates the generally negative response he received.

The crux of the problem was that most of the reforms touched either directly or indirectly on that sacred pair of subjects in the curriculum, Greek and Latin. As Goumy explained in the *RIP*, "The slightest threat to the religion of these priests [Latin and Greek professors] is in their eyes a sacrilege." To these "priests" Latin and Greek were the pillars upon which all French intellectual achievements had been based. To reduce Greek and Latin requirements was akin to destroying part of *la France*. Latin could not even be made optional because to the minds of contemporaries, making a course optional was tantamount to abolishing it. Firmly supporting the professors were both the powerful Association pour l'encouragement des études grecques en

Table 5. Responses to Circulars, April 22 and 23, 1868, on Reform
of the Classical Secondary Curriculum

	Responses		
Reform	Favorable	Unfavorable	Vague[a]
Shorten class length	143	124	27
Increase length of recreations	190	54	49
Suppress *dictée*	57	83	159
Greek-cursive study	85	159	59
Optional Latin verse	102	126	74
Studies optional in general	52	41	222
Suppress chairs[b]	72	67	157
Optional sections on the baccalaureate	65	44	186
Homogeneous grouping of students	72	44	178
Extend special education	63	18	211

Source: Compiled from information in the reports found in cartons
F(17) 6843–48, AN, submitted by 292 *lycées* and *collèges*. Favorable or
unfavorable responses with a qualification (for example, a "no" vote for
reform in 1868 but with the remark that reform could be implemented in
the future) were entered under both "favorable" or "unfavorable" and
"vague." Therefore, the three columns rarely add across to 292.

[a]Most of the responses in this category recommended delaying implementation of the reforms.

[b]Suppress chairs of professors with few students in their classes; the
money saved from these chairs would be distributed to the remaining professors in the form of salary increases.

France and anticlericals, the latter convinced that any modification in
the classical curriculum would redound to the benefit of the Catholic
collèges. Thus when the *Journal de Paris* called Duruy's 1868 proposals absurd, it was speaking for many French educators.[59]

On June 6, 1869, Charles Glachant wrote a memorandum to his
father-in-law suggesting that he content himself with the experiments
at Versailles and abjure their generalization. The University professors

59. *RIP*, 1867, p. 17; F(17) 4363, AN; *RIP*, 1868, pp. 306–308; *JGIP*, 1868,
p. 290.

were in no mood to be coerced; by pushing for further reform Duruy would only damage what sympathies and momentum he had managed to provoke.[60] Duruy did not write his reaction on the memorandum as he often did, so there is no record of what he thought of Glachant's suggestion. Just a few weeks later, Duruy was out of office.

Duruy's reforms in secondary education can be seen against the backdrop of the growing competition between Church and state schools, which Duruy referred to on more than one occasion. But lest Duruy's reputation as an anticlerical cloud the picture, it is important to remember that just fourteen years earlier, there had been no Catholic school system as such at the secondary level, that is, nothing outside of the prosperous minor seminaries. Before 1850, public *lycées* and *collèges* educated a substantial majority of the young men at the secondary level. Between 1850 and 1865, however, the Catholic system of education grew rapidly so that *lycées* and municipal *collèges* had only 46 percent of the secondary pupils, whereas Catholic *collèges* had 24 percent and were still growing. (Lay private *collèges*, a declining sector, had 30 percent.)[61] Catholic *collèges* were becoming serious competitors for the bourgeoisie—the very class from which the state expected to draw its future administrators,[62] and fears were being voiced that two different groups of youths were being reared in France.

Duruy was certainly concerned about the possible creation of such a conflict and the problem of the ultimate control of France. His concern was obvious, for example, in the confidential circular of June 30, 1864, inquiring whether the legitimist feast of Saint-Henry was being celebrated in certain schools, and in his report to the emperor in 1867 on the number of young men from Catholic schools who were being admitted to the *grandes écoles* (Duruy reported happily that the percentage was only 15). But as for competition, Duruy was not unduly alarmed by the growth of Catholic schools because he believed that competition could benefit the nation and that the public schools could

60. F(17) 6872[2], AN.
61. Robert Anderson, "Catholic Secondary Schools (1850–1870): A Reappraisal," in Theodore Zeldin (ed.), *Conflicts in French Society: Anticlericalism, Education and Morals in the Nineteenth Century* (London, 1970), 59.
62. Harrigan, "Social and Political Implications of Catholic Secondary Education," 53.

compete effectively. Indeed, Duruy emphasized that he had no intention of "crushing" the competition.[63] On the other hand, he had no intention of letting the private schools crush the public.

He believed it was imperative for the state to strengthen its own schools. For the classical curriculum, this meant converting the course in logic back to a true course in philosophy, emphasizing conversation and the practical in modern language instruction, teaching young men the very recent history of their country, and generally reducing the tedium and sterile exercises in the secondary curriculum. It also meant reducing the amount of memorization required for the baccalaureate examination and converting the examination into a true test of knowledge gained in school and the ability to think and write. These reforms added up to a pedagogical revolution for France, and they had major repercussions for the nation because the curriculum of the Catholic secondary schools was becoming in the 1860s more and more like that of the public secondary schools.[64] Yet to view Duruy's reforms solely as a response to competition from Catholic schools would be an egregious mistake because Duruy was actually more concerned about the challenges France was facing from growing democratization and industrialization. He would have worked to strengthen the classical curriculum and reform the baccalaureate even if the Falloux Law had never been passed.

And he was convinced that the state had to do more than just improve the classical program. It also had to provide for the "intermediary classes," as Duruy called them, who would form the "future officers of industry and commerce."[65] Fortoul's *bifurcation* was not the answer, particularly because a student had to pass through classical studies before he could begin the technical program. Nor were the *écoles primaires supérieures* the answer because they did not offer the prestige of secondary studies, which many parents sought for their

63. F(17) 9143, AN; Duruy, *Notes et souvenirs*, I, 288, 255.
64. Paul Gerbod, *La vie quotidienne dans les lycées et collèges au XIXe siècle* (Paris, 1968), 125; cf. Harrigan, "Catholic Secondary Education in France," 51–123 and esp. 276–79.
65. Duruy, *Notes et souvenirs*, I, 255. Duruy confided to Alfred Darimon that he hoped that factory directors (*chefs d'usine*) and employers as well as foremen and workers would be prepared by the "*cours supérieurs de l'enseignement spécial*" (Victor Duruy to Alfred Darimon, August 31, 1865, in Alfred Darimon, *Histoire d'un parti: Le tiers parti sous l'empire (1863–1866)* (Paris, 1887), 314.

sons. Duruy hoped that special education would be the solution. Special education was true secondary education. It offered many of the same subjects that the classical program offered, though logically not Latin or Greek, and it had its own *culture général*.

Special education had the virtue of "erect[ing] a bridge" across the chasm between the primary and secondary educational systems.[66] Special education offered status and a modicum of social mobility.[67] And it responded in a very sensitive and sophisticated way—through the concentric circle plan of the curriculum and through the *conseils de perfectionnement* which adjusted the technical curriculum to local interests—to the larger national needs of a country that was daily growing more industrial. Special education was thus liberal and modern, and Duruy judged it one of the most important programs the state had adopted in education.

66. Duruy, *Notes et souvenirs*, I, 257.
67. Harrigan, *Mobility, Elites and Education in French Society of the Second Empire*, 153.

VI · Public Secondary Education for Girls

Secondary education for girls, truly speaking, does not exist in France.
—Victor Duruy, 1867

What I affirm . . . after more than forty years of observation, is that in subjects taught, methods and many other things, the intellectual education of young women is better, more solid, more elevated, more refined, more fertile in definitive and durable results than that offered in schools for young men.
—Félix Dupanloup, 1867

It would be difficult to say exactly when secondary education for women first appeared in France. From at least the time of the Renaissance and during the whole of the Old Regime, countless numbers of women in the upper classes, taught by their fathers, priests, or tutors, knew Greek and Latin and had a fairly wide acquaintance with ancient and contemporary literature. Whether these women in fact possessed a true secondary education is questionable. But certainly their knowledge was much more advanced than that of their sisters who emerged from the elementary schools.

None of the advanced education given to women, however, was well organized. Outside of the school established by Mme de Maintenon at Saint-Cyr in the seventeenth century and the courses organized by Abbé Gaultier in 1786, there was no formal secondary education per se for young women; the latter years of the extant *pensionnats* for young girls were devoted almost exclusively to the "arts of agreement," that is, dance, music, drawing, and needlework. The French Revolution brought little change in this situation, save for the disappearance of many convent schools. Joseph Lakanal was almost alone among the revolutionaries in supporting equal education for girls, but even he supported such equality only at the primary level. The campaign for formal secondary-level female education was not launched effectively until the closing years of the First Empire, when two former educators at the court of Louis XVI, Mme Stéphanie de Genlis and Mme Jeanne Campan, inspired by the initiatives of Abbé Gaultier, began to press for the creation of girls' *pensionnats* that would offer an advanced education. Under their inspiration a number of *pensionnats* began to appear. At the same time, higher schools for daughters of members of the Legion of Honor were founded at Ecouen and Saint-Denis. But few of these initiatives survived the First Empire.[1]

Nonetheless, the tide of opinion favorable to some advanced education for young girls in the upper classes was growing. During the Restoration, female religious congregations made considerable progress in establishing advanced *pensionnats* for young women. Indeed, *pensionnats* became so numerous that the University felt obliged to give them some direction. The *arrêtés* of 1819 and 1820 recognized two orders of education for women, elementary and higher (higher education for girls in the nineteenth century usually meant secondary education).

During the July Monarchy, more *pensionnats* and courses (for day students) were opened—primarily in Paris but in a few provincial cities as well. The now famous courses of the Abbé Gaultier on the rue de Lille in Paris were continued after the abbé's death in 1818 by his students, and in 1836 Alvarès Lévy initiated another series of courses for young women of the affluent classes at Paris. Courses that prepared women for the primary teaching examination also appeared at this time. Once again, the University felt compelled to intervene. On March 7, 1837, the Royal Council of Public Instruction approved an *arrêté* which Octave Gréard has called "the first charter of secondary education for girls." This "charter" established four basic principles. First, it distinguished between inferior-level schools, to which it gave the name *pensions*, and higher-level schools which it called *institutions*. The latter were boarding schools that accepted girls between the ages of ten and sixteen. Second, it articulated the regular elementary curriculum for *pensions* and an advanced curriculum composed of French literature, grammar, and style, geography of the ancient world, ancient and modern history, and cosmology for *institutions*. Third, it

1. Gréard, *Education et instruction*, II, 119, 94–95, 105–110; Paul Janet, "L'éducation des femmes," *Revue des deux mondes*, 3rd period, LIX (1883), 53–54.

imposed more specific regulations for the granting of certificates to directresses of *institutions*; and fourth, it established a regular state inspection for girls' schools. None of these provisions were applied rigorously, however, and none applied to *externats* or day schools.[2]

By the end of the July Monarchy, then, the state had recognized the existence of secondary education for women but was reluctant to intervene seriously and left all initiative for the founding of girls' schools to congregations or lay women. There was little evidence of secondary education for girls in the provinces; indeed, some departments reported none. But the situation in Paris was impressive: there were numerous external courses, *pensionnats*, *institutions*, and literary and scientific "gatherings" for young women. In 1839 the minister of public instruction, Villemain, reported the existence of four hundred *pensionnats* for girls in Paris, and by 1848 estimates were that some fifteen to twenty thousand girls were receiving secondary education. Yet the quality of education varied from course to course and from *internat* to *internat*, and the state was often unable to inspect girls' boarding schools so as to ascertain the true level of studies.[3]

Public opinion was still very divided on the need for secondary-level female education. The majority of Frenchmen and traditionally minded women continued to believe that women did not need a serious intellectual education, considering it a luxury (*enseignement de luxe*), unnecessary for working-class girls, who did not need it for their jobs and upper-class girls, who did not prepare for careers. A serious intellectual education might make young women unhappy in their future roles as wives and mothers. At the worst, it could make them mentally ill, for a woman's mind was not only inferior but weak, incapable of tolerating the strain of serious intellectual study. Conservatives had only to look to George Sand to see what dangers lurked for women who tried to become too intellectual.[4]

Counterposed to this view was that of a growing number of feminists during the July Monarchy, who believed that women had the same capacities as men and were entitled to the same rights and prerogatives. These feminists, many of whom were Saint-Simonians and

2. Gréard, *Education et instruction*, II, 114–15.
3. Mayeur, *L'éducation des filles en France*, 59, 68, 92, 61, 59, 96.
4. *Ibid.*, 49.

Fourierists, were in the forefront of the campaign for higher education for women. In 1845 they founded the *Revue de l'enseignement des femmes* and began demanding both that the state create *collèges* for women and that these *collèges* be operated by female professors.

In 1847 the progressive Salvandy, who sympathized with most of the feminist arguments, established a commission to study the possibility of creating state-directed model *collèges* for women. Before his commission could complete its work, however, the February Revolution intervened and the project was killed by the Second Republic. The Falloux Law did not recognize the existence of a higher level of courses for young women.

During the 1850s, the movement for female higher education came to a halt. Feminists were quiescent, and the inflation in rents in Paris caused by the renovations and the attachment of suburban communes to the city forced the closing of most of the laic *institutions*. The educational program of a few of these *institutions* continued to survive, however, in the form of less costly independent courses. But only the female religious orders, with their more abundant resources, continued to maintain girls' boarding schools.[5]

By the late 1850s and early 1860s there were signs that feminism and the movement for public secondary education for women were reviving. The numbers of young women petitioning for *certificats d'études* and *brevets de capacité* with no intention of becoming teachers grew significantly. In 1862, Julie Daubié, the second Frenchwoman to earn a baccalaureate, roiled the waters by publishing *Du progrès de l'instruction primaire—justice et liberté* and demanding money and professors for *lycées* for girls. By 1865, the press had become involved. Adrien Guerrier de Haupt, inspired by a report on popular education in Great Britain, wrote in the *JGIP* of his regret that France lacked serious higher education for women. And *L'Opinion nationale* demanded that the state undertake the organization of secondary education for women. Thereafter, the press began to feature regular articles on the subject, often comparing the deficiencies of France with the strengths of female education in neighboring foreign countries. Other voices of public opinion joined the debate. Jules Simon at the Corps législatif, deploring the fact that instruction even in the best girls'

5. *Ibid.*, 103–106.

boarding schools was "futile and incomplete . . . containing nothing serious or elevating," demanded the creation of *lycées* for women. Feminists such as Maria Desraimes began to lecture publicly on women's issues, including the need for better education. And even the liberal Catholic spokesman, Bishop Félix Dupanloup, found the situation of women lamentable: "In general . . . they know nothing; they can only speak about personal appearance, fashion, [the steeplechase]. . . . Education, even religious [education] does not give, [indeed] gives too rarely the taste for work to young girls and young women. . . . I attribute this estrangement from work to the education given to them . . . restricted, frivolous and superficial, if not inaccurate." [6]

During all of this discussion, a remarkable change had taken place. No longer did proponents of female education assert solely that education was necessary for female edification and dignity; by midcentury, they began to claim that female education, especially at the higher levels, was necessary for the good of society: modern industrial, social, and economic demands called upon the talents of both sexes. The germ of this idea had been planted by educators such as Mme Campan and Aimé Martin earlier in the century.[7] But it was fertilized by the communists and some of the utopian socialists at midcentury, and it emerged as a dominant argument in the 1860s.

Duruy was most sympathetic to the educational needs of women. In the letter he wrote to the emperor on August 6, 1863, to relay the general plan of reforms he wished to promote as minister, he deplored the contemporary state of women's education, blaming some of the problems on the fact that "we have left this education in the hands of people who belong neither to the present world nor to this country." The remainder of the problems, he believed, were the result of the state's timidity in organizing female education.[8]

6. Janet, "L'éducation des femmes," 48; Gréard, *Education et instruction*, II, 144–45; Mayeur, *L'éducation des filles en France*, 105, 133; *JGIP*, 1865, p. 191; excerpt from *L'Opinion nationale* in *RIP*, 1865, p. 642; *RIP*, 1867, pp. 212–15, and the summer, 1867, issues of *Le Correspondant*, carrying articles on secondary education for women in other countries; transcription of the March 2, 1867, session of the Corps législatif in *JGIP*, 1867, p. 191; *Française*, February 12, 1938; Marie Desraimes, *Les oeuvres complètes* (n.p., 1895); *JGIP*, 1868, p. 722; Félix Dupanloup, *Femmes savantes et femmes studieuses* (Paris, 1867), 27, 29.
7. Rousselot, *Histoire de l'éducation des femmes en France*, II, 352, 425.
8. Duruy, *Notes et souvenirs*, I, 198.

Always seeking advice from others and additional information, Duruy wrote to Jules Simon on August 19, 1863, asking him what he would do for women's education if he were minister. Duruy lamented, "It [women's education] is the great problem of our time; our [national] embarrassment comes especially from this." Several months later, he asked rectors, inspectors, and heads of educational establishments to supply him with vital data on female education—the number of girls' *pensionnats* in each academy, the number operated by lay women, the number operated by religious orders, the academic qualifications of the religious teachers, and the conditions within each *pensionnat*. The majority of the respondents said that most *pensionnats* were operated by *congréganistes* and that only a very small minority of these possessed the *brevet de capacité*. Most had the *lettre d'obédience*. The report from the rector of Lyons was typical: there were 45 lay *pensionnats* and 227 religious *pensionnats*. Only 15 of the directors of the religious *pensionnats* possessed the *brevet*. Everywhere it was reported that education for young women was superficial and frivolous.[9]

Between July, 1864, and early spring, 1867, Duruy was almost completely silent on secondary education for women because he was occupied with the bill on primary education and the development of special education. His one letter on the subject was addressed to Eugénie, who was especially anxious to see women's education improved. The main paragraph of that letter revealed Duruy's thoughts:

> The Empress will notice that in France there is no higher education for women. The evening discussions [*conférences*] on letters, science or art are for them an agreeable and useful distraction from the banalities of provincial life, and [they] fill, in a certain sense, the void in which we leave their minds. However, they are not sufficient. . . . I do not wish to make them into bluestockings. But the influence of the mother on the education of the sons and on the direction of ideas is too great not to worry about seeing women remain strangers to the intellectual life of the modern world.[10]

Finally in March, 1867, while defending the bill on primary education that was promulgated on April 10, Duruy began to prepare pub-

9. A.-M. Ecolan, "Une lettre de Victor Duruy," *L'éducation nationale*, November 27, 1952, p. 12; circular, July 16, 1864, F(17) 6843, AN; replies from rectors, F(17) 6843–48 and 8756, AN.
10. Duruy, *Notes et souvenirs*, II, 190.

lic opinion for the project he would undertake. Contending at the Corps législatif that industrialization in France made advanced education for girls imperative, he suggested that working-class girls needed to continue their education beyond first communion in *classes de perseverance* (higher elementary classes) and in *cours professionels* (vocational courses) and that girls in the upper socioeconomic ranks needed "something else"—a real secondary education without Latin or Greek. This remark prompted Jules Simon to interject and demand *lycées* for girls. But Duruy immediately rebuffed the idea: "I fully accept [secondary] boarding schools for boys; they have the need for a virile education [and] severe discipline . . . because it softens the harshness [*les aspérités*] and gives youth an apprentice[ship] for life. The young girl, herself, [however], is something, I would not say terribly fragile, but delicate and we should surround her with so many precautions and reserves that the idea of separating a girl from her mother is deplorable to me." [11] It was clear by March, 1867, that what Duruy sought was simply to generalize and bring under the direction of the state the enormously successful Parisian practice of offering independent secondary courses for young girls.

In April, 1867, Duruy asked rectors and inspectors to indicate the feasibility of establishing public secondary education for girls in the towns and cities where *lycées* and *collèges* already existed. He also asked them to assess the probable reaction of certain segments of the local population—clergy, mayors, prefects, municipal councillors, professors, directresses of boarding schools, and the public—to such education. Duruy was obviously anxious about the opposition the courses might provoke. On June 30, 1867, he wrote a revealing note to the *proviseur* of the *lycée* of Tours: "Begin very modestly, and without commotion. Allow a privately organized society of professors to propose the foundation of the courses before you become officially involved." [12]

During the next few months only Adolphe Mourier, the head of the academy of Paris, expressed serious doubts. Initially, Mourier had written to Duruy telling him that Orleans was the sole city under his

11. *AIP*, 366–77, and minutes of the Imperial Council for December 9, 1867, F(17*) 1871, AN. Duruy's views were repeated at this session of the council.
12. F(17) 8756, AN.

supervision (outside of Paris) in which the courses might succeed because the mayor there was favorable to their establishment. But after preparations for the courses were launched, and the *Journal du Loiret* had announced their creation, clerical opposition arose. Bishop Dupanloup protested twice to the *proviseur* of the local *lycée* and threatened to incite "great opposition" if the courses materialized. According to Mourier, the problem was that "the diocesan authority cannot allow the University to assume the education of young girls; the young girl of sixteen would risk the greatest dangers to her faith if she received an education that raised doubts; it would excite her to a certain spirit of independence; [and] she would risk additional dangers if she attended courses taught by unmarried professors. . . . The bishop . . . already has warned the curés of the town so that they will discourage the families. . . . If necessary, he will address a pastoral letter and protest to the minister, and if necessary, to the emperor." Mourier urged Duruy to consider limiting the courses to an experimental program at Paris.[13]

But Duruy was not dissuaded. On October 30, 1867, he addressed a public circular to all of his rectors, pointing out the serious deficiencies in French education and claiming that although professional education provided some training for young girls of the working classes, there was no organized form of advanced education for those of the upper classes. He proposed to create the latter because "to fortify her judgment and to enrich her intelligence, to teach her to govern her mind and to place her in a condition to assume, with another person, the tasks and responsibilities of her life without departing from the role nature has assigned to her, a woman needs a strong and simple instruction . . . [one that offers] to the religious sentiment the support of a consciousness of the real, and to the wanderings of the imagination, the obstacle of enlightened reason." Duruy added that a genuine secondary education would have the advantage of occupying young women during the three or four "most difficult . . . years of youth" after they had left their boarding schools, would turn them into "*honnêtes femmes*," and would give them greater personal dignity. As Duruy told the empress, women "demand not to be reduced to the role of

13. Mourier to Victor Duruy, September 30, 1867, *ibid.*

charming creatures." These were progressive ideas for the nineteenth century, but within the context of contemporary liberalism, they were hardly radical. Indeed, it must be emphasized that there was nothing in Duruy's statements that offended liberals in the Church. Duruy was merely suggesting bridging the intellectual gap that often occurred between husbands and wives, preparing young women to be better mothers, and protecting them from the life of frivolity common to many contemporary women.[14]

Duruy boasted that his new program was inexpensive and simple. It did not entail the creation of new personnel because professors already employed in *lycées* and *collèges* could teach the new courses. It did not necessitate the creation of new schools because the professors could teach the courses in an available room in a municipal building. Students would take three or four years of courses from the literary and scientific curriculum that had been mandated for special education; they would be offered no Latin or Greek, but that was not necessary because girls were not destined for the liberal careers. Like Camille Sée later, Duruy would have argued: "Ni femme avocat, ni femme médecin, ni femme parlementaire. Mais il n'est pas interdit d'avoir une femme humaniste."[15] Girls would enter the new program when they were fourteen; they would be expected to attend classes faithfully and to prepare homework regularly, the latter a feature that was not customary practice in the girls' boarding schools or even in the private courses offered for girls by professors. At the end of each year the students would take a final examination. When they completed the program they could petition for one of the diplomas created for special education. They would be seventeen or eighteen years old at the time.

Because the courses were established for the daughters of affluent families, Duruy suggested that young women be charged 15 to 20 francs a month per course, which would free the state from any financial burden. Three-quarters of the tuition money would be used to pay

---

14. Circular, October 30, 1867, F(17) 8753, AN; Duruy, *Notes et souvenirs*, I, 276–77.

15. As quoted in Ponteil, *Histoire de l'enseignement en France*, 299. Duruy did, however, found a medical school—l'Ecole Secondaire Libre de Médecine—for women in Morocco. See [Victor Duruy], "Une conquête de féminisme sous le Second Empire," a.41 *Bulletin de l'enseignement public au Maroc* (October–December, 1954), 51–61.

the professors. The remainder would defray the cost of materials for all students and cover the expense of scholarships for a small group of academically talented girls from less affluent families.[16]

Duruy left the actual creation of the courses to the professors and municipalities. They were to establish the program, act as patrons, control and direct the professors, and provide heat and light for the classrooms. They were also supposed to call upon influential local women to form *comités de patronage* (the female equivalent of the *conseils de perfectionnement* for special education), which would assist in the general supervision of the courses. This local involvement was part of Duruy's plan to "municipalize" the courses, to make them appear to be the result of local initiative. In a confidential circular to the rectors on November 2, Duruy elaborated on his reasoning:

> Insist particularly . . . that we give these courses the character of a municipal creation, of a work begun under your control, by a society of professors acting in complete freedom. Our enterprises will find critics and opponents whose violence I know. It is good to shield ourselves behind two things which will well blunt the darts: the municipal authority which represents the father of the city, and the freedom of the citizens who use the initiative to which they are invited daily by the government itself. You should intervene officially [only] to announce the names of the professors, to smooth difficulties, [and] to facilitate the preparation of programs; you should not spare anything to assure the success [of the courses], on the other hand you should not let it appear that the University is creating a new order of education. It is responding to an appeal, it is attempting to satisfy the needs which are manifested to it . . . but prudence commands it, in a matter so delicate, to efface itself while acting [still] in an effective and preponderant manner.[17]

To complement the aura of paternal sanction he tried to give the courses, Duruy recommended that the representatives of maternal authority—governesses or directresses of boarding schools—or mothers accompany the young women to class.[18] When enacted, this provision helped disseminate the benefits of the courses to older women.

The last section of the confidential circular of November 2 urged

16. Not surprisingly, at least one municipal councillor would later find this provision unacceptable because he believed working-class girls would become *déclassées*. See the extract of the deliberations of the municipal council of Toulon, February 21, 1868, F(17) 8754, AN.

17. Confidential circular, November 2, 1867, F(17) 8753, AN.

18. Circular, October 30, 1867, *ibid.*

rectors to use great care in selecting professors for the courses. Those who were family men, tactful, not too young, and the best teachers available would help to increase both the respect families had for University professors and the moral influence of the University in France.[19]

Proud of being able to create a new educational program by merely rearranging the personnel and facilities already at his disposal and by the almost wholesale conversion of the special education program for the purposes of female higher education, Duruy called the attention of his functionaries to two other potentialities of the courses. First, they could serve as a model for the general improvement of instruction in all women's education (primary, professional, and adult education). And second, they could help prepare young women for the *brevet de capacité* in such places as the department of the Seine, where there were no *écoles normales des filles*.[20]

Almost immediately after Duruy published his circulars, groups of professors following his instructions organized themselves into *sociétés pour l'enseignement des jeunes filles*. At Paris, the members of the societies tended to be leading academicians, especially members of the Institut.[21] Elsewhere, they tended to be professors of *lycées* and *collèges*.

Despite all of the precautions, however, nothing could conceal the official character of the new courses, and trouble began to brew for Duruy at Orleans. On November 11, August Boucher, a substitute teacher at the *lycée* and one of Duruy's former students, confided: "The war began yesterday, Sunday. During the catechism class for teenagers, the pastor of Sainte-Croix denounced the secondary courses for girls as useless and dangerous," and rumor spread that families who supported the courses would be denied absolution. "I learned this

19. In 1863, there were 614 male professors in religious schools for girls and 2,072 male professors in laic *pensionnats* who taught advanced (secondary) courses (*RIP*, 1867, 561; confidential circular, November 2, 1867, F[17] 8753, AN).
20 . An undated note Duruy scribbled on an administrative report to Lavisse, F(17) 8754, AN. In 1867, there were only eleven *écoles normales primaires de filles*, but they were supplemented by fifty-two *cours normales* in various cities. The department of the Seine did not get a normal school for women until 1872, when one was founded at Sevres. Before that time, two women ran private normal institutes in Paris, and the *conseil général* of the Seine organized special courses (attracting about seven hundred students in 1867) that prepared young women for either the *certificat d'études* or the *brevet de capacité* (Gréard, *Education et instruction*, II, 144–46; *RIP*, 1867, p. 577).
21. F(17) 8753, AN.

morning that the bishop [Dupanloup], furious with our prosperity which begins anew, alarmed by the élan of the University . . . is preparing an enormous tract against us."[22]

Indeed, on November 16, the day after the courses opened at Orleans, Dupanloup published a pamphlet entitled *M. Duruy et l'éducation des filles*. Three other pamphlets followed in rapid succession— *Seconde lettre de Mgr. l'évêque d'Orléans sur M. Duruy et l'éducation des filles*; *Les alarmes de l'épiscopat*; and *La femme chrétienne et française*—all of which simply expatiated on arguments advanced in the first pamphlet. Dupanloup attacked only the secondary courses for young women that Duruy had promoted in his October 30 circular; he was silent on the *cours professionel* mentioned in the circular because they were strictly technical in nature. To attack the secondary courses, Dupanloup was forced to contradict practically all of the assertions he had made earlier about female education. Now he expostulated that secondary education for women already existed so there was no need to develop a new program for it. And now, in perhaps his most egregious reversal, he even questioned whether women were capable of advanced studies. Dupanloup then pointed out the inherent dangers in the new program: male professors might corrupt their female students; male professors would become overtaxed by their new burdens and unable to meet their regular commitments; town halls (the site Duruy had proposed for the courses) were dangerous places for young girls because the police detained vagabonds, inebriates, and prostitutes there; and the courses would upset familial relations. "The Saint-Simonian friends of M. Duruy, as we know," he wrote, "have always sought the emancipated woman and they will be delighted."[23]

Dupanloup scrupulously avoided attacking the University; this *franc-tireur* aimed his guns only at Duruy, who, he charged, was the agent of sinister interests and a member of the antireligious conspiracy

22. F(17) 8756, AN. On November 21, 1867, Duruy wrote to Vignat, the mayor of Orleans: "The sophism and violence of your irascible prelate has not impeded you. I congratulate and thank you for that" (copy in *ibid.*).

23. Félix Dupanloup, *M. Duruy et l'éducation des filles, lettre de Mgr. l'évêque d'Orléans à un de ses collègues* (Paris, 1867), 8, 11–12, 15, 17, 18; Félix Dupanloup, *Seconde lettre de Mgr. l'évêque d'Orléans sur M. Duruy et l'éducation des filles* (Paris, 1867); Félix Dupanloup, *Les alarmes de l'épiscopat justifiée par les faits* (Paris, 1868); Félix Dupanloup, *La femme chrétienne et française, dernière réponse à M. Duruy et à ses défenseurs par Mgr. l'évêque d'Orléans* (Paris, 1868).

attacking French society. He was not even Christian, as his history textbooks clearly revealed. After all, Dupanloup pointed out erroneously, had M. Duruy not contended that man had descended from apes? Dupanloup's attack was vicious. Duruy's great aim was to create a corps of "female freethinkers" that would spell the end of religion in France. "Does a minister of public instruction have [that] right of life or death over the public mind?" Dupanloup queried rhetorically.[24]

Dupanloup carried his campaign to the Catholic community at large—the episcopate, the press, the clergy, laymen, and the pope—especially calling upon the episcopate for formal letters of adhesion. Some prelates, backed by laymen and even more enthusiastic ultramontane clergy, rallied immediately;[25] but others, either disagreeing that the courses were a threat or fearing that to join the battle would do more damage than good, hesitated or abstained. Darboy of Paris attempted to moderate. In a homily on November 27, 1867, and in a statement at a session of the Imperial Council of Public Instruction he extolled Duruy's work in general, argued that Bishop Dupanloup did not intend to impugn the reputation of the University or its professors, and blamed the press for misrepresenting the bishop's statements and exciting hostilities.[26]

But then, to the utter astonishment of the press, the pope intervened with a brief on December 21, decrying the antireligious conspiracy that was directed at the schools. The conspirators, Pius IX announced, wanted to capture the minds of women, and that was the quickest way to destroy the social order.[27]

Pius's brief crystallized the opposition. Several prelates whose clergy took the pronunciamento as a *mot d'ordre* were, according to available accounts, subtly pressured into conformity. Donnet of Bordeaux sent Dupanloup a letter of support, but his convictions were questioned by the rector of Bordeaux, who subsequently wrote to Duruy: "There is nothing in his letter which is personal to you, but he was

24. Dupanloup, *M. Duruy et l'éducation des filles*, 20–27; Dupanloup, *Seconde lettre*, 12, 19–21.
25. These letters of adhesion are devoid of any new arguments against the courses: most bishops and archbishops simply parroted the rhetoric of Dupanloup. The letters are reproduced at the end of Dupanloup, *Seconde lettre*.
26. Imperial Council session, December 9, 1867, F(17*) 1871, AN.
27. *JGIP*, 1868, p. 114. The text of the brief is reproduced in Félix Dupanloup, *Nouvelles oeuvres choisies de Mgr. Dupanloup* (7 vols.; Paris, 1873–74), III, 453–55.

obliged by his position to protest in his own turn. I have translated this as 'I have submitted to pressure which, after two months, I no longer know how to stave off.'"[28] In the end all but twenty-eight prelates joined the campaign.[29]

Fully a month before the pope sent his brief to France, however, the press had become involved. On November 21, 1867, the *RIP* announced to its readers, "The battle is engaged and with extreme vigor." Conservative and Catholic papers supported Dupanloup, arguing that the new courses for women were dangerous if not disastrous for the country. *Le Jura* proclaimed, "All seems lost, the family, religion, faith and morality. . . . With the news of this scandal our bishops have torn their robes, veiled their faces, and cried that the abomination of desolation was in the temple"; Duruy is the "esprit terrible du siècle." The controversy exploded into a "holy war" in late spring, 1868, after *L'Osservatore romano* and *L'Univers* demanded that Catholics withhold support from the regime in elections until Duruy was dismissed.[30]

Liberal and anticlerical newspapers such as *L'Opinion nationale*, *Le Charivari*, and *Le Siècle* rushed to Duruy's defense, *Le Siècle* applauding the courses because they would "release women from the yoke of ridiculous superstition and would prepare for new generations." Even the liberal *Le Temps*, "a difficult paper in general, even more difficult for M. Duruy in particular," as the *RIP* put it, sided with Duruy, thus proving how grave the situation was.[31]

28. The rector of Bordeaux to Victor Duruy, January 10, 1868, confidential letter, F(17) 8753, AN.

29. Françoise Mayeur, "Les évêques français et Victor Duruy: Le cours secondaires de jeunes filles," *Revue d'histoire de l'église de France*, LVI (1971), 280. Mayeur correctly attacks Dupanloup's assertion (reduplicated subsequently by several historians, e.g., Maurain, *La politique ecclésiastique du Second Empire*, 845) that the episcopacy formed almost a united front behind Dupanloup. But her three categories of responses to Dupanloup—immediate support, hesitation, and abstention—should be used in only the most impressionistic way. Questions still remain about the dates of the letters and their assignment to the three discrete categories.

30. *RIP*, 1867, p. 529; clipping from *Le Jura*, January 20, 1869, F(17) 8753, AN; Gagnon, *France Since 1789*, 188; *JGIP*, 1868, p. 209. At least one French paper, if not several, had already called for Duruy's resignation. See clipping from the legitimist *La France centrale*, November 22, 1867, F(17) 8753, AN. There was no question that Duruy and his program became an issue in elections. See *JGIP*, 1868, p. 69 (on elections in the Somme), and p. 209 (on elections in the Nord). Charles Louandre, now more sympathetic to Duruy, feared the impact of the clericals' *politique du pire* on the general imperial elections of 1869 (*ibid.*, 435).

31. *Le siècle*, November 16, 1867; *RIP*, 1867, p. 529.

To a limited extent Duruy fueled the controversy by refuting allegations in communiqués addressed to the clerical papers and by "inspir-
ing" an anonymously published tract entitled *Monseigneur Dupanloup devant l'opinion publique* (Paris, 1867). He sent confidential
letters to local republican papers containing information favorable to
the courses and suggested in a circular of October 30, 1867, that a
campaign should be launched to convince the public that the courses
were academically sound and morally irreproachable. Generally, he restricted himself to sending nonpolemical information, and he relied
greatly on regular announcements concerning the courses in the *BAIP*,
but on a few rare occasions he strayed from his resolve and coaxed
universitaires to engage in a "short polemic" for the courses in their
local newspapers. Roustan, now the rector of Toulouse, found cause
to reproach him for the communiqués that he sent to the *Moniteur*,
asserting that the "ignorant" would interpret the publicity as an official war of the University against the Church.[32]

There are almost as many examples of his reserve as of his lack of
restraint, however. In November, 1867, for instance, the *proviseur* of
the *lycée* at Mont-de-Marsan asked Duruy to pressure a notable into
supporting the courses. Duruy refused, claiming that he did not want
to give *L'Univers* grounds for additional criticism. And in February,
1868, Duruy sent *universitaires* specific orders to cease all polemic.[33]

Was this acrimonious controversy only a new and more heated version of the old clerical-anticlerical struggle over schools like the one
that had surfaced in the 1840s, when the right to open Catholic secondary schools was at stake? Duruy thought so, at least initially. On
November 21, he wrote to the emperor, "He [Dupanloup] sees there
[in the courses] a peril for the convents, a menace against the *capta-
tions de testament* and that frightens him." And on November 28, he
wrote confidentially to a friend, "I sense living in me the 30 generations of men that they have burned and tormented, and until my last
breath, I will work for the freedom of conscience. [But] I cannot say

32. Victor Duruy to the inspector of academy at Grenoble, December 26, 1867, copy
of a letter, F(17) 8755, AN; Inspector Roustan to Victor Duruy, November 1, 1868,
F(17) 8756, AN.
33. Victor Duruy to the *proviseur* of the *lycée* of Mont-de-Marsan, November 26,
1867, and to the minister of the interior, February 28, 1868, copies of letters, F(17)
8754, AN. In the February 28 letter Duruy mentioned sending such instructions to all
universitaires.

this publicly in my position." For his part, Dupanloup seems at first to have fought the courses because they made no provision for religious education. Only a solid instruction firmly grounded in religion, he had argued in his earlier writings, would protect young women against pedantry, vanity, and materialism. He believed that the religious education of women was the sole hope of the Church for rechristianizing France because the Church could gain entry into families only through women.[34] This explanation is plausible in the light of similar arguments against state-oriented secondary education for women that Dupanloup used during the next decade.[35]

But why, when he entered the lists against Duruy, did Dupanloup contradict practically all of his earlier writings on women's education? He had, after all, once argued that frivolous women in the wealthy classes were dangerous because they pushed their husbands to cigars, horses, and boredom.[36] And why did Dupanloup's opposition to the courses immediately become transformed into an attack on Duruy personally, five months before Veuillot and *L'Osservatore romano* began calling for Duruy's dismissal? There appear to be two reasons, the one particular to Dupanloup, the other more general. The first is that Dupanloup believed that a stunning victory for the Church in France would place him in a strong position to lead the anti-infallibilists at the forthcoming Vatican Council. He had opposed the calling of a general council in 1865, when the pope had first conveyed his intentions *in modo privatissimo*, but by 1867 he had had a change of mind. Unlike the doomsayers of the Church who predicted that Pius IX would be the last pope and that the Church was nearing its demise, Dupanloup believed that the council could usher in a new dawn in the long saga of the Church.[37] But he had to go to the council sufficiently strong to win over the pope and conservatives to a dialogue with the

34. Duruy, *Notes et souvenirs*, I, 276; Victor Duruy to Caraguel, November 28, 1867, copy of a letter in possession of Mme Albert Duruy; Dupanloup, *Seconde lettre*, 19–21; Dupanloup, *Femme chrétienne*, 7. Dupanloup's concern with women's role accords with his great solicitude for the decline of Christian practice in France. See Christianne Marcilhacy, *Le diocèse d'Orléans sous l'épiscopat de Mgr. Dupanloup, 1848–1878* (Paris, 1962), 195.

35. Charles Hanriot, *Mgr. Dupanloup et l'enseignement secondaire* (Troyes, 1873), 81–83.

36. Françoise Mayeur, "Les Catholiques libéraux et l'éducation des femmes," Actes du Colloque international d'histoire religieuse de Grenoble des 30 Septembre–3 Octobre, 1971, *Les catholiques libéraux au XIXᵉ siècle* (Grenoble, 1974), 426.

37. Cuthbert Butler, *The Vatican Council* (2 vols.; London, 1930), I, 66.

contemporary world. This strategy dictated to Dupanloup conservative politics (a reconciliation with the ultramontanists) at home followed by liberal politics abroad. It was a plan with considerable potential.

Second, and closely related to the first reason, the French defeat of Garibaldi at Mentana on November 3, 1867, followed by the December 5 attack of the democratic opposition in the Corps législatif and Rouher's famous "*Jamais*" speech gave clericals renewed hope for a rapprochement with the regime. But as long as Duruy, the most outspoken opponent in the government of Mentana, remained in office, Catholics would be unable to effect a secure *modus vivendi* with the state. This conflict explains Dupanloup's actions as well as those of Louis Veuillot and *L'Osservatore romano*. It was "la campagne de Rome à l'intérieure" as *Le Temps* put it. Duruy would have to be stopped just as Garibaldi had been. "The religious and political questions are indissolubly united," *Le Charivari* proclaimed.[38]

The Roman issue also explains the immediate and profuse support of the French liberals for the women's courses. Frustrated by Mentana, they viewed their support for Duruy as one of the best, if not the only, means of doing battle with the Church. *Le Charivari*, always more interested in satirizing the naiveté of Duruy, now faced the Church head-on. It predicted a totally new regime for France if the clericals won; Dupanloup would become either the next minister of public instruction or minister of state. The liberal press viewed Duruy as the last barrier to the "ultramontane invasion." But by the spring of 1868, it concluded that its cause was ruined and that Duruy's end was imminent. On April 4 *L'Independence belge* ruefully announced, "M. Duruy est *perdu*."[39]

But Duruy's end had not yet come. The emperor obviously appreciated his value as a cutting edge against the clericals, and he retained Duruy at the ministry. And he did not order Duruy to dismantle the controversial courses. Instead, he silenced Duruy's critics curtly by replying that he was an "*honnête homme*."[40]

38. Debidour, *Histoire des rapports de l'église et de l'état en France*, 603; excerpt from *Le Temps* in *L'Opinion nationale*, November 23, 1867; *Le Charivari*, December 6, 1867.

39. *RIP*, 1867, p. 563; *Le Charivari*, April 4, 1868.

40. Thomas W. Evans, *The Second French Empire* (New York, 1905), 44.

Despite the agitation, the courses were established in forty cities and towns during the first academic year. Plotted on a map of France, the locations of the courses would form a giant letter X with a juncture just southwest of Paris. The greatest successes were achieved in the academy of Bordeaux, the eastern and western parts of the academies of Montpellier and Aix, respectively, and the academies of Paris, Douai, and Nancy. Provincial cities with significant non-Catholic populations were among the notable triumphs for Duruy. Predictably, Paris had the best record because there the precedent for secondary courses for young women had already been firmly established. The most popular courses were those held at the Sorbonne, where 226 girls and women attended the opening session. The Sorbonne, however, was not the only site of the courses in Paris: the first, third, eleventh, and sixteenth arrondissements also had them. The ministers of foreign affairs and finance sent their daughters to the courses at the Sorbonne, and Eugénie, who was undaunted by the clerical attacks and who was interceding in another case to help a woman get her doctorate in medicine, sent her two nieces.[41]

The courses were also relatively successful at Orleans in spite of Dupanloup's hostility. Boucher, Duruy's former student, sent regular reports on the situation. In one he announced, "Our success renders him [Dupanloup] mad. At the end of our class, he happened to find his way among our students; we saw him yesterday for the third time prowling on the sidewalk." Curiously, the chaplain at the *lycée* remained neutral throughout the commotion. In July Dupanloup had him replaced.[42]

From the reports of the functionaries, it is clear that there was considerable variety in the courses offered. Some, like those offered at the Sorbonne, resembled university-level courses; others were elementary. But most appear to have been true secondary courses in French grammar and composition, the history of French literature, French history and geography, mathematics and astronomy, physics, chemistry, and biology. Each class met for one hour a week, and on the average girls went to class six hours a week. Few towns offered all of the courses,

41. Mayeur, *L'éducation des filles en France*, 114; *RIP*, 1867, p. 618; Kurtz, *Empress Eugénie*, 196; Duruy, *Notes et souvenirs*, I, 275.
42. Boucher to Victor Duruy, December 14, 1867, and July 5, 1868, F(17) 8756, AN.

but some offered special ones. Nancy, for example, offered a course in vegetable physiology and Bordeaux one in mineralogy. The twenty-nine towns and cities that reported courses they had offered during the first year listed a total of 167, or an average of 5.7 courses per location. Montpellier and Paris (the Sorbonne location) had the greatest number, 9, and Auxerre, Mont-de-Marsan, and Nîmes followed with 8 each.[43] Paris, Marseilles, and Bordeaux would soon institute a three-year cycle of courses based on the special education curriculum, and Rouen, Amiens, Lyons, Limoges, and Mont-de-Marsan would institute a two-year cycle.[44]

The majority of young girls taking the courses seem to have been Protestants or Jews. Some Greek Orthodox and Roman Catholic (both French and foreign) girls attended the courses, as well as some "of doubtful or undetermined religious affiliation." One-third of the girls at Montpellier were Catholic, but less than one-fifth at Nîmes were Catholic, and they were all foreigners. Most of the girls belonged to the middle classes, being especially the daughters of teachers, functionaries, men in the liberal professions, and wealthy industrialists and businessmen.[45] And most, according to a report Duruy sent to the empress, had spent several years previously in *pensionnats*.[46]

Unfortunately, it is not possible to present accurate statistics on enrollments in the courses. Even the ministry was disappointed in its efforts to do so.[47] One problem was that the rectors seldom reported in a uniform manner. Sometimes they distinguished between the students and the older women (*institutrices*, directresses of boarding schools, governesses, or mothers) who sat in on the courses, and sometimes they did not. The other problem was that the enrollment figures for any one location fluctuated from one report to the next. An extreme example is provided by the report of inspector Chabert in the academy of Aix: initially, a fair number of registrations had been taken by the authorities, but then bad weather and a virus plagued the town, one

43. Tabulated from documents in F(17) 8753, AN.

44. Mayeur, *L'éducation des filles en France*, 120.

45. I plan to publish data on the social origins of these girls and detailed information on what happened in each town—reaction of the clergy, functionaries, and press, public opinion, and specific results—in a specialized article.

46. *AIP*, 668–73 (report of October 25, 1868).

47. Ernest Lavisse, then twenty-three years old and Duruy's special assistant for the program, attempted a tabulation but gave up in frustration (F[17] 8753, AN).

girl ran off to Rouen, another got married, and before long the entire student body had disappeared.[48] Most of the courses outside of Paris, however, averaged between fifteen and fifty students.

Obviously, hostile clergymen were responsible for a large share of the attrition in enrollments. And from five cities and towns—Poitiers, Avignon, Saint-Etienne, Colmar, and Bar-le-Rue—there were specific complaints that the Jesuits were campaigning against the courses. At Lille, "ultramontane forces" worked against them. Whenever possible, the clergy used religious retreats, their pulpits, and the confessional to preach against the courses. Some priests even threatened to refuse absolution to uncooperative families. A particularly fierce wave of attack was launched in the Lenten pastoral letters of 1868.[49]

Although the clergy frequently used religious arguments against the courses, they also, like lay critics, used nonreligious arguments. Unfortunately, because the clerical element was the most identifiable and noisy element among the opposition, historians (with the recent exception of Françoise Mayeur) have either neglected or failed to realize the role these nonreligious arguments played. The most prevalent were of a misogynist nature. Opponents argued that women did not need an advanced education and that they should not transgress the role nature assigned to them. One municipal councillor argued that advanced education for women militated against "the destiny of woman, who should especially live an inner life."[50] Even well-educated men expressed strong reservations. Louis Gaulot, *procureur-general* of the imperial court of Lyons, for example, feared that *enseignement secondaire des jeunes filles* would create a revolution in the family. He believed that in cities like Lyons, where, he said, the majority of women were more intelligent than their husbands, it was necessary for family stability to maintain the *femme pôt-au-feu* (stay-at-home wife) until husbands could find more dignified work at better salaries.[51] Arthur Loth in an article in *L'Univers* assailed the courses because

48. Report of inspector Chabert, January 18, 1868, F(17) 8754, AN. Similar occurrences were repeated elsewhere.

49. F(17) 4362, 8753–56, F(19*) 1131 (the case of Mlle Amblard), and F(19) 3972, AN.

50. Report, February, 1868, F(17) 8754, and report from Lyons, November 26, 1867, F(17) 4362, AN.

51. Louis Gaulot to Victor Duruy, January 16, 1868, F(17) 8755, AN.

they would create liberated women. Most of the misogynist clamor dwelled on three themes: girls would become odious blue-stockings, they would lose their taste for domesticity and motherhood, and they would have difficulties finding husbands.[52] The latter was the subject of an amusing cartoon in *Le Charivari* on May 7, 1868, showing a mother discovering her unmarried daughter with a baby. Indignantly questioned by the mother for an explanation, the daughter replied that because of Duruy's courses, having a child was the one remaining way of snagging a husband. The fact that young Protestant and Jewish women suffered from these same slurs proves the extent to which anti-feminism was part of the opposition to the courses.

Girls were intimidated by the press, by anonymous mail, and by hecklers. The hostile press published the names of girls enrolled in the courses and coined terms of opprobrium: *cours-Duruy* for the courses; *Duruyfication* for the process of corruption; and *Duruyfiée* or *Durysée* for the result.[53] At Périgueux girls attending the courses received copies of a malicious song, and at Clamecy all mothers received copies of Dupanloup's brochures and a vitriolic attack on the courses by Veuillot. From a number of towns came reports that the girls were harassed regularly by hecklers who crowded the entrances to classes.[54]

The other nonreligious antagonism developed from jealousies or fears certain people had of the courses. Some directresses of boarding schools for girls, for example, feared that the new courses would compromise the success of their own schools or that if they supported the courses they would have to admit that they had not been providing secondary education for girls within their own walls.[55] Some municipal authorities, such as those at Dijon, were opposed to voting heat and light costs for courses that would benefit, they said, only the

---

52. Clipping from *L'Univers*, March 23, 1869, F(19) 3972, AN; *L'Opinion nationale*, November 6, 1868; the *proviseur* of the *lycée* of Troyes to Victor Duruy, November 25, 1867, F(17) 8754, AN; confidential letter from inspector Bertrand to Victor Duruy, undated, F(17) 8755, AN.

53. Clippings from several newspapers in F(17) 8754, AN.

54. F(17) 8753–55, AN. In a letter dated February 10, 1868, the rector of Montpellier described the hecklers as "clerical and legitimist youth" (F[17] 8755, AN).

55. The *proviseur* of the *lycée* of Troyes to Victor Duruy, November 25, 1867, and the *proviseur* of the *lycée* of Avignon to Victor Duruy, November 27, 1868, F(17) 8754, AN; confidential letter from inspector Bertrand to Duruy, undated, F(17) 8755, AN.

daughters of the upper bourgeoisie and aristocracy.[56] And many professors already engaged in private tutoring feared they would lose their students.[57]

There was no question that resistance to the courses was strong. Glachant in a confidential report noted that rectors, inspectors, and organizers of the courses had little confidence in their success. Glachant was no more optimistic in light of the fact that they had been "put on the Index" by the clergy. But Duruy refused to be defeated. Although he had originally envisioned the creation of secondary courses for young girls in all 340 towns and cities where there were public *lycées* and *collèges,* and although he had to diminish his ambitions substantially, he was persuaded that the more important matter was to establish a principle. As Duruy had told the rector of Caen earlier, "The essential is to succeed on a certain number of points." The new courses were good, and they responded well to the needs of contemporary France: "The example of success will be contagious."[58]

By early 1868 Duruy was cautioning his functionaries against forcing the courses: "Failure will only compromise the new institutions for a long time in any one town," he told them.[59] While Duruy remained in office the forty original courses continued and some new ones—especially in the academy of Nancy, where rector Louis Maggiolo was very active—opened. The Franco-Prussian War, however, brought an abrupt end to them. A few reopened after 1871; only ten continued until 1878. (The courses at Orleans ceased in 1872.) Yet the young women who had attended the courses in the closing years of the empire did so primarily to obtain an education that was unavailable in the contemporary *pensionnats.* After the Franco-Prussian War many of the *pensionnats* began to offer a standard complement of nonclassical secondary courses, and the need for independent courses such as Duruy had established decreased in certain towns and cities. Also, by

56. The rector of Dijon to Victor Duruy, December 17, 1867, F(17) 8754, AN.
57. Confidential letter from Vieille of Aix to Victor Duruy, July 15, 1868, F(17) 8754, AN; report of Maggiolo, January 30, 1868, F(17) 8755, AN.
58. Glachant's confidential report, July, 1868, F(17) 9096, AN; Victor Duruy to the rector of Caen, December 27, 1867, copy of a letter, F(17) 8754, AN.
59. Victor Duruy to the rector of Clermont, January 3, 1868, copy of a letter, F(17) 8754, AN, and Duruy's annotation at the top of a letter from the rector of Poitiers, February 15, 1869, F(17) 8756, AN.

the late 1870s, it was common knowledge that republicans and especially Camille Sée were preparing a bill that would create *lycées* and
collèges for women. Many municipalities therefore decided to wait
until the state acted.[60]

It is somewhat surprising that Duruy's courses were not more successful than they were, especially given the care with which he fashioned
the courses and the program. As he noted in the November 2 circular,
the state was not establishing a new order of education. It was simply
responding to a "social demand" and was proposing a traditional program for young girls from the wealthy classes. Although the courses
were to be genuinely of the secondary level and the professors were to
be the same men who taught the students' brothers, there was to be no
Latin, Greek, or philosophy in the program, and science was to be limited to the rudiments; in short, the program was very similar to those
in some religious and laic *pensionnats* in Paris. But the Church feared
that young girls would be "laicized" (which is why it feared losing its
monopoly over women's education); clericals saw opposition to the
courses as a means of promoting Duruy's downfall and, conversely, a
new rapprochement between the Church and state; directresses of
pensionnats feared they would lose students; and misogynists feared
the creation of a race of bluestockings.

Still, although Duruy lost in the short run, he scored a major victory
in the long run. He set an important precedent for the state's taking an
active role in the fostering of higher education for women throughout
the country. And he helped to secure the notion that young women
were entitled to a humanistic education whether or not a career
awaited them. Duruy appreciated the influence of women in society,
and he believed that the entire educational system of France, and certainly the nation itself, could profit from a strengthening and expansion of women's education. Indeed, Duruy believed that the state
needed more highly educated women. The industrial world and the
competition it brought necessitated the employment of women as well
as men. France had to "open, since it is necessary, honorable careers
[for woman] and multiply the professions she is capable of filling."[61]

60. Gréard, *Education et instruction*, II, 155–56.
61. Duruy, *Notes et Souvenirs*, II, 201.

Duruy did not live long enough to see any meaningful development in the number of "honorable careers" and professions open to women. This did not happen until well into the twentieth century. But he did live to see his immediate educational efforts for women bear fruit. In the late 1870s, republicans began borrowing his ideas and programs in order to develop a more structured program of secondary education for girls, and by the 1880s, after Camille Sée's law was passed, the first *lycées* and *collèges* for women in France began to appear. To honor Duruy's important work, educators eventually gave his name to one of the *lycées* for young women in Paris. The Lycée Victor Duruy still flourishes today.

VII · Higher Education

Divided into four faculties, juxtaposed, none in communication with the others, not even a common principle uniting them; . . . schools of medicine and law . . . the former teaching an art, the latter, the management of scholastics; faculties of letters without students, vulgarizing [their studies] for an anonymous audience . . . ; faculties of science without students, vulgarizing, also, without laboratories or with empty laboratories; everywhere an incredible shortage of instruments and books; the rector of Strasbourg denouncing the poverty of the [local] faculty of letters which had an annual budget of 100 francs; Claude Bernard at the Collège de France, ashamed to introduce foreign visitors drawn by his great name to the humble closet where he worked; everywhere the ignominity of ugly buildings; nowhere was science organized; there were no means of information; . . . the very rare admirable efforts of some were isolated; indifference, apathy, lethargy were widespread.
—Ernest Lavisse, *Un ministre—Victor Duruy*

The tableau sketched by Ernest Lavisse on conditions in higher education when Duruy took office in 1863 could have applied almost equally to any earlier period in the nineteenth century.[1] The great prestige France had enjoyed in higher education since the Middle Ages had largely evaporated before the Revolution, when its old universities sank into profound decadence. New institutions created during the Revolution or First Empire unfortunately did far too little to resurrect that prestige. Indeed, the Napoleonic system of higher education and the unwillingness of various French governments in the early decades following Waterloo to take steps to solve the problems of higher education served only to perpetuate France's inferior situation.

1. Excellent background surveys on French higher education include Liard, *L'enseignement supérieur en France*; d'Irsay, *Histoire des universités françaises et étrangères*, vol. II; Theodore Zeldin, "Higher Education in France, 1848–1940," *Journal of Contemporary History*, II (July, 1967), 53–80; Prost, *Histoire de l'enseignement en France*, 223–40; Moody, *French Education Since Napoleon*, 8 and *passim*; Ringer, *Education and Society in Modern Europe*, 113 and *passim*; and René Baillaud, "L'insuffisance de la recherche scientifique en France sous le Second Empire," *P. V. M. Académie des Sciences et Belles-Lettres* (Besançon), CLXXVII (1968 [1966–67]), 77–96.

At the highest level, France had its *grandes écoles* such as the Ecole Normale Supérieure, the Ecole des Chartes, and the Ecole des Langues Orientales; the fragmented system of faculties—law, medicine, theology, sciences, and letters—and a few specialized institutions such as the Collège de France, the Museum of Natural History, the Paris Observatory, and the Bureau of Longitudes. The *grandes écoles* and the faculties of law and medicine were the professional schools created to train the nation's civil and military elite. The faculties of theology, divided into faculties for Catholic theology (Paris, Aix, Bordeaux, Lyons, and Rouen) and for Protestant theology (Montauban and Strasbourg), were the token religious schools; they were mainly superfluous because the Catholic priesthood was trained almost exclusively in the major seminaries run by the bishops and one of the Protestant faculties (Montauban) had produced only two *licences* since 1811.[2] Science and letters faculties had a somewhat ambiguous existence. Created largely to give examinations and award the three main University degrees—the baccalaureate, the *licence*, and the doctorate—they had no students in the true sense of the word, only auditors, because their courses were not required for the passing of examinations.[3] But they did have professors who, to attract an audience, vulgarized their lectures. Although research and excellence in teaching were not totally absent in these faculties, the traditions had largely been lost, except at Paris.[4] The Collège de France, the Paris Observatory, the Bureau of Longitudes, and the Museum of Natural History, therefore, were the only institutions in which pure and disinterested research was actively fostered.

Nevertheless, progress was made in French scholarship and science within the Napoleonic system. History got its early start as an academic discipline, great scientific journals were created, and mathematics developed into a precise science. French science enjoyed an international reputation at least until the 1840s. And even in the 1850s and 1860s brilliant scholars such as Claude Bernard, J.-B. Dumas, and Louis Pasteur were still able to make advances in theoretical science in spite of the relative lack of resources and the crowded and nearly im-

2. Duruy, *Notes et souvenirs*, II, 60–61.
3. The exception was Montpellier, where medical students took courses at the faculty of science (Liard, *L'enseignement supérieur en France*, II, 123).
4. Bruneau, "French Faculties and Universities," 45.

possible conditions under which they were forced to work. Nonetheless, by the middle of the nineteenth century it was painfully clear that France had fallen far behind other nations in research and scholarship, and by 1863 nothing short of a major reorientation and expansion of higher education was necessary.[5]

The famous historian and Third Republic reformer Gabriel Monod believed that this was why Napoleon III elevated Duruy to the Ministry of Public Instruction in June of 1863. A few months earlier, Theodor Mommsen had visited France and had impressed on the emperor that French institutions were in a lamentable state of inferiority compared to their German counterparts. Mommsen, a student of ancient Rome like Duruy, may have even suggested Duruy's name to the emperor because Duruy, with his background in the humanities and simultaneous commitment to science and research, could be especially effective in reforming the system. That the emperor had a specific and relatively sweeping mission in mind for Duruy is supported by the transfer to his jurisdiction of all of the academic and scholarly institutions that had previously been under the jurisdiction of the minister of state: the Institut, the Academy of Medicine, the Ecole des Chartes, the libraries—Impérial, Mazarine, Arsenal, and Sainte-Geneviève—the *Journal des savants*, and responsibility for encouragements and subventions to savants, men of letters, and scientific missions.[6]

Duruy's earliest ideas on the need for reform in higher education came from his own educational experiences at the Ecole Normale and the Ecole Polytechnique as well as from contacts with his teachers and a limited circle of scholars. For example, he first learned of German erudition from Michelet. After he became minister, Duruy sought actively to augment his knowledge of problems in the French system. He quizzed various academic friends, attentively read reports from his subordinates, consulted reform proposals of earlier education ministers, and called upon the diplomatic corps to send him information on

---

5. Guillaume de Bertier de Sauvigny, *The Bourbon Restoration*, trans. Lynn M. Case (Philadelphia, 1967), 332; d'Irsay, *Histoire des universités françaises et étrangères*, II, 293; and Fox and Weisz, eds., *Organization of Science and Technology*, 23. See *ibid.*, 21–28, for an excellent summary of the debate over the decline in nineteenth-century French science and the current revisionist interpretation of the decline.

6. Monod, *Portraits et souvenirs*, 123–24; *JGIP*, 1863, p. 489 (decree of June 23, 1863).

higher education abroad. Indeed, these sources were not enough for him; soon he commissioned the publication of several reports on higher education in foreign countries and the lengthy and extremely important statistical study of French institutions, which was published in 1868 as *Statistique de l'enseignement supérieure.*[7]

According to inspector Roustan, who may have discussed the subject with Duruy as they rode back to Paris after Duruy was named minister, Duruy's determination to reform the system of higher education was present from the moment he took office. His enthusiasm was also fueled by developments during his ministry. Ernest Renan's famous critique on higher education in France written for the *Revue des deux mondes* in 1864 and fears about France's scientific inferiority expressed by scholars after the Universal Exposition of 1867 further impressed on him the compelling need for reform.[8]

Duruy's diagnosis of what was wrong with French higher education was almost always illuminated by comparisons with the German system, from which he wanted to take lessons but not copy exactly. Duruy was concerned about the lack of emphasis on science and the "scientific method," by which he meant, along with some of his contemporaries, as George Weisz notes, an emphasis on what the Germans called *Wissenschaft,* "all real knowledge that emerged from a critical, rational and methodological examination of concrete reality." He was concerned about the relative dearth of scholars in France based on his judgment that France had lost its former preeminence in science and scholarship. His misgivings about "this democracy which overflows its banks" had convinced him of the need for an "aristocracy of intelligence." Duruy feared not social mobility but (like Tocqueville) complete social leveling and consequent vulgarization of all knowl-

7. Some of the studies Duruy commissioned on higher education abroad include J. F. Minssen, *Etude sur l'instruction secondaire et supérieur en Allemagne* (1866); Jacques Demogeot and Henry Montucci, *De l'enseignement supérieur en Angleterre et en Écosse* (1870); and Adolphe Wurtz, *Les hautes études pratiques dans les universités allemandes* (1870).
8. M. Roustan, "L'enseignement primaire de Fortoul à Duruy: Le ministère Rouland (1856–1863)," *Revue pédagogique*, LVIII (1911), 155; Duruy, *L'instruction publique et la démocratie,* 259; Robert Fox, "Scientific Enterprise and the Patronage of Research in France, 1800–1870," in G. L'E. Turner (ed.), *The Patronage of Science in the Nineteenth Century* (Leiden, 1976), 9–10; George Weisz, "Le corps professoral de l'enseignement supérieur et l'idéologie de la réforme universitaire en France, 1860–1885," *Revue française de sociologie*, XVIII (1977), 206.

edge and art.[9] Duruy regretted the lack in the faculties of sciences and letters of true students such as were present in the universities in England and Germany. French letters and science faculties had only auditors. In a memorable passage, Duruy described the differences between an auditor and a student. An auditor, he explained, was "someone who comes in [to the classroom], sits for an hour to listen to an elegant, witty and sometimes eloquent lecture, and who carries from it an impression of what he heard, sometimes with the desire of opening a book to pursue the topic further. Students are young men attached to the word, the train of thought, the work of the teacher, meeting with him in his office or laboratory, becoming familiar with the methods of investigation and research, even aiding the teacher in the making of discoveries." French science and letters faculties needed students. He also regretted the limited range of courses offered and restricted number of professors in the faculties (mainly though not exclusively problems in the provincial faculties). German states had ordinary and extraordinary professors and the *privat-docent* or assistant professor. France had only titulary professors because substitutes and *chargés de cours* (lecturers) did not count as a separate level and could not offer additional courses. Financial and intellectual incentives for professors were also too few. German students paid their professors directly for their courses, and German states competed among themselves for the most distinguished professors, practices that seemed to encourage better teaching. In France, professors had only the lure of Paris and Parisian posts as incentives. Duruy did not want to abolish the state system of appointment, but he thought that if provincial institutions could be strengthened and given some voice in appointments there would be greater professional incentives for professors. Finally, Duruy deplored the fragmentation of faculties, the lack of funds for higher education, and the poverty and paucity of libraries, collections, laboratories, and buildings.[10]

9. Weisz, "The Academic Elite and the Movement to Reform French Higher Education," 107; Duruy, *Notes et souvenirs*, I, 198; Monod, *Portraits et souvenirs*, 124. Duruy's phrase, "this democracy which overflows its banks," was borrowed almost verbatim from Royer-Collard; it was fashionable liberal terminology and reflected the particular and rather conservative brand of liberalism developed in nineteenth-century France (Theodore Zeldin, "English Ideals in French Politics," *Historical Journal*, II [1959], 47).
10. *AIP*, 782, 717–20, 731.

In light of Duruy's comprehensive understanding of the problems in French higher education, his knowledge of the English and German systems, and his early commitment to reform, it is surprising that in his 1868 report to the emperor he would state, "It appears, for the moment, that the organization of our higher education does not need great reform. The edifice is old but solid in its bases; all we require are appropriations for new needs." This statement, however, cannot be taken at face value. Duruy did believe, like most French reformers, that the basic structures of French education reflected specific French circumstances and exigencies and that they should command a certain respect. Existing structures could not be eliminated wholesale. But Duruy seems to have had the problem of how to deal with vested interests and conservatism foremost in mind when he wrote to the emperor because certainly, as Louis Liard, the great reformer of higher education in the late nineteenth century, attested, and as Duruy's programs indicate, he intended to pursue a "vast program" of reform in higher education.[11] The statement to the emperor, therefore, was a calculated attempt to assuage the fears of those most opposed to change on the eve of some of his most ambitious initiatives in higher education.

Resistance to reform was enormous. Paraphrasing Louis Liard, the greatest difficulty was that almost everywhere Frenchmen were so used to the existing system that they could not conceive of significant alterations; they complained readily about the lack of adequate buildings and money, but they had relatively little complaint about the purposes of and attitudes toward higher education in France. William Bruneau has confirmed this assessment by pointing out that despite Duruy's suggestions in his inquiries of 1866–1868, "not a single institution of higher education proved willing to undertake research training for students or to encourage research among its staff." For most Frenchmen, even those such as Gabriel Monod who were interested in introducing German methods, to alter the structure of higher education significantly was to go against the *moeurs* of the people.[12]

Thus in light of the stubborn resistance to change and the perennial

11. *Ibid.*, 676. Bruneau, "French Faculties and Universities," 159; Chevallier and Grosperrin, *L'enseignement français de la Révolution à nos jours*, II, 235.

12. Liard, *L'enseignement supérieur en France*, II, 283; Bruneau, "French Faculties and Universities," 33, 167.

unwillingness of tightfisted legislators to allocate adequate funds for higher education, Duruy realized he would have to proceed cautiously and develop subtle and clever strategies for reform. To attract greater resources to higher education, diversify course offerings, and improve teaching, particularly by providing competition for state faculties, Duruy proposed that the state monopoly over higher education be terminated and that freedom to teach be granted to all academically eligible persons, thus enabling private institutions to do what the state would not or could not do. To strengthen state schools, he proposed that a research dimension be added to teaching everywhere in France and that universities be created in certain regional centers. Finally, to stem the prevalent apathy, he proposed that wide publicity be given to the deficiencies in French higher education and to the need for reform. This third strategy particularly explains why he commissioned *Statistique de l'enseignement supérieure* (1868) and several studies of higher education abroad and contributed as much as he could to the national debates over higher education in the 1860s.

When Duruy took office in 1863, he was not able to give his attention immediately to reforms because first he was forced to settle the famous Renan affair that had caused a public outcry during the closing months of Rouland's administration. Rouland had suspended Ernest Renan from his teaching post at the Collège de France for having denied the divinity of Christ in a public lecture. Most Christians were placated temporarily by the suspension and by the apparent defeat of the new biblical exegesis, which was still considered a dangerous German import, but they and the emperor wanted Renan not only suspended but dismissed from his post. Non-Christians, freethinkers, and Renan, of course, were outraged by what they considered a denial of academic freedom, and the matter posed a terrible dilemma for Duruy. Although he was a staunch supporter of academic freedom, he opposed any teaching that threatened religious or political peace. He also understood fully that his resolution of the affair would affect his future relations with scholars and teachers in higher institutions. His memoirs demonstrate that Duruy spent many anguished hours trying to determine an appropriate course of action. He claims that he finally decided to give the emperor two options: he would either dismiss Renan from the Collège, giving him his former post at the Bibliothèque Impérial as compensation, or, if the emperor did not find that acceptable, he would resign and allow the emperor to appoint a successor who could handle the matter differently. It is difficult to imagine Duruy giving the emperor such an ultimatum, but we have only Duruy's assertion. In any event, the emperor agreed to the reappointment of Renan to the Bibliothèque Impérial, and Duruy passed over the clerical candidate for Renan's vacant post in Hebrew at the Collège to name the distinguished Hebrew scholar, Salomon Munk. Duruy considered this appointment his revenge for the injustice that had been done to Renan.[13]

Unfortunately for Duruy, the Renan affair was not over. Renan continued to protest his treatment, arguing that he could not be dismissed because he had been elected to the Collège de France by vote of its faculty. The liberal press, especially *L'Opinion Nationale* and *Le Siècle*, took up Renan's cause, decrying the abridgment of academic freedom by a liberal minister. The most critical journalist was Lucien Prévost-Paradol, who proclaimed in the *Courrier du dimanche* that a truly liberal minister would have threatened to resign if the government proceeded with its plan to dismiss Renan. Duruy chose not to answer Prévost-Paradol and instead, he attempted to silence Renan and the press by issuing a statement reminding them that the decree-law of March 9, 1852, had given the minister final authority over all University appointments and revocations. The controversy quietened although it continued to smolder for the rest of the decade.[14]

While Renan's case was being argued, but after Duruy was able to distance himself from it, he began working on his first major reform in higher education, the introduction of *liberté de l'enseignement supérieur*. In October, 1863, Duruy wrote to the emperor asking for permission to prepare a bill, justifying his request on the grounds that such legislation had been promised in article 85 of the Falloux Law. The creation of private faculties would stimulate a sense of competition at the highest level, which would rejuvenate the languishing faculties of the state. Essentially, the bill was to be an extension of the *liberté de l'enseignement secondaire* provisions of the Falloux Law.

13. Roustan, "L'enseignement primaire de Fortoul à Duruy," 155; Duruy, *Notes et souvenirs*, I, 37.

14. *JGIP*, 1864, p. 359; Jules Baroche to the Bishop of Meaux, April 5, 8, 1869, F(19) 3972, AN; report of the Carnot Commission, F(17) 2654, AN.

Private higher establishments would be subject to regular state inspection to verify that nothing in their teaching was, as article 21 of the Falloux Law specified, "contrary to morality, the constitution or laws." Duruy had no fear, as some did, that the granting of *liberté* would lead to a growth in clericalism; he was confident that truth, justice, and a respect for differing beliefs would ultimately triumph. Within a few days after he made his request, however, he realized that his timing was wrong and moving too hastily could jeopardize the future success of the reform. Men closest to Napoleon III had revealed their opposition, making the reform more a matter of politics than of academics.[15]

Instead of pressing ahead, Duruy decided to promote an interim measure that would accustom legislators and public opinion to the idea of liberty in higher education and also provide some of the diversity in course offerings that he so zealously sought. This measure was the expansion of a small and informal program that had been extant since the Old Regime, the practice of offering extension courses (*conférences litteraires et scientifiques*) in higher education. These *conférences*, which became known more popularly as *cours libres*, a label Duruy helped to impress on them, were independent courses offered by scholars to the leisured classes who had no desire to win University degrees but who wanted intellectual distractions and the social legitimization attendance at such lectures bestowed. Duruy believed these courses were a marvelous opportunity for making the bourgeoisie and aristocracy more moral.

On October 1, 1864, Duruy sent a circular to his rectors asking them to encourage but not force the creation of *cours libres* in all of the populous towns of their academies. There were faculties in eighteen towns and cities in the provinces, and professors at these schools could supplement their incomes through the paying courses. Of course, professors could also offer their courses in outlying towns by traveling to them on the railroads. Duruy observed that the provinces provided a natural audience, especially among women, who were barred from the higher institutions of the state. The teachers, however, were not to be restricted to University professors; Duruy urged rectors to recruit members of learned societies (there were forty-six around the coun-

15. Duruy, *Notes et souvenirs*, II, 1–4.

try), magistrates, eminent engineers, and "men of culture and knowledge" who could share "the treasures of their experience" with audiences. *Agrégés* of *lycées* likewise were to be encouraged to offer courses; Duruy envisioned that the use of *agrégés* to teach the *cours libres* would be tantamount to creating a *privat-docenten* system for France such as the German states possessed. The lecturers were to select small topics, especially ones not normally treated in higher institutions, that could be exhausted in one or two evening sessions so that University teaching would not be reduplicated. Several related topics could be strung together if a lecturer wished to teach for several weeks or even a few months. Courses offered in the faculty towns would be loosely attached to the offerings of the faculties as *cours complémentaires.*[16]

Response to the minister's circular was rewarding. The number of *cours libres* grew rapidly, becoming popular "beyond all expectation," even in Corsica.[17] Learned societies instituted 169 courses, industrial societies, 18. A total of 751 courses were offered in 1864–1865; those attracting the largest audiences were in applied science, economics, literature, and history. Duruy was overjoyed. In Paris the courses were so well received that they had to be held at four different sites: in the lecture halls on the rue de la Paix, the rue de Cadet, and the rue Scribe and in the classrooms at the Sorbonne. Crowds at the Sorbonne eventually necessitated the establishment of an annex amphitheater on the rue de Gerson, which, Duruy noted, soon offered such a variety of courses that it was serving as a quasi-university.[18]

The liberal press applauded the new courses enthusiastically at first. Opposed to the concession of *liberté de l'enseignement supérieur* out of anxiety that Catholic higher institutions would become potent centers of clericalism and ultramontanism, it saw in the *cours libres* a legal way of expanding higher education while circumventing the problems *liberté* might present.[19] As the number of *cours libres* rose from twenty in 1863 to three hundred in early 1864–1865, *La France*

16. *BAIP*, II (1864), 401–404; Liard, *L'enseignement supérieur en France*, II, 291; *JGIP*, 1866, p. 250.

17. *AIP*, 733–34; confidential first trimester report, April 1, 1865, from the rector of Aix, F(17) 2650, AN.

18. *AIP*, 215–25; Victor Duruy to Edouard Laboulaye, December 5, 1874, in Duruy, *Notes et souvenirs*, I, 323.

19. *JGIP*, 1864, pp. 792, 644, 893.

(Catholic but pro-regime) proudly announced that the courses were promoting "a veritable reawakening of intellectual life" in the countryside. Indeed, some were drawing crowds of three and four hundred.[20] Only the conservative Catholic press was disturbed by the courses, and its opposition rested on two considerations: it did not approve of many of the orators authorized by the government to give lectures, and it resented partial measures such as *cours libres,* which would delay passage of a law providing for complete *liberté de l'enseignement supérieur.*[21]

Despite the criticism, however, Duruy did not authorize the courses carelessly. They were subjected perforce to the imperial law on associations, which gave the government discretionary power to prevent political lectures, and they were restricted to academic topics. Additionally, all of the lecturers were warned personally by Duruy to refrain from religious and political polemics, and all were surveyed closely by the rectors, who had to submit confidential reports to Duruy on the statements made at each lecture.[22] Thus when Saint-Marc Girardin criticized Russia excessively, Duruy reprimanded him. When the republican polemicist Prévost-Paradol requested permission to give courses on Montaigne at the salle Barthélemy in Paris, Duruy denied him. And when several other potentially troublesome individuals petitioned for the right to lecture, Duruy turned them down. The liberal and republican press argued that such actions were making a sham out of the putative liberty of the courses.[23] But Duruy argued that his restrictions were preventing more seriously damaging political controversies.

For the time being, the courses remained popular and increased in number. In the fall of 1865 Duruy granted 1,003 authorizations for 304 courses in Paris and 699 in the departments. Table 6 shows their dispersion by subject, as tallied by the ministry. Of the 955 different lecturers teaching these 1,003 courses, 349 were University professors

20. *RIP,* 1864, p. 818. Complete information on the courses is in F(17) 6635–6705, AN.
21. *JGIP,* 1864, p. 893.
22. Victor Duruy to Napoleon III, January 18, 1865, in Duruy, *Notes et souvenirs,* II, 17; confidential circular, January 28, 1867, F(17) 1475, AN.
23. Victor Duruy to Saint-Marc Girardin, March 22, 1864, fragment of a copy of a letter in possession of Mme Albert Duruy; *RIP,* 1866, p. 21.

Table 6. Cours libres Offered in 1865

Subject Areas	Number of Courses		
	Paris	Departments	Total
Theoretical science	59	61	120
Applied science	42	61	103
Literature	96	298	394
History	22	81	103
Political economy	6	12	18
Law	31	38	69
Archaeology	4	11	15
Fine arts	12	36	48
Hygiene	8	32	40
Agriculture	5	19	24
Geography	11	25	36
Philosophy	8	25	33
Totals	304	699	1,003

and 38 were public functionaries. The remainder were a mix of lycée agrégés and specialists from a variety of fields.[24]

After the academic year 1865–1866, the number of authorizations began to decline, however, and by 1867–1868 there were only 732 cours libres in the empire. In part the decline resulted from the transformation of many of the courses into advanced courses for adults attending night school. But in part it was the result of the increasing deployment of the courses by journalists and politicians as political forums, despite Duruy's specific instructions to the contrary. Duruy was forced to curb authorizations, and in his circular of January 23, 1865, he announced that in the future requests would be denied not only for potentially controversial topics and lecture locations but also to persons of specific political or religious "notoriety." He later justified this decision in a memorandum in which he argued that politics and religion already had a sufficient supply of tribunals and news-

24. JGIP, 1867, p. 187; 1866, p. 746.

papers to argue their opinions; public education was no place for such matters.[25]

Thus Duruy denied permission for courses to a variety of eminent political figures, including Jules Simon, Camille Pelletan, Adolf Guéroult, Jules Labbé, Albert duc de Broglie, and even François Guizot. He reversed some authorizations weeks after they had been granted (a particularly notorious case involved Guizot), and he closed courses that had become controversial months after they had been initiated. The most famous case of the latter involved lectures for Polish exiles in France, which were closed after being taken over by dedicated republicans including Jules Simon and Jules Favre.[26]

Gradually, all of the opposition deputies in the Corps législatif and anyone who could cause difficulties for the regime were placed on the ministry's proscribed list. Unfortunately, however, some of the justifications Duruy gave to the would-be lecturers and the press for his actions either had little relevance to the guidelines he had established in the January 23, 1865, circular or were so confused and contradictory that the press began to mock him.[27] But the liberal press and liberals in general had a more serious complaint in that ever since Persigny had promised further liberalization of the regime (once political parties ceased attacking the principles of the government), they had been looking to the *cours libres* for a sign of the sincerity of the government's promises. When they did not see this sign, and when Duruy, supposedly the representative liberal in the government, began to impose greater restrictions on the courses and play verbal gymnastics with the petitioners and the press, they began to cry fraud and to chastise him. Jules Simon flatly accused him of having abandoned liberalism.[28]

Criticism from the political right was as fierce as that from the left. The conservative clergy and clerical press attacked both the courses and Duruy personally. Dupanloup denounced them in his *Les alarmes*

25. *AIP*, 734; *JGIP*, 1865, p. 60; and undated notes in Victor Duruy's hand in possession of Mme Albert Duruy.
26. *JGIP*, 1864, pp. 241–42, 245; 1865, pp. 767, 89; memorandum, probably from Charles Glachant to Victor Duruy, November, 1864, Duruy Papers, 114AP-1-XV, AN. The response at the bottom of the memorandum is in Duruy's hand.
27. *Le Charivari*, June 21, 1868.
28. *JGIP*, 1865, pp. 89, 501, 78; *Le Charivari*, July 21, 1868.

de l'épiscopat for perpetuating atheism and impiety; and Bishop du Pont des Loges condemned them in his lenten message for 1868, asserting and deploring that in certain places Charles Darwin's theories were being taught under the cloak of *cours libres*. Sometimes the clerical attacks were effective in getting authorizations refused or withdrawn, as in the case of the Protestant minister Athanase Coquerel, editor of the newspaper *Le Lien*, who had desired to give a course on the primitive church. In other cases, however, Catholics were not so successful. Emile Deschanel's courses on the rue de Paix in Paris, which were tainted with anticlericalism and hostility to Christianity, for example, continued to exist and to draw large crowds despite lively protests from the clergy.[29]

Surprisingly, some *universitaires* opposed the courses, although most of these opponents were men of letters who objected to the apparent favoritism Duruy gave to the sciences among the *cours libres*. They failed to perceive, however, that Duruy was just as solicitous of the humanities as he was of the sciences. To be sure, he had attempted to persuade Baron Georges Haussmann, the prefect who was responsible for rebuilding Paris during the Second Empire, to construct a huge amphitheater for the literary courses in the center of Paris, and when Haussman refused, Duruy took his case to the emperor, protesting: "Your crown lacks its most brilliant *fleuron* . . . the radiance of letters. No new talent has been produced, and we still rely on the movement of 1829. Your Majesty cannot, despite his power, be a great writer; but you can, Sire, hasten the birth of some unknown genius by preparing the most favorable milieu for his development."[30] But in truth, Duruy alone was responsible for the ire of the humanists because it was science and the scientific method that he extolled most often in his official circulars and speeches.

While this multifaceted controversy ensued, Duruy was trying by means of small and piecemeal reforms to strengthen state institutions for the competition he expected they would soon face from private institutions. There had long been concern over the numbers of students

29. Dupanloup, *Les alarmes de l'épiscopat*, 28; F(19) 2537, AN; letters from clericals, especially those from Monsignors Parisis and de Bonnechose, November, 1864, Duruy Papers, 114AP-1-XV, AN; Bourgain, *L'église de France et l'état au dix-neuvième siècle*, II, 174.
30. Duruy, *Notes et souvenirs*, II, 9.

entering the profession of law and what new courses should be offered; here he made three improvements. In 1864, to respond to the
influx of students entering the legal profession since 1860, he created a
new law faculty at Nancy.[31] Then, to respond to a pressing need and to
satisfy the theoretical economists and Saint-Simonians grouped around
the liberal *Journal des économists* with whom he sympathized, he created a chair of political economy at the faculty of law in Paris in November, 1864. Finally, to provide general stimulus for the quality of
legal studies, he instituted a competitive examination (a *concours général*) for all third-year law students in the empire in January, 1869.
Of the three reforms, Duruy considered the second his most important
for it introduced an academic discipline that would help inoculate
young men against the "dangerous utopian dreams" that had attracted
so many in 1848. Additionally, it would give the French some strength,
even if limited, in a social science that had gained much ground in the
German institutions of higher learning. Duruy wished to create new
chairs for political economy at all law faculties in the empire, but
available funds prohibited doing so. Nonetheless, a few months after
his dismissal from office, chairs of political economy were created at
three more faculties of law—Nancy, Grenoble, and Toulouse—in part
because of Duruy's initiatives.[32]

For medical education, in which the number of students had doubled since the beginning of the empire, Duruy added new chairs and
courses: a chair for the history of medicine and a course in organic
chemistry at the Collège de France and two chairs of clinical pathology
at the faculty of medicine in Strasbourg. The press rumored in 1866
that Duruy was contemplating the conversion of four *écoles secon-*

31. According to a survey completed in 1867, 40 percent of these students were seeking a legal career; 40 percent were seeking employment in government (and had, of
course, no *école d'administration* to attend); and 20 percent were simply seeking a
higher degree for generalists (Geiger, "Prelude to Reform," 350). For the law faculty at
Nancy, *BAIP*, I (1864), 28–29 (decree of January 9, 1864).
32. Guy Palmade, "Le journal des économistes et la pensée libérale sous le Second
Empire," *Bulletin de la Société d'histoire moderne et contemporaine*, no. 22 (1968),
9–16; *BAIP*, II (1864), 267–70; XI (1869), 127 (decree of January 27, 1869); Lucette
Le Van-Lemesle, "La faculté de droit de Paris et l'introduction de l'économie politique
dans son enseignement, 1864–1878," in Baker and Harrigan, *Making of Frenchmen*,
329; Bruneau, "French Faculties and Universities," 34. The city of Bordeaux also
wanted a law faculty, but Duruy, opposed to multiplying university facilities carelessly,
judged it unnecessary and rebuffed the request (Minutes of the academic council of
Toulouse, June, 1865, F[17] 4360, AN).

daires de médicine into full-fledged faculties of medicine, but there was no further mention of the idea. Opposition to such a move from the three existing medical faculties (Paris, Strasbourg, and Montpellier) certainly would have been overwhelming. But Duruy publicized his efforts to provide places for theoretical studies in medical education and more practical experiences for medical students, which was part of his effort to respond to the call for reform in medical education that had been raised in 1848.[33]

Duruy also made a few changes in the faculties of sciences and letters. He forced errant cities to establish preparatory schools to these faculties as they had been directed to do by the decrees of August 22, 1854. He created a chair of physiology at the faculty of science in Paris, which was rapidly becoming more research-oriented.[34] Up to this time the Collège de France had been the only institution in the empire to conduct pure research in human physiology (under the direction of Claude Bernard). Finally, by a series of circulars, some of which were confidential, he attempted to guarantee the continuation of daytime classes at faculties that, in contrast to evening classes, had a more didactic character and to regulate both the length of lectures and student attendance in class.[35] He did nothing for the faculties of theology that lay beyond his domain, but he did urge Catholics to petition Rome for canonical sanction, a status enjoyed by Catholic faculties of theology in other countries. Admittedly, these measures helped the faculties only in small ways. Abolishing some of the faculties of letters and sciences which had been created so enthusiastically during the July Monarchy and the early Second Empire would have been more useful for it would have guaranteed a greater share of the notoriously derisory higher education budget for the surviving faculties. But

33. *JGIP*, 1869, p. 260; *BAIP*, XI (1869), 127; F(17*) 1870, AN (decree of November 19, 1864); *JGIP*, 1866, p. 74; *AIP*, 693; Liard, *L'enseignement supérieur en France*, II, 226.

34. Craig Zwerling, "The Emergence of the Ecole Normale Supérieure as a Center of Scientific Education in the Nineteenth Century," in Fox and Weisz (eds.), *Organization of Science and Technology in France*, 31–60.

35. *AIP*, 83–84; Ministère de l'Instruction Publique, *Statistique de l'enseignement supérieur*, 331; d'Irsay, *Histoire des universités françaises et étrangères*, II, 296; Victor Karady, "L'accès aux grades et leurs fonctions universitaires dans les facultés des sciences au 19ᵉ siècle; examen d'une mutation," in Baker and Harrigan, *Making of Frenchmen*, 401–10; confidential circulars, October 24, 1863, April 21, 22, December 13, 1864, F(17) 1474, and January 15, March 28, 1866, F(17) 1475, AN.

abolishing these faculties was neither politically feasible nor amenable to the larger role Duruy would designate for them later.

At the Ecole Normale Supérieure Duruy created a new chair in the history of philosophy to complement his reestablishment of philosophy in the secondary schools. And to test student progress more carefully, he added semester and end-of-the-year examinations.[36]

Duruy extended higher instruction in languages by adding new courses in general grammar and comparative philology at the Collège de France and, in hopes of making instruction more pertinent to the new needs of the empire abroad, courses in Maghrebi Arabic, Japanese, and the languages of Tibet, Mongolia, and Amman at the Ecole des Langues Orientales. To correct the relative lack of emphasis on conversation in foreign languages at the Ecole des Langues Orientales, a deficiency which meant that French ambassadors and agents abroad often had to rely on foreign nationals to serve as translators, he created a commission consisting of himself, the minister of foreign affairs, and the minister of commerce to prepare proposals calling for the employment of native speakers on the faculty and requiring students to demonstrate a certain speaking facility before graduation.[37] The proposals were still under discussion when Duruy left office, but they were implemented shortly thereafter in a November, 1869, decree. Duruy's plans to send students from the *grandes écoles*, equipped with a knowledge of foreign languages, abroad for a year to take advanced courses from eminent scientists unfortunately never succeeded.[38]

The material as well as the educational situation at the great scientific institutions of France deeply troubled Duruy. In his great report on higher education (1868), he would write: "Foreigners are justly shocked by the crowded quarters allotted to certain fields of research, but lack of space is not the only problem: in this place or that, the health of the professors is being compromised by the insalubrities of their surroundings . . . [which] admit no air and are poorly lighted." Duruy did what he could to improve these and other conditions for

36. *JGIP*, 1864, p. 776; *BAIP*, III (1865), 91–93 (*arrêté* of February 7, 1865).

37. Albert Duruy, "La statistique de l'enseignement supérieur," *Revue des deux mondes*, 3rd period, 32 (April 1, 1879), 556–91.

38. Announced by Duruy at the November 10, 1864, meeting of the Imperial Council, F(17) 1870, AN; *JGIP*, 1867, p. 170; Duruy, "La statistique de l'enseignement supérieur," 568; *RIP*, 1868, p. 50.

scientists. He facilitated the construction of a laboratory for Pasteur in the courtyard of the Ecole Normale. By the decree of December 29, 1863, he created a commission of inspection for the Museum of Natural History to improve its material situation, and he extended the term of its director from one to five years to promote planning on a longer basis. Claude Bernard and his course in general physiology were moved from the Sorbonne to the museum, where there was more room for the development of a laboratory, and a model laboratory was established at the museum from funds donated to Duruy by the rich industrialist Menier. Duruy also created a program of applied science for agronomy at the museum.[39]

A few minor organizational changes were made at the Ecole d'Athenes and the Ecole des Chartres, but they had no significant impact on the nature of the schools.[40] At the Institut, Duruy suppressed the sixth section of the Académie des Sciences Morales—politics, administration and finance—and attached its scholars to the fourth section, renaming it "political economy, finances, and statistics" and justifying his action as an attempt to bring structure and titles into line with actual functions. The *JGIP* accepted this explanation at face value, noting that Duruy had a "mania" for bureaucratic organization. The *Revue des deux mondes*, however, suspected that there were ulterior political motives behind the measure inasmuch as most of the scholars in the old sixth section were still loyal to Orleanism and legitimism; in the fourth section they would be outnumbered by scholars of other sympathies. The evidence suggests that both periodicals were correct: Duruy's measure was the proverbial one stone that killed two birds. What Duruy would have done had he been able to create a *grande école* of public administration as he wished to do remains open to speculation. His bill for this school was submitted to the Imperial Council twelve days after he left office and was forgotten in the confusion that struck the country after the fall of the empire.[41]

In his report to the emperor on higher education, the *Statistique de l'enseignement supérieur* (1868), Duruy argued for the need to in-

39. Ministère de l'Instruction Publique, *Statistique de l'enseignement supérieur*, 22; *JGIP*, 1864, p. 18; 1868, p. 817; 1864, p. 777; 1869, p. 177.
40. See Rohr, *Victor Duruy, ministre de Napoléon III*, 108.
41. *JGIP*, 1866, p. 329; *RIP*, 1869, p. 275.

crease the number of chairs in the natural sciences, to augment budgets for libraries and learned societies (particularly to stimulate the production of scholarly journals), and to allow scholars to travel more, especially so they could complete their education by studying abroad at distinguished universities. Unfortunately, he accomplished very little along these lines while he was minister, but among the more intriguing activities he was able to foster in his capacity as supervisor for encouragements to scientists and savants were the scientific expedition to Mexico, the creation of a prize of 50,000 francs for a practical application of Volta's battery, and the erection of meteorological observatories. One of the observatories was established in the park of Montsouris in Paris after Duruy persuaded Haussmann to lease the palace of the bey of Tunis (which had been sent to Paris for the Universal Exposition of 1867) to him for one franc a year, instead of using it as a lodge for groundskeepers or a refreshment stand. The other observatory, scheduled to be erected at Le Puy in Puy-de-Dôme, was never realized, despite the careful plans Duruy made for it. Duruy's support for savants and scholarship elsewhere, through his rhetoric, his programs, and the small subsidies he was able to distribute paid handsome dividends in the rejuvenation of learned societies. According to Paul Gerbod, increased numbers of the teaching corps sought membership in these societies; a new enthusiasm for doing research and for publishing erudite works was stimulated; and "the vocations of local scholars emerged and took shape." [42]

Duruy considered all of these reforms important, if sometimes only small steps forward, but none could compare with his greatest achievement in higher education: the creation of the Ecole Pratique des Hautes Etudes. The Ecole Pratique was designed as a superstructure to coordinate advanced research in Paris and to supply France with the research scientists and scholars it lacked. Its creation was a prime example of Duruy's ability to employ logic and imagination to solve major educational problems in a state whose legislature was little inclined to spend money on education. And in this case, his success reflected his effort to surmount the resistance of vested interests in the *grandes écoles* and faculties to substantial reform. [43]

42. *AIP*, 699–704; *JGIP*, 1864, pp. 129–30, 177, 593; Duruy, *Notes et souvenirs*, I, 309–13; Gerbod, *La condition universitaire en France*, 458.
43. As with most "new" ideas, there is a question about who first conceived the idea

As Duruy told the emperor in a lengthy letter in January, 1868, "In no other city of the universe [other than Paris could] . . . one find united in so small an area [the hill of Sainte-Geneviève] such a collection of institutions of the highest order." There were five faculties: law, medicine, theology, letters, and sciences; two institutions of pure research: the Collège de France and the Museum of Natural History; the School of Pharmacy; the Paris Observatory; the *grandes écoles*; seven great libraries: those of Sainte-Geneviève, Mazarine, the Arsenal, the Sorbonne, the Institut, the Museum of Natural History, and the Ecole Normale; and three important museums: the museum for ancient art at the Ecole des Beaux-Arts, the museum for medieval art at Cluny, and the museum for modern art at Luxembourg. The facilities of each could be joined together to form one very distinguished institution of higher learning in France, an Ecole Pratique des Hautes Etudes.[44]

The word "Pratique" in the title of the school had been carefully chosen, and Duruy took pains both in his letter to the emperor and in all subsequent information he disseminated to emphasize that the school would be dedicated to the pursuit of research and theoretical studies. "Pratique" meant that students would be given practical experiences in research and theory. More specifically, students would work in *conférences* or small discussion groups and seminars similar to those developed in Germany. If they were in the humanities sections of the school they would analyze texts and manuscripts at the school, museums, libraries, and archives, they would prepare bibliographies, and they would be sent to foreign countries to perfect their language skills; or, if they were in the scientific sections they would have practical laboratory experiences—dissections, use of sophisticated scientific instruments, and verification of scientific laws and precepts, and they would take field trips to places of interest. Both groups of students were to spend most of their time doing original research; Duruy stressed that the inductive method was to predominate.[45]

---

for the Ecole Pratique. Geiger, "Prelude to Reform," 359, mentions that the idea first came from Michel Bréal, although it resembled a suggestion made by Ernest Renan in 1864. Duruy, of course, gives the impression that the idea was his (*Notes et souvenirs*, I, 301–24, esp. 305). But there is no doubt about who put the school in place and gave it its precise form.

44. Duruy, *Notes et souvenirs*, I, 304.

45. Duruy was planning to establish a periodical that would contain students' *mémoires*, *analyses*, and extracts of scholarly works and translations—especially from

The faculty of the new school—many young men independent of University tradition and some recently trained in German seminars— would be given complete freedom to teach what they wished and how they wished as long as they adhered to the essential nature of the school as Duruy created it. "Work as you think best" was the message Duruy sent to them. There were to be no special programs, no assignment of teachers and students, and no bureaucratic "red tape." Duruy did ask that the subjects taught be highly unusual, ones not yet taught in the regular institutions of higher learning, and he required professors to submit annual reports to him, but he made no further demands on them. Proof of the freedom he gave them resides in the anecdote that Gabriel Monod related later: Duruy had left so much latitude to the professors in establishing the school that a minor dispute between them over the nature of the institution actually caused a delay in its opening. It was resolved a few days later when the professors decided to use the German *Hochschulen* as their model.[46]

The school was to be open to anyone who wished to enroll, Frenchmen and foreigners alike. There were no qualifying degrees and no entrance examinations, although students were rigorously screened after they entered, and the academically inferior ones were subject to weeding out. Nor were there any particular terminal degrees because Duruy wanted to avoid the excessive emphasis on examinations and procurement of degrees prevalent in French higher education. But students wishing evidence of their work at the school could petition for either a *diplôme de l'Ecole* or a *doctorat-ès-sciences*. As a result of these liberalities, Lavisse relates, one worker with little formal education entered the school and ultimately rose to become a professor at the Collège de France and a member of the Institut.[47]

Initially, the Ecole Pratique des Hautes Etudes was divided into four sections—mathematics, physics and chemistry, biology, and history and philology. Later, by the decree of January 30, 1869, a fifth section,

German. Ultimately, students' works were presented in a journal entitled *Bibliothèque de l'Ecole des Hautes Etudes* (F[17] 13617, AN).

46. Thompson and Holm, *History of Historical Writing*, II, 268; Lavisse, "Victor Duruy," 49; Duruy, *Notes et souvenirs*, I, 305; Victor Duruy to the directors of the laboratories and study centers of the Ecole Pratique des Hautes Etudes, March 1, 1869, F(17) 13614, AN; Gabriel Monod to Victor Duruy, November 6, 1878, Duruy Papers, 114 AP-1-VII, AN.

47. Lavisse, "Victor Duruy," 50.

political economy and administration, was added.[48] Each section was given its own advisory commission. Each was staffed by faculty from the higher institutions of Paris, which became annexes of the school and were required to maintain either an office of studies or a laboratory that was directly attached to the Ecole Pratique. Higher institutions and professors in the provinces were allowed to link themselves to the school if they wished, an elastic measure that Duruy purposely devised. And indeed, higher institutions at Lille, Marseilles, Caen, and Saint-Maur availed themselves of this opportunity forthwith. A sense of unity was provided, according to Duruy, by four elements: the achievement certificates that could be awarded to the students, the advisory commissions created for each section, the single budget from which all members drew, and finally, and perhaps most important, the Conseil Supérieur which had broad power and could coordinate all activities related to the school and ensure its research orientation.[49]

The Ecole Pratique was officially brought into existence by the decree of July 31, 1868. To the skeptical Gabriel Monod, who doubted whether France needed any more institutions of higher education and who suggested that it would be wiser to reorganize the faculties, Duruy replied that an *école des hautes études* "can be created with a pen and a sheet of paper. I will obtain the money for it which they [the legislators] will not give me for the faculties. To make the French understand something, one has to have a name which really strikes the mind."[50]

And strike the mind he hoped it would do because he wanted the school to become a model for the pedagogical reform of other higher institutions, particularly the faculties of letters and sciences. The Ecole Pratique was intended to provoke a preference for the scientific method and research (reminiscent of the German tradition of *Lehr- und Lernfreiheit*) among all institutions with which it had contact. As Duruy put it succinctly, "The Ecole Pratique des Hautes Etudes is a germ which I am depositing in the cracked walls of the old Sorbonne; in growing, it will crumble it [the Sorbonne]."[51]

48. F(17) 13614, AN (decree of January 30, 1869).
49. *BAIP*, X (1868), 110, 334–36.
50. A. Lebey, *La lutte scolaire en France au XIXe siècle: Le ministre Duruy* (Paris, n.d.), 34; *BAIP*, X (1868), 104.
51. Thompson and Holm, *History of Historical Writing*, II, 267, quoting from

By the decree of July 31, 1868, Duruy also distinguished between the types of laboratories that should be maintained by member institutions. Deciding not to follow the current German trend toward the integration of teaching and research in laboratories (because it was too radical a change for the French), Duruy specified that the Ecole Pratique laboratories be divided, as French tradition dictated, into teaching laboratories and research laboratories. Thus affiliating institutions would have either to designate existing laboratories or to create new ones. (Many institutions, including the Sorbonne, which got new laboratories for physics, chemistry, and physiology, profited from this requirement.) Affiliating institutions would have to identify carefully the nature of each laboratory. In the teaching laboratories, students would be introduced to established scientific principles under the tutelage of the best scientists in France. Later, in research laboratories, which would have a special budget for research funds and student scholarships, students would work on original projects in pure science under the direction, again, of eminent scientists aided by several highly skilled research assistants. Duruy specified in his decree that the function of the teaching laboratories was to diffuse scientific knowledge while that of the research laboratories was to advance scientific knowledge. Together, they would provide France with the facilities she had lacked previously. "It is with institutions of this type," Duruy noted, "that Germany has been able to achieve the great development of experimental sciences which we study with anxiety." And certainly, it was with institutions of this type that Duruy was able to satisfy both the emperor, who feared that industry was drawing off the best science students to the disadvantage of pure research, and scientists such as Louis Pasteur and Jean-Baptiste Dumas, who had decried the poverty of scientific facilities in France. Dumas would sadly mourn later to Duruy that he had been born too early: "This decree reminds me of the lost time, the futile efforts, the difficulties I encountered trying to find a laboratory, instruments, the financial resources, in short, everything you are going to give to my successors. What I could have done with such resources." [52]

Albert duc de Broglie, "Notice sur la vie et les oeuvres de M. Victor Duruy," *ASMP*, CXLIX (1898), 569–602, cf. 729–45.

52. Fox, "Scientific Enterprise and the Patronage of Research in France," 29; *Rapport à l'empereur et décrets relatifs aux laboratoires d'enseignement et de recherche et à*

Duruy envisioned that the new laboratories would provide, as he put it, "arsenals of science" for France. They were to produce scholars, not teachers. Several laboratories were organized in 1868 by some of the most distinguished scientists of the day: Marcellin Berthelot (organic chemistry) and Claude Bernard (physiology) took charge of the new laboratories at the Collège de France; Louis Pasteur (chemistry) directed one at the Ecole Normale; Henry Milne-Edwards (zoology), Joseph Decaisne (botany), Vicomte Adolphe d'Archiac (paleontology), and Gabriel Delafosse (mineralogy) headed laboratories at the Museum of Natural History; and Pierre Duchartre (vegetal anatomy), Edmond Hébert (geology), and Jules Jamin (physics) became directors at the Sorbonne. By the academic year 1869–1870, forty-two laboratories and *conférences* were operating under the aegis of the Ecole Pratique, and more than 215 students were enrolled. By his own assessment, Duruy had created a "noiseless revolution" in French science and had helped to engineer a scientific renaissance.[53]

The other major ancillary reform in the decree of July 31, 1868, was the creation of an advanced program of study for *agrégés* of the Ecole Normale Supérieure who might wish to continue their scholarly pursuits beyond the required curriculum of the school.[54] The purpose of this measure was both to associate the Ecole Normale more closely with the Ecole Pratique and to help make the Ecole Normale, which had been established mainly to train *lycée* professors, a more elite institution, one that concentrated on the preparation of research-oriented professors for faculties of letters and sciences.

As the Ecole Normale was taking on its new character, Duruy envisioned that the task of training teachers for secondary schools would be shifted to and assumed by the studentless departmental faculties. He had already anticipated this change in the decree of January 11, 1868, by creating the position of *maître répétiteur auxiliaire* (student teacher) at all of the departmental faculties of letters and sciences. *Maîtres répétiteurs auxiliaires* were to spend two hours each day as-

la création d'un Ecole Pratique des Hautes Études, in *BAIP*, X (1868), 102, 106; Williams, *World of Napoleon III*, 158; Fox, "Scientific Enterprise and the Patronage of Research in France," 9; Duruy quoting Dumas in *Notes et souvenirs*, II, 239.

53. *Arrêté* of January 2, 1869, and a report on the school, both in F(17) 13614, AN; Duruy, *Notes et souvenirs*, I, 319.

54. *BAIP*, X (1868), 115.

sisting master teachers at the local *lycée* and the rest of their time taking special research-oriented courses at the faculties. If they were in letters, they were to concentrate on analyzing texts and manuscripts; if they were in sciences, they were to focus on laboratory work. In exchange for their time at the *lycées*, the student teachers received room, board, and the generous stipend of 400 francs.[55]

On the basis of the decree of January 11, 1868, complemented by the decree of July 31, 1868, on the Ecole Pratique, Duruy proudly boasted that he had created veritable *écoles normales secondaires* (secondary normal schools), schools which some of his predecessors had tried unsuccessfully to create.[56] They were supposed to help solve a number of problems in higher education. First, he claimed, the Ecole Normale Supérieure would be relieved of some of its overcrowding. Because of financial considerations, students interested in attending the Ecole Normale would be encouraged to earn their *licence* degree at one of the faculties in the provinces before moving to Paris. Second, their built-in convenience would encourage more young people to enter teaching and to earn the *licence* degree, which was not specifically required but was considered highly desirable. Third, by clever use of existing personnel and buildings, the state got a new institution, secondary normal schools, without charge beyond the cost of some stipend money for students. Fourth, provincial faculties of letters and sciences would be populated with true students, who would receive practical learning experiences, thus altering the pedagogical nature of the provincial faculties. Fifth, faculty professors would be placed in contact with the future teachers of candidates to the baccalaureate examination, which would, in turn, help improve that "master-key" of the University. Finally, an avenue of advancement would be created for student teachers who wished to continue studies at a higher level after they received their *licence*. Their practical experiences at the faculties would equip them handily for future work at a branch of the Ecole Pratique.[57]

The *écoles normales secondaires* were initiated in 1868 at fourteen faculty centers in the provinces. By the end of that year, 249 students

55. *BAIP*, X (1868), 102–27.
56. *AIP*, 721.
57. *Ibid.*, 730; *BAIP*, X (1868), 104–105.

were enrolled in the program studying for their *licence* or *agrégation*, and by 1869, there were nearly 500 such students.[58] Given the paucity of funds available for such a program, the fact that secondary school-teachers were not specifically required by the state to hold the *licence* or *agrégation* degrees, and the lack of career options for graduates of the letters and sciences faculties, Duruy's accomplishment was impressive.

In addition to the creation of the Ecole Pratique des Hautes Etudes, the teaching and research laboratories, and the secondary normal schools, Duruy also hoped to create a *grande école* of agronomy and a *grande école* of horticulture to serve as capstones to the agricultural education courses and programs being introduced at lower levels. In correspondence with the empress, Duruy proudly pointed out that no other country in Europe had yet conceived of schools of this nature and that their establishment would win much prestige in the scientific world. Eventually, Duruy managed to secure funds for the creation of a higher school of agronomy at the Museum of Natural History. But his plans to establish a higher school of horticulture as well as several more chairs for natural science foundered. The legislature continued to resist augmenting his budget for higher education.[59]

Duruy worked assiduously to get his bill on *liberté de l'enseignement supérieur* enacted because it would cost nothing, but it would promote a significant expansion in the total facilities available in higher education. As we saw earlier, overtures made in 1863 were brought to an abrupt halt following Duruy's conclusion that the political climate was inopportune. In 1867, however, after the emperor announced that the regime would be liberalized further, Duruy thought the moment ripe for a fresh start. Freedom of higher education would be, he believed, "a magnificent conclusion" to the other new liberties the emperor intended to grant. Duruy began his campaign by taking his bill to the Senate, which had jurisdiction over the fundamental laws of the empire, and by urging senators to approve it and send it to the legislature for action. The Senate, however, demurred for several

58. *AIP*, 783.
59. Victor Duruy to the empress, August 3, 1868, in Duruy, *Notes et souvenirs*, II, 185; Victor Duruy to Edmond About, April 18, 1868, copy of a letter, Duruy Papers, 114 AP-1-IX, AN; Duruy, *Notes et souvenirs*, I, 323.

months, not wishing to open debate on such a controversial issue. Finally, on December 7, 1867, an exasperated Duruy begged Rouher to intercede before the "clerical party" stole the initiative and forced the government to concede freedom of higher education on its own terms.[60] Five days later, the Senate reluctantly complied.

Duruy's bill for freedom of higher education was short. It would have allowed any man, Frenchman or foreigner, who was at least twenty-five years old and who held at least a *licence* in the appropriate field of learning to open an institution of higher learning. It said nothing about state examinations or the awarding of degrees, but it made abundantly clear that private institutions were to have no authority in these areas.[61] Perhaps unfortunately, deliberations on the bill were speedy. Senators failed to appreciate that they had an ideal opportunity to grant a small concession without substantially jeopardizing the state's monopoly in higher education. They voted instead to reroute the bill to the Imperial Council, where an ad hoc commission of ten members was to be selected to review it with Duruy.

Back at the Imperial Council, Duruy defended the bill valiantly. He argued that because *liberté* had been established at the primary and secondary levels, it was contradictory to refuse it at the highest level, especially since a modicum of *liberté* already existed there in the form of the *cours libres*. He also argued that the government needed a law on *liberté* in order to control the cadre of "clandestine" professors—private individuals who tutored students preparing for state examinations—which tended to attract students away from the faculties. But committee members were not persuaded. They feared that the granting of *liberté* would open higher education to the teaching of doctrines such as socialism and ultramontanism that were dangerous or subversive to the state. They told Duruy bluntly they had no confidence that state inspection of the schools would prevent the teaching of such doctrines. After all, were not the Jesuits on the rue des Postes infamous for eluding state inspection? And was it not true that officials of religious schools prepared carefully for the visits of the state inspectors, who, wishing to avoid conflicts, failed to press for detailed information on the teaching? Duruy replied that this assertion was not true, but "if . . . the means of control, of action, of repression are not sufficiently

60. Duruy, *Notes et souvenirs*, II, 2, 22.
61. *AIP*, 831–33.

defined, we should make them [more] precise." Duruy himself had no fear, certainly not while he was minister. As he had told the emperor earlier, the government was "armed to the teeth" to prevent problems, and he was "well disposed" to use the power the government gave him. Despite his defense, however, the committee voted to table the bill and thus effectively killed it.

Perhaps not surprisingly, Duruy found little support for the bill from the University community. Most faculty deans and academic councils and nine out of fifteen rectors feared that state institutions would suffer irreparable damage from the competition of the new private institutions. And some functionaries, such as the councillor on the academic council of Bordeaux, protested that since the graduates of higher institutions would have a particularly large influence on the whole of society, society needed the special protection that only state faculties could provide. Later Duruy admitted to Guizot that he had been "foolhardy" to have proposed *liberté de l'enseignement supérieur* in 1867 because the climate of opinion was still not ripe for it.[62]

Actually, Duruy did make one more plea, on March 14, 1868, to the emperor, arguing that the newly passed press law and law on meetings dictated a law providing freedom of higher education. Only the latter could give full meaning to the other two laws. But evidently the emperor offered no special encouragement or assistance.[63]

In the meantime, Catholics picked up where Duruy left off and flooded the Senate with petitions demanding that *liberté de l'enseignement supérieur* be granted because state institutions were riddled with materialism. The argument was not unfamiliar; it had been used in the 1840s when Catholics campaigned for the right to open secondary schools. But in the 1860s, certainly, materialism was a greater reality and threat, given the new moral laxity of society under the Second Empire, the growth of socialism, the success of the International, the appearance of aggressive antireligious student groups, and the continuous press coverage of these developments.[64] Dupanloup became so

62. Duruy, *Notes et souvenirs*, II, 33 (the complete account of the meeting is on pp. 23–38), 8; academic council reports, F(17) 4374, AN; minutes of the academic council session in Bordeaux, June, 1868, F(17) 4363, AN; Victor Duruy to François Guizot, March 23, 1870, letter 18, François Guizot Papers, 42 AP 268, AN.

63. Duruy, *Notes et souvenirs*, II, 40.

64. Seignobos, *Le déclin de l'empire et l'établissement de la Troisième République*, 41, 60. In 1865, the Imperial Council had taken up the case of a group of students from the faculties of law and medicine in Paris who had attended an international students'

concerned that in 1866 he conferred with the pope, who, equally dismayed, urged Dupanloup and other French prelates to devote all of their talents "to the energetic defense of religion." As a result of this exchange, Dupanloup wrote and published his pamphlet *Les alarmes de l'épiscopat* (1868), and Catholics began submitting petitions to the Senate demanding freedom of higher education.[65]

Each of the petitions sent to the Senate was rerouted to Duruy because each made specific charges against teaching in the state institutions. Duruy investigated them thoroughly. Almost all proved to indict either phrases taken out of context or words misunderstood by auditors in large lecture halls. The one petition that caused some difficulty for Duruy was submitted by Leopold Giraud, editor of the Catholic *Journal des villes et campagnes*. This petition cited certain statements in a recently accepted doctoral thesis at the Paris faculty of medicine which amounted to a denial of the existence of the soul and life after death. The petition incriminated the entire faculty of medicine and demanded *liberté de l'enseignement supérieur* as "the sole corrective to the propagation of dangerous doctrines."[66] Duruy ordered that the thesis be sent to him, and when he discovered the offending passages he annulled the thesis and reprimanded the mentor. Nevertheless, he was required to appear before the Senate to answer for the faculty.

The morning the Senate was to begin deliberations on the Giraud petition (May 19, 1868), the *Moniteur* ran a long article carefully establishing Duruy's orthodoxy. Later, in the Senate, Duruy, aided by Charles Adolphe Wurtz, the dean of the faculty, Pasteur, and Dumas, defended the faculty against Giraud's charge. There had been two unfortunate incidents at the faculty, Duruy admitted—the student's thesis and the profession of atheism in one lecture given by a Professor Robin—but the people involved in both instances had been punished. Catholics had no further reason to fear offenses because teaching at

---

conference in Brussels and who had allegedly made certain offensive attacks on religion. This so-called Liège Affair brought considerable public and press attention to the growth of atheism among students (F[17*] 1870, AN [session of December 26, 1865]; *JGIP*, 1865, p. 798, and 1866, p. 5).

65. Schwab, "Victor Duruy et les premiers pas de l'enseignement laique," 5–6; report of Chaix d'Est-Ange to the Senate, March 27, 1868, reproduced in *JGIP*, 1868, p. 217.

66. Duruy, *Notes et souvenirs*, I, 363; petition of April 6, 1867, F(17) 2511, AN.

the faculty was otherwise morally and religiously irreproachable, and special efforts were being made to avoid appointing professors who were materialists. Nonetheless, bishops in the Senate became increasingly exercised over the episodes. Eventually, in the heat of debate, Saint-Beuve intervened to defend free speech and attacked "the aggressive and encroaching attitude assumed . . . with increasing audacity by the clerical party."[67]

These sessions continued for three additional days, becoming progressively more stormy. Antireligious statements made by French students from the faculty of medicine in Paris at Liège in 1865 were dredged up as proof that there had been materialist teaching at the school, and Duruy was blamed for the Liège incident because it had occurred during his ministry. Comments concerning the theory that man had descended from an ape made in one of Duruy's history textbooks were taken out of context and employed to suggest that the teaching of materialism in state institutions had Duruy's covert blessing.

On May 23, Duruy was given another chance to defend the faculty and himself. He began by reading a letter from a student who, after having been an outright materialist at the age of twenty-five, found himself naturally returning to belief as his scientific research progressed to more advanced stages. Duruy argued that this letter recounted a typical phenomenon, that most students evolved through a period of questioning or rejection of faith as part of the normal intellectual growth process. The University could do nothing about this, nor should it. The University was justified only in guaranteeing that the content of courses and lectures was not antireligious. Indeed, the University had, according to Duruy, not only the right but also an obligation to do so for materialism was antithetical to the philosophy of education. As he put it, the University could not exist without "spiritualism"—that is, the "belief that man is something more than chemical elements . . . that creation is something other than matter and force." Without "spiritualism," the University could not preach the moral dignity of mankind nor encourage its students to work for moral development in society. Duruy's speech was moving testimony

67. *JGIP*, 1868, p. 261; Duruy, *Notes et souvenirs*, I, 360; *RIP*, 1868, p. 130.

that Catholics could have applauded. But then, in anger and frustration over the insinuations and complaints of the previous three days, Duruy attacked the intrigue he believed lay behind the recent flood of petitions and complaints. Reviewing the steps of this scheme, he observed that on June 6, 1867, Cardinal Prospero Caterini had sent a letter from Rome to all French bishops lamenting that the public schools were generally deprived "of the moderating authority of the Church" and asking that within four months the bishops send him suggestions on how this problem could be corrected. Eleven days later, shortly after the bishops had received the Caterini letter, the Giraud petition began to circulate. On November 16—at the end of the four-month period prescribed by the Cardinal—"there took place, the first attack, an excessively violent attack, against a part of public education." Thus the Giraud petition, Duruy concluded, was part of a crusade that "responded to orders from the court of Rome." It was perhaps the thought of Italian intervention in French affairs that irritated Duruy most. He wished to terminate the affair immediately and completed his remarks briefly with a final defense of the religious character of University teaching. Shortly thereafter, the Senate voted on the two propositions before it. The first, demanding *liberté de l'enseignement supérieur*, was defeated 84 to 31. The second, charging the faculty of medicine with materialism, was defeated 80 to 43.[68]

The affair was settled for the moment, although the press continued to debate the issues. The Catholic press, still bristling from Duruy's creation of secondary courses for young girls, was stimulated anew by Dupanloup's brochure, *La liberté de l'enseignement supérieur* (1868) and by his latest argument that Catholics did not wish to pay taxes that would go for salaries of materialistic professors. And the liberal press, especially the more radical liberal press, fulminated against Duruy's annulment of the culpable thesis, which it saw as an abridgment of academic freedom and a concession to the clericals.[69] Its disappointment in Duruy was undisguised.

Throughout the controversy there were rumors, triggered by the

---

68. *RIP*, 1868, p. 130; the full text of the Senate's deliberations was reproduced in *ibid.*, 131–59. The number of votes cast for the two propositions differs because more senators voted when the second proposition was presented.

69. Especially *Le Courrier français* and *L'Avenir national. JGIP*, 1868, pp. 225–41, 275.

revelation that Rouher had visited the emperor three times in one day to discuss Duruy's status, that Duruy's dismissal was imminent.[70] But if the normally vacillating emperor entertained the thought of asking for Duruy's resignation, he concluded against it.

During the academic year 1868–1869, charges of materialism against state institutions lessened significantly and the clergy turned to the more pressing matter of Vatican I. Still, demands for *liberté de l'enseignement supérieur*, emanating essentially from Catholic deputies in the Corps législatif, continued. As late as April 16, 1869, the legislature heard a demand for *liberté*, followed by a plea from Duruy that his bill be debated before the body. But national elections intervened, and shortly thereafter, in a changed political atmosphere, the emperor dismissed Duruy.

Duruy's fall from office did not end his efforts to reform French higher education. In 1870, when an extraparliamentary commission headed by Guizot was established to consider demands of the liberal-conservative coalition for liberty of higher education,[71] Duruy, appointed to the Senate after his dismissal from the ministry, made one last essay to complete the program he had designed for the renovation of higher education. Acting quickly, he submitted two bills directly to the Senate.

The first, sent to the Senate on July 28, was a slightly modified version of his 1867 bill on liberty of higher education. The major change it contained was a compromise on the issue of the awarding of degrees (*grades*), which he believed would better satisfy new political forces and provide a more agreeable balance between public and private interests. In his own words, the revised bill would be more in keeping with "the new ideas that must be incorporated into our legislation." The bill reserved for the state exclusive rights over degrees in all positions of public trust, defined as teaching, law, and medicine. The power of certification for careers in the private sector, however, was to be enjoyed by both state and private institutions. The only restrictions were that, according to article 2 of the bill, private schools could not take the name "faculty" (they had to call themselves *écoles libres*) and

70. *JGIP*, 1868, pp. 261–62.
71. Albert Duruy, "La liberté de L'enseignement supérieur," *Revue des deux mondes* (1871), no. 1, cited in Weisz, "The Academic Elite and the Movement to Reform French Higher Education," 258; Liard, *L'enseignement supérieur en France*, II, 304.

could not employ the titles of the state for their degrees. Duruy had great hopes for the passage of the bill because the political passions raised in 1867 had been appeased, thirteen petitions with a total of forty thousand signatures favoring liberty of higher education had been received by the government, and the legislature had recently voted favorably on the principle itself.[72]

A week after submitting the first bill, Duruy submitted a second, which he felt was a vital partner to the first if competition was to work beneficently in the sphere of higher education. It reflected the desires Duruy had articulated in the Senate on June 28—"the absolute necessity of maintaining the great laic corporation created by the genius of Napoleon I, the University, by giving it a greater autonomy and by fortifying its institutions of higher education instead of multiplying them."[73] It was, in fact, Duruy's attempt to fulfill the other outstanding promise made by the framers of the Falloux Law: to provide a new organic law for public higher education.

Public higher education was to be offered in four different genres of faculties: letters; sciences; law, economics, and administration; and medicine and pharmacy. The state would no longer be responsible for the faculties of theology, which were to be returned to the supervision of the minister of religion.

Very little was said in the bill about the letters and science faculties. But article 7 provided for the creation of scholarships to help populate these faculties; article 14 specified that *agrégés* would lead seminars or small group discussions or offer practical exercises to students; and portions of other articles set certain standards that would have improved the quality of education in these faculties. For example, a provision in article 9 required candidates for faculty chairs "to give proof, in a public lecture, of their ability to teach." These provisions would have helped transform the nature of letters and sciences, particularly in making them true teaching institutions.

The law faculties, of which there were eleven, were grouped under the general category of faculties of law, economics, and administration. Only the faculties of law at Paris and Toulouse would have been affected specifically, but Duruy hoped that the other law faculties soon

72. Duruy, *Notes et souvenirs*, II, 49–51, 44–46.
73. *Ibid.*, 42–59.

would be similarly modified. At Paris and Toulouse the law faculties were to have two divisions, one for the traditional law curriculum, the other for economics and administration. Particular courses for the second division were not enumerated in the bill because Duruy noted that they would have to be designated in concert with the Imperial Council of Public Instruction. But he observed that the idea for these courses came both from a plan devised by Georges Cuvier a half century earlier and from the longstanding German example. Students in one division would be allowed to take courses in the other. Indeed, Duruy wished to encourage students in the traditional section to take economics courses to immunize them against the lures of utopian schemes. The economics and administration division at the two law faculties was to be Duruy's substitute for the *grande école* of public administration he had been unable to secure earlier. It was intended to create a new branch of professional studies, a kind of *enseignement supérieur spécial* as Duruy dubbed it, that would prepare men for new careers in government, industry, and business.

Former *écoles de pharmacie* would be given faculty status and would fall administratively within the fourth category, faculties of medicine and pharmacy. There is nothing in the bill to explain this change other than the implication that it made the organization of medical education a little more rational. Duruy specified that medical education was to be both theoretical and practical, and he increased the amount of training students would have in physics, chemistry, and biology laboratories. To cope with the decreasing proportion of doctors relative to the population, a problem that deeply troubled Duruy, tuition-free medical education was to be made available to young men *sans fortune* who had a *licence* in medicine and who were willing to pledge ten years of service after graduation in a small rural locality that lacked a doctor. Duruy explained this provision in a letter to Guizot, confiding that his intention was to "organize a *service medical* in each commune just as there was a *service scolaire* in each commune."[74]

74. Victor Duruy to François Guizot, letter 17, Guizot Papers, 42 AP 268, AN. Increased training for medical students in physics, chemistry, and biology laboratories was mandated by the decree of June 20, 1878 (Prost, *Histoire de l'enseignement en France*, 233).

The most exciting part of the bill was Duruy's plan to create autonomous provincial universities from groups of these four categories of faculties. Article 21 provided that "in academies which have at least three of the four faculties, the ensemble would carry the name 'university,' and this university was to take the name of the chief city of the academy." Other articles would have given the universities a civil personality (hence almost complete control over all self-generated income, including gifts and endowments); a faculty council comprised of the deans of each faculty; and control over curriculum, which Duruy hoped "would enable the faculties to follow the changes of their discipline and to respond to all the needs of education." To reinforce the sense of autonomy and to liberalize French higher education further, faculty professors would be given greater voice in the nomination of titularies to vacant chairs (they would pick three finalists, and the emperor would make the ultimate selection), and they would be granted such considerable guarantees against the revocation of their appointment that their removal, especially for political or religious reasons, would be almost impossible. Finally, to assist and encourage the universities in the development of new courses and disciplines, article 15 authorized titularies and *agrégés* to offer extra courses (*cours complémentaires*) of their own choosing at the faculties. These courses could be free or paying, depending on the wishes of the professor. But if they were paying, the professor could keep all money generated.

The last portion of the bill treated the preparatory schools to higher education. These were schools established by the departments or communes, which could offer the *licence* degree in such fields as law and medicine at a more modest cost than the faculties. Duruy was concerned that these institutions were sadly neglected at a time when they could be of great use in helping to reduce the surfeit of students and the burden on resources at law and medical faculties. Articles 35 through 38 of the bill, therefore, were designed to make them more attractive to young students by subjecting them to the same restrictions and academic guarantees that full-fledged faculties enjoyed.[75]

Six weeks after the presentation of these two bills, a republic was declared and the empire was gone. Duruy's bills, although not his

75. Duruy, *Notes et souvenirs*, II, 59–74.

ideas, were forgotten in the political and military turmoil that visited France in the succeeding months.

In December, 1874, Deputy Edouard Laboulaye, a leader of the Center Left and a former administrator at the Collège de France, rose in the legislature to condemn the record of the Second Empire in higher education and to argue that little had been accomplished under Napoleon III. This charge was patently untrue, and Duruy was quick to refute it. He sent Laboulaye a long letter in which he detailed a full list of his achievements and explained the difficulties under which he was forced to work, difficulties which one had to know intimately to appreciate. Then, in a patronizing tone, he concluded with the rejoinder: "You see, Monsieur, when it is necessary to renovate the whole organization of education in a country where there is an old system, one must proceed logically, wisely, and slowly. The time given to the empire was well employed to benefit primary and secondary education. And [complete] plans for reforming higher education were advanced; they only needed the vote of the legislature to be realized."[76]

Duruy's defense was entirely valid. He had worked with great effort and with significant success to reform French higher education.

Duruy was painfully aware of the superiority of other countries in science and research, and he spoke regularly of the need to refurbish the "intellectual glory of France." He admired the German system of higher education, and in 1868 he sent Lavisse to make a detailed comparison of the French and German systems, but he wanted only to borrow key concepts and methodologies from German higher education.

Duruy realized that there was formidable resistance to reform in French higher education. There was a basic inertia against reform within the system and little concern for a level of education that was politically and socially insignificant on the outside, particularly among legislators. Yet paradoxically, as the bitter controversy over the *cours libres* poignantly confirmed, reform even in the politically and socially insignificant area of higher education could be threatened by politics.

The minister's approach was to attempt to disarm the opposition by

76. Victor Duruy to Edouard Laboulaye, December 5, 1874, in Duruy, *Notes et souvenirs*, I, 324.

proceeding slowly—by working for incremental change—and by avoiding a direct confrontation with vested interests. Thus almost all of his major programs and proposals—the Ecole Pratique des Hautes Etudes, the *cours libres*, the *écoles normale secondaires*, *liberté de l'enseignement supérieure*—were designed to be attractive, low-cost additions and enhancements to the existing system.

The Ecole Pratique took few students and offered no practical careers to young men, but in both of these ways it resembled other higher research institutions in France. The school did give France serious students in several important academic disciplines, history and philology among them, and it introduced the German research model into France.

The *cours libres*, although subject to political complications, complemented Duruy's addition of new subjects and new chairs in various higher institutions. And before Duruy left office, the courses began to do what they would do so well later in the century: provide an avenue for innovations in subject areas. Duruy was unable to get freedom of higher education approved, but the *cours libres* represented an important step in that direction.

The *écoles normales secondaires* gave the provincial faculties of letters and sciences their first taste of true students. Liard, who knew of Duruy's intentions and ideas through Lavisse, confides that Duruy did not want to abolish the public or popular lectures in the faculties. He wished to keep them because they provoked "a certain '*agitation intellectuelle*' in the towns where, without them, 'there would be nothing.' But he intended that instead of being '*le principal*' they would become '*l'accessoire*' to the main concern of higher education." [77]

The emphasis on true students for the letters and science faculties and the attempt to assist the Sorbonne to become an institution that would train research-oriented professors for the faculties of sciences and letters by attaching it to the Ecole Pratique can be seen as part of Duruy's broader effort to strengthen French higher education. Duruy's addition of new courses to various higher schools, the most famous of which was the addition of political economy to the law schools, his creation of new chairs for the sciences, and his many efforts to

77. Liard, *L'enseignement supérieur en France*, II, 289.

strengthen the teaching of science and scientific research within higher institutions were among other important measures taken toward restoring the "intellectual glory of France."

The most comprehensive plan for strengthening French education came in the proposal to provide a new organic law for higher education and especially to create universities. This step was not cautiously limited as were the other proposals, but when Duruy proposed it, he had run out of time. He was no longer minister and could not hope to shepherd the proposal through in a number of less controversial stages. Yet the proposal had to be all-embracing if it was to be a worthy complement to the proposal on freedom of higher education, which now had a good chance of passing.

Louis Liard, analyzing the significance of Duruy's reforms in his widely respected book on higher education in nineteenth-century France, argues that they had two main thrusts: first, to develop *enseignement supérieure enseignant* or true teaching, which was, at least for the faculties of letters and sciences, a revolution, and second, to develop theoretical studies in higher education. With Duruy, Liard maintains, "higher education . . . was finally held for something other than a chemist's shop in which to produce lawyers, doctors and pharmacists. For the first time in the course of half a century, a minister declared that he 'responded to the great interests'"—a taste for vigorous study, the need to encourage and recruit an intellectual elite, and the strengthening of higher education as it was understood generally in Europe. It was Duruy, Liard concludes, who truly sent "shock waves" through the French system of higher education in the 1860s.[78]

78. *Ibid.*, 286–92.

VIII · Teachers and the Teaching Profession

He gave back to teachers confidence in themselves and faith in their mission.
—Emile Tersen, "L'instituteur de la Ière république à l'aube de la IIIe."

Duruy's concerns as minister of public instruction were not limited to the education of students. He was also vitally interested in the formation of teachers and the condition of the teaching profession, particularly since reports from functionaries pointed to serious problems. Inspectors complained of poorly trained teachers and inferior teaching methods. They also noted the difficulty of recruiting teachers owing to the low prestige of the profession and the depressing possibilities for professional or economic advancement.

Some of these problems dated from the Second Republic, when normal schools for primary education were radically transformed by conservatives, but normal schools had never had an easy time in France. From their inception they were seen as a German Protestant institution imported by republicans to substitute for the novitiates of the teaching orders that had been abolished during the Revolution. But in 1849 and 1850 they stood accused of having infected young *instituteurs* with radical ideas that spilled over in the 1848 revolution.[1] Adolphe Thiers, president of the Falloux commission, hated normal schools; he and many others wanted to abolish them in favor of the so-called *stage* system (on-the-job training). But the Falloux Law of 1850 preserved the normal schools, albeit with a proviso stipulating that a normal school could be suppressed and replaced by a system of *stage* if serious complaints were leveled against it.

In 1851, a regulation enacted by Fortoul replaced the ordinance of

1. The study completed subsequently by the Ministry of Public Instruction demonstrated that only a small percentage of *normaliens* and *instituteurs* were actually involved in the *journées* of 1848. See Maurice Gontard, *La question des écoles normales primaires de la Révolution de 1789 à nos jours* (Paris, 1962), 60.

1832, which was the "charter" regulation for normal schools. The minimum age for entrance to the schools was raised from sixteen to eighteen years, the competitive departmental examinations for admission were suppressed, and the curriculum was divided into required and optional subjects and greatly reduced. Only a few students each year were allowed to take the optional subjects, and tight restrictions were placed on the number of classes the schools might offer in certain subjects. In the optional history course, for example, a professor had only four classes during which to lecture on the Revolution and First Empire. The emphasis in the curriculum was on religious and moral training.[2]

It is not surprising, therefore, that many contemporaries believed that the purpose of the Fortoul regulation was to produce the "maître ignorantin." As one put it, the *instituteur* was supposed to be "half domestic, half verger, someone from whom one demanded complete humility and discretion. His appearance had to reflect what he was; circulars flooded him with advice: humble like a vicar, clothed in simple dress like a peasant, it was good that he was out of date in his clothing because this suggested that he was not progressive in political ideas." The normal schools were minutely regulated and surveyed to ensure that they would not produce students with "dangerous ideas."[3]

By late 1854, the quality of normal school students had fallen so low that Fortoul had to issue circulars insisting that serious attention be given to the academic abilities of applicants. Then in 1856, the government, concerned about agricultural productivity and the depopulation of the countryside, added agricultural and horticultural education to the required curriculum. The regulation of 1851 had now been breached. "Beginning in 1860," writes Maurice Gontard, "the imperial state resolved to reanimate the moribund normal schools and fortify laic education." Between 1860 and 1863 the government set about liberalizing the interior regime of the schools, broadening their curriculum, and showing its firm support for them. No substantial reform was promulgated, but the political climate became much more favorable to the schools.[4]

2. *Ibid.*, 30.
3. Roustan, "L'enseignement primaire de Fortoul à Duruy," 160.
4. Gontard, *La question des écoles normales primaires*, 66–75.

Duruy's first attempt to help the teaching profession came in the October 17, 1863, circular in which he urged prefects to persuade municipalities to prefer *normaliens* over teachers prepared outside the normal schools. Duruy stressed that *normaliens* had proven themselves to be "the elite of our teachers." Taught in complete and regular courses by good methods, they in turn disseminated to their own students good and accurate knowledge by the best methodology. *Normaliens* offered "incontestable guarantees of capacity and morality." And if this was not enough to persuade the officials, Duruy called the prefects' attention to two considerations of justice: first, that "it is appropriate to affirm to student teachers that their work and good conduct are a guarantee of immediate nomination [to a teaching post]," and second, "that student teachers entering the normal school take the obligation of devoting themselves to teaching for ten years and that in accepting this obligation which ties them to the state, the state ties itself equally to them." Directors of the normal schools would, in the future, send to prefects a list of all graduating *normaliens*, along with a description of the aptitudes and abilities of each.[5]

In 1864, Duruy commissioned an inquiry into the quality of education at the *écoles normales* and found that the intellectual level and the breadth of instruction were still sadly deficient. Indeed, the *normaliens* of the 1850s, the elite *instituteurs* of the day, were inferior to those of the 1830s. To help correct this situation, Duruy elaborated the agricultural education program, introduced instruction in meteorology, added pedagogical lessons (*conférences de sortie*) for students just before they left school, and required music education.[6]

The meteorology course was closely tied to the agricultural education program introduced in 1856. The *écoles normales primaires* would not only train students to evaluate meteorological data for farmers but they would also become centers for the collection of atmospheric data. Prefects were invited to solicit municipal council appropriations for barometers, thermometers, rain gauges, psychrometers, and weathervanes to be placed in the teachers' colleges. The students would then gather statistics on atmospheric conditions, dis-

5. *BAIP*, IX (1863), 372–73.
6. Gontard, *La question des écoles normales primaires*, 76; *BAIP*, V (1866), 564–65. The pertinent circulars are September 1, 1865, and May 17, 1866.

turbances, and meteorological phenomena, all of which would be sent to a collection center in the Imperial Observatory. The program became so effective that three years later the Association scientifique de France, entirely on its own volition, decided to award gold medals worth 100 francs each to various *écoles normales primaires*.[7]

The music education course was instituted largely because Duruy was convinced that music familiarizes the mind with the "more gentle ways" of life. The decree of January 30, 1865, based on recommendations Duruy received from a special commission on music education which he had constituted a few months earlier, specified five hours of music each week. A later decree (February 3, 1869) created the position of special teachers of music in all the normal schools.[8]

The *conférences de sortie* represented only a partial return to the regular pedagogic instruction that had been required by the regulation of 1832, but they were widely welcomed. As Guerrier de Haupt effused in the *JGIP*, "We see with pleasure this return [in part] to the old programs. . . . These pedagogical conferences, in a sense catechetical sessions, [are] where the moral education of the future *instituteurs* is given." At the conferences the students' vocation would be developed, "that is, the taste, the sentiment of duty, in a word, the special aptitude for a mission which will demand all their zeal, their devotion, their life and abnegation."[9]

But more important than these earlier reforms was Duruy's decree of July 2, 1866, which revived the normal schools by restoring some of the most important provisions of the 1832 regulation. By the decree of July 2, the minimum age of entrance for candidates to the school was lowered from eighteen to seventeen years of age so the schools could attract younger candidates who might otherwise be lured from the teaching profession by industry and the promise of an immediate salary. The provision was so favorably received that in 1868 Duruy further reduced the age requirement to sixteen years.[10] The July 2 de-

---

7. *BAIP*, II (1864), 199 (circular, August 13, 1864), and 240–41 (circular, September 3, 1864); VII (1867), 635.

8. Duruy Papers, 114 AP-1-XII, AN; *AIP*, 325; Gontard, *La question des écoles normales primaires*, 78.

9. *JGIP*, 1865, p. 655.

10. *BAIP*, VI (1866), 2–8 (decree of July 2, 1866); *AIP*, 326; F(17) 4362, AN; *BAIP*, IX (1868), 433.

cree also restored the competitive departmental examination (*con-cours*) for candidates to the normal schools so the schools could discriminate among the alleged "best" candidates from the various arrondissements of the department. The distinction between required and optional courses that had been inaugurated by the regulation of 1851 was abolished, and "modern" courses—gymnastics and bookkeeping—were added to the curriculum. Duruy was eager to help the teacher become, as he frequently put it, "a missionary of all useful and healthy ideas in his commune." He was anxious to give teachers another skill, bookkeeping, which they could teach and could also exploit to supplement their meager salaries. Duruy incorporated the music and agricultural education programs implemented earlier into the decree of July 2, 1866, and prescribed a full-fledged "science of pedagogy" course for the third year of the *normale* curriculum. Finally, he further mitigated the austere internal regime of the normal schools which had been mandated by the regulation of 1851. Most important, surveillance over students was loosened, thus giving the professors in the normal schools more time to prepare their classes, and vacation periods were lengthened.[11]

Of the various reforms in the decree of July 2, 1866, the restoration of the departmental competitive examination and the reintroduction of methods courses had the most far-reaching consequences. The importance and effect of the first reform are obvious. The importance and effect of the second reform, the introduction of courses on pedagogy, however, will become clearer after we review the other programs Duruy associated with them.

Duruy had been very displeased by the use of mechanical rote memorization for the baccalaureate examination at the secondary level. But he was also troubled by reports that memorization was the dominant form of learning at the elementary level.[12] Duruy believed that for true, lasting learning, a student had to rely primarily on his native intelligence and reasoning powers, and he often tried to convince teachers of this theory. He told teachers of French, for example, that they were not doing their job if they were content to have students memorize vocabulary and a multitude of grammatical rules. Instead, children

11. Gontard, *La question des écoles normales primaires*, 78.
12. F(17) 4358–64, AN.

should be given practice writing and speaking their language in creative classroom situations. Indeed, both teachers and students should concentrate on ridding themselves of "vicious pronunciations and bad accents." Similarly, he counseled teachers of history not to burden their students with the memorization of a plethora of facts. Students should be given the opportunity to discover their political and economic heritage, and they should have a chance to derive certain moral lessons from history, particularly that "the law of work dominates all society; that it is work which produces wealth, the spirit of order which preserves it, [and] the spirit of beneficence which honors it; that, finally, our modern society, founded on justice, is still animated with . . . [a] love of good which makes it . . . [strive for societal happiness, justice and economic welfare]." [13]

But Duruy believed that if there was to be a major change in methodology, it would have to be by way of a "revolution from above," that is, teachers would have to be taught the correct way to teach from the very beginning. Thus the methods courses—the *conférences de sortie*, which were retained for students working only for the *brevet simple* and leaving after two years, and the pedagogy courses for third-year *normaliens* who were working for the full-fledged *brevet de capacité*—were the most essential elements for the revolution.

Normaliens were to practice the new pedagogical methods in the campus school (*école annexe*), which Duruy hoped would become the great model for primary education in each department. But the practice-teaching exercise was not to be the end of teacher education, for Duruy also instituted in-service education for teachers. In the circular of October 7, 1866, he directed *inspecteurs primaires* to hold teachers' conferences two or three times a year at the *école normale*. The *école normale* was to become, in Duruy's words, a "motherhouse" of primary education. [14]

His belief in the value of conferences devoted to pedagogy led Duruy to develop the idea of school fairs. The first school fair and the greatest one of his ministry was held at the Universal Exposition of 1867 in Paris. Duruy and his subordinates prepared for the exposition an elaborate display on French education which stressed the progress

13. *BAIP*, VI (1866), 11; *AIP*, 321.
14. *AIP*, 328; Rohr, *Victor Duruy, ministre de Napoléon III*, 159.

being made and the innovations being developed. The intention was both to impress the public and to provide an exchange of pedagogical information among visiting teachers. The administration not only encouraged teachers to attend the exposition but subsidized travel expenses to and from Paris for eight hundred teachers living in the provinces and arranged for a special conference on pedagogy at the Sorbonne. Then, at the end of October, 1867, Duruy sent a circular to prefects inviting them to establish departmental school fairs (*expositions scolaires*) to be held at the conclusion of each academic year and instructing them to make certain that the best work produced by students during the school year was placed on display. Finally, in the circular of May 9, 1868, he established prizes for the two or three schools in each department that seemed to have achieved the best results from their instruction.[15]

Beyond establishing model primary schools (in the form of campus schools), *normale* "mother-houses," and local educational fairs, Duruy established a model primary school system in the department of the Seine. All of the new pedagogy was carefully implemented, and three new practices were commenced there. Students were divided into three tracks as determined by their native intelligence and cultural background so they could follow courses at their ability level; final examinations were instituted for each course; and a newly created *certificat des études* was issued to graduates of the schools. Duruy hoped to extend the "Seine program" to the provinces, but inspectors at a conference called in the spring of 1869 at Paris discouraged him. They pointed out that there were not enough teachers in rural schools to implement the reforms and that even if there were, rural schoolchildren were considerably more homogeneous as a group than were urban schoolchildren.[16]

Duruy not only further elaborated the pedagogy program of the July 2 decree and provided occasions for teachers to discuss and view the results of good pedagogy, but he also continued to develop the agricultural education program. In the *arrêté* of December 30, 1867,

15. Dejob, "Le reveil de l'opinion dans l'Université sous le Second Empire," 122; *BAIP*, VIII (1867), 143–46, 460; IX (1868), 427.

16. Mourier to Victor Duruy, April 15, 1869, F(17) 9376, AN, and *Exposé* of the vice-rector of Paris [Mourier], June 15, 1869, F(17) 4364, AN.

Duruy conceded that the normal schools were not created to train farmers but argued that teachers could reasonably be expected to offer agricultural education in the classroom and to act as a source of information for local farmers. The following day, he publicized in a circular several proposals for agricultural education which had come from a special committee he had previously established. The proposals included suggestions that class time schedules in the elementary schools be correlated with children's chores on their fathers' farms, that agricultural programs vary departmentally, according to the specialties and problems of each, that each department hire a special professor of agriculture to supervise its agricultural education program, that each normal school have a garden or farm annexed to it, that students take weekly trips to farms, that students everywhere be encouraged to write essays on aspects of farming and husbandry, and finally that prizes be established to reward teachers for their participation in the program. In 1868, the ministry issued a special report sketching the programs of agricultural education that had been devised for the various regions of France. By 1869 many of the proposals and programs were being implemented.[17]

In focusing on agricultural education, specific attention was given to the education of young girls in rural areas. Duruy lamented in the December 31, 1867, circular the antiagricultural and antirural spirit that dominated educational institutions for girls. "These schools," Duruy charged, "are true novitiates for desertion. . . . the damage has gone so far, according to the findings, that today, gentlemen wishing to devote themselves to farming can no longer find [suitable] wives in the countryside."[18] Thus a complete program of agricultural education for girls which affected teaching in the normal schools was outlined by the circular (see Appendix C) and recommended for implementation.

17. *BAIP*, VIII (1867), 907–22; X (1868), 306–12; *AIP*, 858–59. In the latter source, the *Exposé de la situation de l'instruction publique en 1868* reported that all *écoles normales primaires* had a course in agriculture and that the vast majority had gardens. Five departments had appointed the special professor of agriculture. Many teachers had already received awards for their efforts, and many communes reported that teachers were rendering invaluable services trimming and grafting trees and giving rural inhabitants good strains of plants to raise. The draft for the 1869 *Exposé* in F(17) 2677, AN, noted, on page 16, that more than fifteen thousand institutions were training students to prune, graft, and grow fruit trees and that agricultural education at the primary level, now offered in the majority of rural schools, took a practical approach.

18. *BAIP*, VIII (1867), 932–40.

Duruy's several reforms for teacher education, warmly praised in
many quarters, led to a renaissance in the teaching of the *écoles normales*. Indeed, considering that four of the normal schools suppressed
in favor of the *stage* system were restored in 1862, that two new normal schools (Var and Haute-Vienne) were opened in 1863 bringing the
total number to seventy-eight, that the number of *normaliens* grew by
16 percent (to 3,500 students) between 1865 and 1869, and that by
the end of the empire the number of applicants to the normal schools
had increased to an impressive 3,600 candidates for 1,200 vacancies,
Duruy's reforms were an important part of what Gontard has called
the "triumph" of the normal school in France in the 1860s.[19]

In women's education, religious orders traditionally satisfied the
need for teachers, either supplying their own members or lay women
taught in the *cours normaux* attached to their *pensionnats* or the
écoles normales primaires which they directed. The "cascade" of authorizations of religious orders in the latter part of the July Monarchy
and during the first decade of the Second Empire meant that "the religious source flowed with abundance." In 1863, Ministry of Public Instruction officials deemed that only 383 lay *institutrices* were needed
to fill jobs which religious orders could not cover.[20]

Most lay women were trained in the normal courses. In 1863 there
were only nine normal schools for lay women, the majority of them
created during the July Monarchy, particularly after critics began to
complain about the growing gap between boys' and girls' education.
Religious orders held a virtual monopoly over the preparation of lay
institutrices because they directed eight of the nine *écoles normales
primaires* for women and forty-two of the fifty-three *cours normaux*.[21]

Of the three sources from which female teachers emanated—the religious orders, the normal schools, and the *cours normaux*—it appears that the first two provided at least a satisfactory education. The
cours normaux, or at least most of them, apparently did not.[22]

---

19. For an example of praise, see *JGIP*, 1866, p. 457. Gontard, *La question des
écoles normales primaires*, 76, 78; *BAIP*, XII (1869), 36. I have used Duruy's tally for
the number of men's normal schools, not Gontard's.
20. Gontard, *La question des écoles normales primaires*, 37, 79.
21. *Ibid.*, 79–80; *BAIP*, XII (1869), 36. Again, I have used Duruy's figure for the
number of normal schools, not Gontard's.
22. Furet and Ozouf, *Lire et écrire*, I, 171; Robert Gildea, "Education and the
Classes Moyennes in the Nineteenth Century," in Baker and Harrigan, *Making of
Frenchmen*, 222; *BAIP*, XII (1869), 36–38.

Since the 1830s a number of proposals had been advanced in favor of creating more women's normal schools. Boulay de la Meurthe proposed in 1846, for example, that all departments be required to create normal schools for women.[23] But a majority of legislators and politicians were content to leave women's education in the hands of the Church. Some years later, when Duruy's law of April 10, 1867, was being discussed in the legislature, supporters of women's normal schools again became hopeful because Duruy's law required the creation of eight thousand new girls' schools. Jules Simon, among others, insisted that the April 10 law require departments to open schools for *institutrices*. But the government refused to launch a bold challenge to the Church's hold over women's education, particularly since many municipal councils had just recently accepted the idea of normal schools for men.[24]

Duruy agreed that the moment had not yet arrived to require each department to create a normal school for *institutrices*, and he refrained from including such a provision in his new law. But he saw no reason why he could not try to encourage more departments to create women's normal schools on their own. Just thirteen days before he was dismissed from office (July 6, 1869), he sent prefects a circular informing them that many girls' schools did not meet the academic standards of boys' schools, attributing the problem to the quality of teachers available for girls' schools. Normal schools for young women were generally good, but the same was not true of the *cours normaux*. "Eight or ten [out of fifty-three] . . . are up to the standards of the normal schools; . . . the others, for the most part are simple annexes to private *pensionnats* where they occupy a place of secondary importance." Citing the growing number of girls' schools in response to the law of April 10, 1867, Duruy urged that the situation be changed. Some of the new schools would necessarily be confided to the religious orders, but others would be entrusted to lay teachers, following the wishes of families in various areas. Duruy asked prefects to calculate the number of lay *institutrices* who would be needed to accommodate the growth in the number of girls' schools and to determine which of the sites offering normal courses could sustain a normal school for women. Then prefects were advised to "study, with all the

23. Mayeur, *L'éducation des filles en France*, 93.
24. Gontard, *La question des écoles normales primaires*, 22, 39, 73–76, 80–81.

care that such a subject demands, what propositions you might submit
to the departmental council [*conseil général*] at its next session in order to obtain on the question I have just raised a favorable solution to
which I attach the greatest price [*sic*]."[25] Unfortunately, Duruy left
office before the departmental councils had a chance to respond, and
the request went unanswered.

Normal school education was one great concern; the certification of
teachers was another. *Instituteurs* all held a state certificate to teach—
the *brevet*. When Duruy reorganized the normal school curriculum on
July 2, 1866, and abolished the distinction between required and optional subjects, he restored to the curriculum subjects that had been
mandated by the regulation of 1832 such as history, geography, notions of physical and natural sciences, grammar, geometry, music, and
surveying (*arpentage*) and made them all, once again, required courses
for the *brevet*. By the *arrêté* of July 3, 1866, however, Duruy distinguished between a *brevet simple*, which a student could earn at the end
of two years at a normal school,[26] and a *brevet de capacité*, which
could be earned at the end of the third year. In the third year the student took not only the course in pedagogy but also several new "optional" courses, which derived from the special education program
legislated for the secondary schools in 1865: commercial art and design, the elements of geometry, modern foreign languages, and bookkeeping.[27] Thus Duruy made it easier and faster for a student headed
for teaching to get his certification, and he made it possible for *normaliens* to gain a modicum of social mobility by preparing for teaching in the special education program (even though they could not attend Cluny).

Institutrices had to hold the *brevet* just as *instituteurs* did, unless
they were members of a teaching congregation and held a so-called
letter of obedience from their order. This arrangement stretched back
to 1819, when, because the novitiates of the religious orders committed to teaching were veritable normal schools, the letter of obedience was declared the equivalent of the *brevet*. Even male religious

25. *BAIP*, XII (1869), 36–38.
26. The 1851 regulation had required all students to stay for a full three years to
guarantee that they had developed the right attitudes and habits of thinking.
27. *BAIP*, VI (1866), 20–27.

enjoyed the "privilege" under the Restoration. Under the anticlerical July Monarchy, the Christian Brothers were required to hold the *brevet de capacité*. Female religious, however, were still allowed to teach with the letter of obedience, and this situation was untouched by the Falloux Law.

By the 1860s republicans and anticlericals, concerned by the great growth in the number of female teaching orders after 1850 and troubled by reports that some female religious holding only the letter of obedience were poor teachers, began clamoring loudly for an end to the substitution of letters for *brevets*. Duruy was sympathetic to complaints about the quality of teaching among female religious, but he ultimately decided not to try to overturn the policy on the letters of obedience because the Falloux Law had unequivocally stated that they were veritable *brevets de capacité* for female teachers.[28] To be sure, Duruy wanted *institutrices* of high quality, but he obviously concluded that it was better to concentrate his efforts on laic teachers trained in the normal schools and on women's normal schools.

As for secondary schoolteachers, we have already reviewed Duruy's creation of Cluny for special education and his attempt to establish *écoles normales secondaires*. The Ecole Normale Supérieur in Paris was still the premier institution for the formation of secondary schoolteachers. The sole changes Duruy made there were to introduce semester and end-of-the-year examinations and to prohibit students without a *licence* from entering the second year of studies in the humanities section.[29]

Changes in teacher training and a modification in certification could only partially solve the problems for teachers, however, because teachers did not enter a comfortable existence. At best, standards in the teaching profession were mediocre.[30] There were problems in recruiting teachers, and professional merit often went unrecognized. Salaries and pensions were low, and living conditions were poor.

The problems of recruitment were multiple and dependent upon the status of the profession. At the highest level of education, the minister

28. Memorandum, March 8, 1867, F(19) 6246, AN.

29. Rohr, *Victor Duruy, ministre de Napoléon III*, 76; *BAIP*, III (1865), 91–93 (arrêté of February 7, 1865); XI (1869), 209 (*arrêté* of February 15, 1869).

30. See Adrien Dansette, "Le corps enseignant au XIXᵉ siècle," *La Revue de Paris*, October, 1966, 117–20.

attempted to improve recruitment through the *agrégation* examination. He reestablished the *agrégation* for philosophy and for modern foreign languages and abolished the minimum age limit of twenty-five years for an *agrégé* so that successful younger competitors would not have to wait for their degrees. He also established *écoles normales secondaires*. At the primary level, Duruy entertained a proposal from the emperor that elementary teachers could be recruited directly from men leaving the army. There were some eighteen hundred new openings yearly, but the *écoles normales primaires* were able to fill only about a thousand or twelve hundred of these. Duruy insisted, however, that the deficit could be filled only by men who possessed the appropriate certificates or *brevets*.[31] Recruitment was also facilitated by the creation of the *brevet simple* and the lowering of the age of admissions for candidates to the normal schools.

Clearly, two of the major reasons why it was difficult to recruit for the teaching corps were low and irregularly paid salaries. Duruy noted these problems in the plan he sent the emperor in 1863 for his administration, arguing: "It is necessary to pay *instituteurs* regularly for many are not so paid. [And] we should not let thousands of *institutrices* exist on less than 400 francs." Shortly thereafter, he commissioned a detailed survey of the situation. Meanwhile, the *Situation de l'empire* for 1863 showed that public *instituteurs* earned an average of 790 francs annually and that *institutrices* earned considerably less. If *institutrices* taught in an *école mixte*, they were guaranteed a minimum salary of 400 francs; otherwise they were left to the mercy of the municipal councils. In 1863, about half of the lay *institutrices* received between 100 and 350 francs. Salaries were so insufficient that Duruy sadly referred to elementary teachers as "la misère en habit noir." He used subsidies to supplement unusually low salaries, and his circular of April 16, 1865, released teachers from the need to supply a certificate of employment triennially to the state, which was the principal cause of the outrageous delay in salary payments. But female schoolteachers were really helped only with Duruy's law of April 10, 1867, which established minimum salary levels of 500 and 400 francs, de-

---

31. *BAIP*, XIV (1863), 118 (decree of June 29, 1863); II (1864), 588–89 (decree of November 27, 1864); XI (1869), 186; Duruy, *Notes et souvenirs*, I, 249.

pending on which of the two new divisions *institutrices* fell into, and which guaranteed the minimum salary levels set for *instituteurs* (600 francs as mandated by the Falloux Law) and for *institutrices* against losses incurred in tuition money which was used to pay teachers' salaries. Duruy never won an increase in salaries for *instituteurs* even though he argued that salary increases were imperative to keep schoolteachers loyal to the regime and to keep rural schoolteachers from deserting the countryside for the city. But he could take some solace in knowing that because the cost of living in France remained remarkably stable throughout the 1860s, the salary adjustments and increases he did win were real gains for teachers.[32]

Salaries for *lycée* personnel, although considerably higher, were still inadequate. Duruy was not able to increase *lycée* salaries in general, but he did make several minor revisions that ameliorated the lot of some professors. To understand the improvements, one should keep in mind that professors were divided into two categories, one for the *lycées* of Paris and Versailles, the other for the *lycées* of the departments. Within each category, they were further subdivided into titulary professors and nontitulary (*divisionnaire*) professors. Finally, each group of professors was assigned a seniority rank (*classes*, between one and three in each subdivision), which ultimately determined salary. In addition to the titulary and nontitulary professors, there were *chargés de cours* (lecturers, who filled about one-third of the departmental posts), *maîtres élémentaires* (elementary-level teachers), and *répétiteurs* (students teachers), who were also subdivided by geographical location and seniority. The salaries of professors were composed of two parts: the so-called minimum (*traitement fixe*), determined by the state, and the variable amount (*éventuel*), which depended on student enrollment at each *lycée*.

Duruy's modifications were mostly adjustments. The decree of De-

<hr />

32. Dansette, "Le corps enseignant au XIXe siècle," 119; Victor Duruy to Napoleon III, August 6, 1863, in Duruy, *Notes et souvenirs*, I, 197; F(17) 9142, AN (includes the responses to Duruy's survey); F(17) 4358–64, AN (demands concerning salaries in the minutes of academic councils and examples of Duruy's granting of subsidies); Rohr, *Victor Duruy, ministre de Napoléon III*, 58; circular, April 16, 1865, on the triennial certificate, F(17) 9146, AN; Chevallier and Grosperrin, *L'enseignement français de la Révolution à nos jours*, II, 169, 212 (articles 4, 9, 10, and 11); Victor Duruy to Napoleon III, September 9, 1866, copy of a letter in possession of Mme Albert Duruy; and B. R. Mitchell, *European Historical Statistics, 1750–1970* (New York, 1975), 742.

cember 31, 1863, regularized the ratio of divisionary professors to titulary professors in the proportion of two to one, thereby increasing the number of titulary professors to correspond to the growth in secondary school population. The decree also created three classes or seniority ranks for *chargés de cours*, thus allowing for salary increases after long periods of service to the state. Then the decree of June 19, 1867, established a uniform *traitement fixe* salary schedule for professors in the departmental *lycées* and guaranteed them the minimum *éventuel* of 800 francs originally established in 1858. This minimum was revised upward to 1,000 francs by the decree of December 26, 1867, which also created a fourth class for the titulary professors of Paris and Versailles with a *traitement fixe* of 3,000 francs. Divisionaries who had been in the first class for three years were thereafter to enter automatically into the new fourth titulary class. Divisionaries at Paris and Versailles saw their salaries raised by the December 26, 1867, decree: their minimum *traitement fixe* was increased from 2,400 to 2,500 francs in the first class and from 1,800 to 2,000 in the second class. Unfortunately, comparable adjustments were not made for the departmental divisionaries, but a new article granted them a 300-franc salary increase after fifteen years of service.[33]

Although professors in the departmental *lycées* were guaranteed a minimum *éventuel* of 1,000 francs, there was considerable opposition to continued dependence on the variable amount. Two basic arguments were made against the *éventuel*. First, it provided for anomalous situations; for example, a young *agrégé* professor could earn an exaggerated salary if he was placed in an important *lycée*. Second, fluctuations in the *éventuel* at *lycées* left the financial situation of professors unstable. More generally, the *éventuel* was disliked because it was at odds with the time-honored principle of merit. Duruy's son-in-law and principal private secretary, Victor Glachant, argued against the variable amount in a confidential report he presented to Duruy in 1867. He also capitalized on the occasion to criticize the general effect of the December 26, 1867, decree on salaries: "It gives satisfaction to the aristocracy and the bourgeoisie of secondary education; but the democracy appears to be forgotten." But Edmond Goumy writing in

33. *BAIP*, XIV (1863), 513; VII (1867), 598, 811–12.

the *RIP* was more sympathetic; he focused on what Duruy actually accomplished. Goumy noted in January, 1868, that Duruy's recent dispositions were followed by "numerous promotions," which had "the important advantage of clearing away in the hierarchy of secondary education a circulation troubled for a long time by the deplorable stagnation in their places of a great number of divisionary professors."[34]

Salaries for professors in the state faculties were likewise divided into a base payment and a variable *éventuel*. Here again, the *éventuel* differed widely between localities and faculties. Article 1 of the second decree issued on December 26, 1867, guaranteed a minimum *éventuel* of 1,000 francs to professors in the faculties of science and letters, who, owing to their connection with the baccalaureate examinations, experienced the greatest discrepancies in remuneration. Then the decree of December 21, 1868, corrected the salaries of professors at the faculty of law at Paris with a 500-franc increase to put them on a par with titularies at the Sorbonne.[35]

For the personnel at the normal schools, Duruy secured modest salary increases in September of 1863. The minimum salary for directors of the schools was raised from 2,200 to 2,400 francs and the maximum salary from 3,000 to 3,600 francs. Salaries for the three *classes* of *maîtres-adjoints* were raised 200 francs each. Overall, salary levels at the *écoles normales primaires* reflected the humble mission of the schools. The 3,000-franc maximum salary for directors, for example, was still 400 francs below the base or fixed salary of professors at the provincial faculties of letters and sciences.[36]

And Duruy sought to help teachers in other minor financial ways. He lent his unofficial support to the work of teachers' mutual aid societies, which with their regular members and their honorary benefactors (2,078 in 1866) were immensely valuable in supplementing the woefully inadequate pensions of retired schoolteachers in the provinces.[37] The first mutual aid society for teachers dated back to 1846;

34. Inspector Vielle to Victor Duruy, August 31, 1867, and Charles Glachant's confidential report, December 22, 1867, F(17) 8702, AN; *RIP*, 1868, p. 618.

35. *BAIP*, VIII (1867), 812–13; Rohr, *Victor Duruy, ministre de Napoléon III*, 101.

36. *BAIP*, XIV (1863), 228; Weisz, "The Academic Elite and the Movement to Reform French Higher Education," 89.

37. F(17) 8847, AN; *JGIP*, 1866, p. 107. Provincial pensions ranged between forty

between 1853 and 1862 thirty-five new societies were organized. But during just the first three years of Duruy's ministry, their number more than doubled.[38] Duruy also promoted the practice of subprefects and mayors employing teachers as part-time secretaries, although he discovered that because mayors were either keeping the secretarial salaries for themselves or forcing teachers to share their salaries with them he also had to correct basic abuses in the system.[39] Duruy urged teachers, their wives, and children to raise silkworms at home for another supplement to the family income. He solicited information about the raising of silkworms from Louis Pasteur. Unfortunately, Duruy was so anxious to help teachers that he pestered Pasteur for instructions on the growing of silkworms until an exasperated Pasteur finally exploded: "Tell your *instituteurs* to raise them [the silkworms] as beasts like everyone else [does]. [Either] one knows or does not know how to raise them. If they do not know how to raise them, they should not ask for the grain [to feed them]!"[40]

Duruy also carefully supervised the granting of prizes and honors for meritorious effort and service. His success in securing award medals for teachers volunteering to teach night school courses and public secondary courses for girls and for the outstanding teachers judged in exposition competition has already been mentioned. Less well known was his creation of decorations to be worn by honoraries of the University. Two Legion of Honor titles, Officier de l'Instruction Publique and Officier d'Académie, had been created at the time the University was founded, but no decoration for academic robes had ever been introduced. Convinced of the value of displaying such distinctions at academic convocations, Duruy created a purple and gold decoration for the higher title and a purple and silver decoration for the more modest. He contended later in a confidential circular to the prefects that Legion of Honor decorations were a matter of considerable political importance for the government, which was anxious to reaffirm to the

---

and sixty francs per annum when Duruy became minister. Duruy managed to raise pensions to a uniform seventy-five francs in 1864 and ninety-five francs in 1865 (Zévort, "Victor Duruy," 484).

38. *JGIP*, 1867, p. 107: *Exposé de la situation de l'empire* for 1866; thirty-nine new societies were established.

39. Confidential circular, January 15, 1865, F(17) 2680 (incorrectly listed as F[17] 2678 in the Archives Nationales *Inventaire*); F(17) 2681, AN.

40. F(17) 9147, AN.

instituteurs that their services to the country were not forgotten. Duruy also wanted secondary teachers in the *collèges* to know that the government greatly valued their services. Consequently, with the law of January 12, 1867, he abolished the title of *regent*, which had an inferior connotation, and substituted the title of *professeur*. Gabriel Monod remarks that these were among his most noble efforts, for teachers sensed that their work was noticed and that advancement could be achieved on the just basis of individual merit.[41]

In the realm of pensions, there were serious inequalities. Teachers' pensions were based on previous earnings and regulated by the law on civil pensions. The regulation of June 9, 1853, assured public *instituteurs* and *institutrices* an annuity of one-half of their withholdings, but the full benefits of this law would not be realized by retired teachers until 1884. In the meantime, many pensioners were living on less than a franc per day, and many had no other income. In the early years of his administration Duruy designated modest subsidies for pensions. Then, in a confidential letter circulated to prefects in December, 1867, he asked for complete and detailed information on retired teachers. In 1868, he more boldly petitioned the legislature for a budgetary grant to subsidize retired teachers up to 350 francs per year until 1884. Unfortunately, the minister of finance was strongly opposed. By the time an amendment from two deputies for a subsidy to bring teachers' pensions to 500 francs a year reached the floor of the legislature, Duruy had been forced with the rest of his colleagues to agree not to support any proposal that would disturb the "financial harmony" of the 1869 or 1870 budget and he was unable to endorse the amendment. Duruy unjustly got much bad press for a painful situation that was not of his doing.[42]

Limited chances for promotion were another problem of recruitment and another of Duruy's concerns. Adrian Dansette, in "Le corps enseignant au XIXe siècle," describes the basic situation: there was little status mobility but relatively great geographical mobility in the

41. *BAIP*, V (1866), 460–62; confidential circular, July 25, 1867, F(17) 1475, AN; Victor Duruy to Charles Augustin Saint-Beuve, July, 1866, Duruy Papers, 114 AP-1-XXIII, AN; *BAIP*, VII (1867), 16–17; Gabriel Monod, "Victor Duruy," *Revue internationale de l'enseignement*, XXVIII (1894), 488.
42. Confidential circular, December 19, 1867, F(17) 1475, AN; *JGIP*, 1869, pp. 225, 290 (excerpt from the *Journal de Paris*); and memorandum regarding the budget of 1869, in possession of Mme Albert Duruy.

teaching profession. According to Dansette, the average teacher could expect five changes of place during the course of his career—a considerable number for the nineteenth century. Duruy's ideal solution was to work for the widespread adoption of *avancement sur place* (promotion within the same school).[43] But before *avancement sur place* could be achieved, a set of seniority classes had to be established for each group of functionaries. Such a set existed at the secondary level, and Duruy enlarged the structure slightly by creating a fourth class for the titulary professors of Paris and Versailles (decree of December 26, 1867). But when he proposed *avancement sur place* as part of the 1868 reforms for secondary education, teachers warned him that few municipal councils would respond favorably, and he decided not to press the measure. Duruy also envisioned establishing seniority systems and *avancement sur place* at the primary and tertiary levels, but budgetary considerations once again forced him to abandon his plans.[44] At the end of six years in office, despite his sincere efforts, Duruy had had practically no success with schemes for promotion.

Teachers, to Duruy's mind, and he was thinking particularly of the *instituteur*, "la misère en habit noir," who fought the great enemy ignorance in the countryside, formed a national "army of peace." Therefore, it was the responsibility of the state to help teachers in every way possible. One of Duruy's earliest acts was intended to relieve the *instituteur* from an unjust financial burden—that of procuring furnishings for his living quarters. The decree of September 4, 1863, required the commune to share with the state in providing *instituteurs* and *institutrices* with personal furniture, which was to remain the property of the commune to be used by successive teachers. On September 26, 1863, he gave the prefects a list of all furniture to be provided. In subsequent communiqués with functionaries he checked the progress communes were making. The press unanimously approved of Duruy's decree, the *JGIP* noting that it gave teachers an advantage that the *congréganistes* enjoyed.[45]

With regard to teachers and the teaching profession in general, Du-

---

43. Dansette, "Le corps enseignant au XIXᵉ siècle," 119; report to the emperor preceding the decree of December 31, 1863, *AIP*, 53–55.

44. F(17) 6853, AN; *JGIP*, 1868, p. 290; Rohr, *Victor Duruy, un ministre de Napoléon III*, 100, 58, note 10.

45. Duruy, *Notes et souvenirs*, I, 241; *BAIP*, XIV (1863), 226–28 (decree of September 4, 1863), and 308–10; *RIP*, 1863, p. 385; *JGIP*, 1864, p. 777.

ruy had to deal with various problems and controversies that involved clergy and religious who were teachers in public institutions and with the issue of teachers' loyalties vis-à-vis the regime. The main issue in this area involved dispensations from military service, a problem with origins in the First Empire. At the time the University was founded, the state's educational forces were greatly limited. Consequently, the Christian Brothers were given a national mandate to dispense primary education. Napoleon recognized the important service the religious order would render, and he thus granted the Brothers a special exemption from the military (article 109 of the decree of March 17, 1808). During the Restoration the dispensation was extended to include "students of the *école normale* and other members of public instruction who contracted before the University council to devote themselves for ten years to this service."[46] On March 21, 1832, the dispensation was specifically limited to *instituteurs* in public institutions, but it was not until the law of 1833 that a clear distinction was made between private and public schools.

Although the vast majority of *congréganistes* enjoying the exemption were within the requirements of the law, there were some transgressions during the July Monarchy. One case even came in 1846 before the Cour de Cassation (the French supreme court of appeal), which upheld both the laws of 1832 and 1833.

The Falloux Law of 1850 extended the military exemption to the secondary level. Article 79 stated: "The *instituteurs adjoints* of the public schools, the young men who are preparing themselves for public primary school teaching in schools ordained for that purpose, the members or novices of religious associations devoted to education and authorized by law or recognized as institutions of public utility, students of the Ecole Normale Supérieur, *maîtres d'étude, regents* and professors of the *collèges* and *lycées* are dispensed from military service if they have, before the time fixed for the draft, contracted with the rector the commitment to serve for ten years in public education and if they complete this obligation." The clause exempting "the members or novices of religious associations devoted to education and authorized by law or recognized as institutions of public utility" sug-

46. Law of March 10, 1818, article 15, section 5. Most of the information on military dispensation is in F(17) 9115, AN.

gested that the Second Republic was revising the policy of the July Monarchy. But in January, 1851, when Minister of Public Instruction de Parieu was asked to interpret the clause, he replied that the exemption was enjoyed only by those who taught in public schools. Clearly, the law and the Ministry of Public Instruction were in conflict. Therefore, it is not surprising that de Parieu's specification was not enforced everywhere.

De Parieu's successor, Fortoul, did not concern himself with the matter. Fortoul's successor, Rouland, did, but he only complicated the issue by seeking an opinion from and consensus with the minister of war. The minister of war thus formed the impression that he had some authority in the interpretation of the Falloux Law.

Laxity continued until 1865, when Duruy's attention was drawn to the case of Bernard Raffi and Pierre Trinquier, members of the Frères de Saint-Vioteur and *instituteurs* in their order's schools in the department of Aveyron. Both brothers had contracted the decennial engagement. But the exemptions were seriously questioned by the prefect, Castelnau, who wrote to the minister of war asking for advice. Indications are that Castelnau, prefect of a department renowned for its clericalism, was motivated more by anticlericalism than by a sense of duty. When the minister of war responded, he upheld Raffi and Trinquier, basing his decision on the now controversial clause in article 79 of the Falloux Law.[47]

The affair probably would have rested there if the prefect had not complained subsequently to Duruy. After considerable delay, and after Duruy received requests from Protestant and Jewish associations asking that their members teaching in their private schools be made eligible for the military exemption, Duruy sent a confidential letter to the prefect (now Isolard, not Castelnau), saying simply that the private schools to which the religious orders attributed the character of "public utility" were almost free from state surveillance and were "used sometimes to struggle energetically against the communal school." On July 31, Duruy publicized these sentiments in a circular to the rectors and prefects.[48]

47. The minister of war to the prefect of Aveyron, February 13, 1865, copy of a letter, *ibid.*
48. See Charles Robert's timetable of developments in the military dispensation issue and the letters from Protestant and Jewish groups, all in *ibid.*

By this time, Duruy had excited the wrath of the minister of war, who accused him of wanting to give a new interpretation to the law. A heated correspondence ensued between the two. Duruy pointedly reminded his colleague that the law of March 15, 1850, was, in fact, a *loi scolaire* and that he, as minister of public instruction, had the exclusive right of interpreting the law. He supported this claim with the argument of precedence: the de Parieu letter of 1851 and the fact that the two ministries had never conferred before in regard to article 79 except in 1859, when Rouland conferred with the minister of war in a "very special instance." Duruy urged an immediate resolution of the controversy in his September, 1865, letter to his colleague: "I should not let it be ignored by Your Excellency that this grave question extends very far, and that, under pain of disrupting the whole scholastic organization of our country, it is necessary to hold rigorously to the principle. Diverse and numerous pretensions are appearing in the bosom of the Protestant and Jewish communions." Duruy believed that exemptions to members of religious orders who did not teach in public schools or who did not teach at all were an "excessive privilege." Conversely, the minister of war claimed that "privilege" to the Catholic orders was the intent of the Falloux Law. He accused Duruy of attempting to score a major defeat for the religious orders because the vast majority of their members taught in their own schools.[49]

The conflict between the two ministers became more tense in early 1866, when both men issued divergent instructions to their subordinates. The minister of war upheld his interpretation of the law in a circular issued on February 1. Two weeks later, on February 14, Duruy issued his own more narrow interpretation of article 79. Article 79 had granted the military exemption to men who contracted to devote themselves to teaching in a public institution, and Duruy's circular clarified that public instruction meant instruction given in a public institution (*établissement public d'instruction*). Furthermore, it specified that public education was that "which is given at the expense of the municipality, the department, or the state, in the public schools of the communes, by *instituteurs* who are named, suspended, transferred and revoked by the administration and who thus fulfill, under the di-

---

49. Victor Duruy to the minister of war, August 30, September, 1865, copies of letters, *ibid.*; minister of war to Duruy, October 16, 1865, F(17) 9115, AN.

rection, control and inspection of academic authorities, a paid public function."[50] The new stipulation, however, purposefully was not retroactive. In March supplementary instructions based on precedents established during the Restoration by Pierre-Paul Royer-Collard and Antoine de Vatimesnil were issued: an open dossier was to be kept on the dispensed teachers in each *académie* in the office of the rector. Inspectors of academy (for lay teachers) or religious superiors (for their charges) were to keep the rector informed of all changes in the status or location of the teachers involved. Any teacher leaving the realm of public instruction would be viewed as having broken his contract.[51]

As might be expected, the press jumped into the fray. *L'Avenir nationale* on February 21, 1866, praised Duruy, advocated a complete revision of article 79, and ventured that while the Corps législatif was at it, it should modify all of the Falloux Law. The opinions of the anticlerical *Le Siècle* and *L'Opinion national* were similar. The legitimist *Le Monde* (February 25, 1866), not surprisingly, took a different view: "The measure taken by the minister has no other goal than to create an evident situation of inferiority for private teachers, especially *congréganistes.*" *L'Union de l'Ouest* (April 18, 1866), another legitimist paper, was in full accord. Frédéric Lock in the liberal *Le Temps*, though siding with Duruy, offered one of the few objective appraisals: It was regrettable that "on a point which for thirty years has not been seriously contested, two administrations of the state enter publicly into conflict. It is rather curious also that, breaking with a constant tradition, the administration of war abandons the defense of the military interest." Duruy would later wonder about this himself in a letter to the emperor.[52]

At the height of the crisis, Duruy wrote a note to Mourier, the vice-rector of Paris, maintaining that the new act "has for a goal not to change, but to explain the law," which was confusing. Shortly thereafter, he issued a confidential circular to the rectors and asked for

50. *AIP*, 266–72; *BAIP*, V (1866), 198–203 (circular, February 14, 1866). A communal school was defined as either a school maintained by the municipality, or, if no such school existed, a private school maintained for the municipality as a public school and usually subsidized by the municipality.

51. *BAIP*, V (1866), 296–98 (regulation of March 17, 1866).

52. Newspaper clipping in F(17) 9115, AN; *JGIP*, 1866, p. 139; and Victor Duruy to Napoleon III, August 21, 1866, copy of a letter in possession of Mme Albert Duruy.

more data on the situation. This circular, dated March 10, 1866, gives the impression that Duruy had sudden doubts about the extent of the abuse and wished to have a true picture of the situation. But Duruy remained fully convinced of the justice of his interpretations, and in a letter to the prefect of police he mused: "I wish it were possible for you to consult the workers and peasants on this matter. You would observe . . . men indignant at seeing the head of a congregation have the routine right of granting a military exemption to any three folds of black, gray or white robe. All questions have two sides. I believe that a country of equality must not preserve a privilege, especially a privilege which bears a tax of blood [*impôt du sang*]. This seems to be the broadest and most politic view of things." At this point, the archbishop of Rennes, taking up the Catholic cause, sent a petition to the Senate. Simultaneously, he assured Duruy that he had no malicious intent; he believed that the minister of public instruction was being seriously deceived and desired only to initiate a just solution. Probably seeking further moral support, Duruy consulted subsequently with Adolphe Mourier (head of the academy of Paris), Jules Baroche (minister of justice), Pierre Paul de Royer (a member of the Imperial Council of Public Instruction), and the archbishop of Paris; all agreed that Duruy's measure was "legal and just."[53]

Meanwhile, the government began to investigate this issue. It was examined in the Council of State, a special committee of the Corps législatif, and the Senate. Simon Genteur was busy working for the cause in the Senate, and to this end he wrote Duruy confidentially asking for a list of the number of authorized male religious orders and their strengths so that he could impress senators with the number of conscripts the government was failing to recruit as a result of the military exemption privilege.

Four days later, on May 13, 1866, Duruy wrote to the emperor telling him of "the secret hostility which exists between the forty thousand laic *instituteurs* and the twelve thousand religious *instituteurs*" and which was confirmed by the reports of the prefects. Duruy was

53. Confidential circular, March 10, 1866, F(17) 9115, AN; Victor Duruy to the prefect of the police, April 9, 1866, in Duruy, *Notes et souvenirs*, I, 352–53; Jules Baroche to Victor Duruy, July 13, 1865, and the archbishop of Paris to Victor Duruy, January 5, 1866, F(17) 9115, AN.

not proposing "that the government act against the small army for the profit of the large," but he did wish to see the resolution of an injustice. Even domestics (*gens de service*) attached to the religious orders received the exemption yet laymen in similar positions in the *lycées* did not. This was the basis of Duruy's constant complaint that three folds of a robe should not be sufficient qualification for a military exemption.[54]

By June, the Senate had three petitions to consider, each protesting Duruy's circular of February 14. A special commission chaired by Baron Charron reviewed the controversy and reported that Duruy had not misinterpreted the law. Dismayed with the conclusion, the Cardinal Comte Henri de Bonnechose informed the Senate that Duruy's action had the effect of making a difficult recruitment of men to religious vocations even more difficult and that this would prove that the government wished to harm the *congréganistes*. But "a very great majority" of the Senate voted to accept the commission's conclusion, although the ministers of public instruction and war were encouraged to reexamine the possibilities of extending the categories of schools in which the commitment could be contracted. By then Duruy could analyze his "victory" for the emperor: the Chamber of Deputies and the Council of State had cleared him of any fault, as did the Senate, which had registered "a bloody and very significant defeat" for the Cardinals Césaire Mathieu and de Bonnechose.[55]

But the desire of the Senate commission that the privilege of military exemption be extended would soon be realized in the April 10, 1867, law on primary education. When Duruy defended his bill on primary education before the legislature on March 11, he had to counter three suggested amendments. The first, advanced by Baron L. F. D. de Ravinel, proposed that all religious be exempted from the military. The second, advanced by the marquis d'Andelarre and vicomte de Grouchy, ventured to make an engagement of ten years in any school worth an exemption. And the third, brought forth by Pierre Chesnelong, pro-

54. Undated confidential note, Simon Genteur to Victor Duruy, F(17) 9115, AN; Duruy, *Notes et souvenirs*, I, 353; *AIP*, 375 (from Duruy's March 11, 1867, speech to the Corps législatif).
55. Maurain, *La politique ecclésiastique du Second Empire*, 773; *RIP*, 1866, pp. 193–94; *BAIP*, V (1866), 910–11; and Victor Duruy to Napoleon III, January 5, 1866, in Duruy, *Notes et souvenirs*, I, 356–57.

posed to grant exemptions to all members of religious congregations recognized as having public utility. To counter the proposals, Duruy used a set of statistics to argue that many men entered religious orders only as a shield against the draft; when they completed their "engagement," they left the religious orders hastily. He also argued that "the country with its old Gallic good sense would never understand a privilege in this area, that with three folds of a black or gray robe the head of a community could give, outside public service, a military dispensation." The arguments against the amendments held, and the new law of April 10, 1867, as Duruy wished, extended the decennial engagement only to semipublic schools, defined as those that received a subsidy from the commune. In his instruction of January 31, 1868, Duruy further specified that subsidization alone was not sufficient proof that a school was "public." Thus he added such considerations as the sufficiency of public schools in a department and the indigency among children served by the schools.[56]

Duruy's circular of January 31 was met by angry protests from Frère Philippe, Superior of the Christian Brothers. But Philippe's protests were soon lost in the midst of a new concession to religious teachers: the new military law of February 1, 1868, as applied by the circular of March 20, 1868, exempted from the National Guard both *instituteurs* already excused from military service and those attached to "a private school extant for at least two years and having at least thirty students."[57]

The military exemption issue as it turned out was the only general issue in the realm of relations with clergy and religious with which Duruy had to deal. All other issues in this realm involved various individual authorizations to teach or to open schools, and their details do not merit discussion. Nonetheless, it is worthwhile considering how the cases were resolved and what, if any, guidelines Duruy followed in their resolution. Analyses which I have presented elsewhere reveal that Duruy refused authorizations to clergy and religious no more often than he did to laymen; that in cases in which curés requested permission to open schools, Duruy usually refused authorizations on the

56. *AIP*, 387–95; Zévort, "Victor Duruy," 483–84; Rohr, *Victor Duruy, ministre de Napoléon III*, 207 (text of the law of April 10, 1867); and *AIP*, 554–57.
57. F(19) 3972, AN; *BAIP*, IX (1868), 252–54.

grounds that the tasks of pastor and schoolmaster were incompatible; and that whenever a clergyman or religious was refused the right to teach, Duruy saw to it that that person was replaced by another man of the Church.[58] There is nothing in these findings to tarnish Duruy's reputation as a moderate anticlerical who continued to show a basic respect for religion and, indeed, the Church.

As for the second political issue—teachers' loyalties toward the regime—Duruy believed that the best ways to stimulate loyalty were to improve the salaries of teachers and to reward teachers for meritorious service. Duruy was not particularly enamored with the Second Empire practice of using schoolteachers to help official government candidates in elections. He was willing to let academic administrators instruct teachers verbally on whom to support in elections, but he cautioned them that in dealing with teachers they should "carefully avoid acts and words which are or could be interpreted as pressure." Duruy told his subordinates further that such acts and words were neither in the attributions nor character of the functions of *universitaires*. As a basic policy, "it is not wise for the University overtly to take an active role in aggressive politics." [59]

Duruy remained consistent in applying his policy throughout his years in office. Not even a request for assistance from the minister of the interior caused him to modify his stand. But although his policy was known early in his career as minister, at least as late as 1867, he still found it necessary to reprove a prefect for having pressured an inspector of academy into writing a letter for the press supporting the government's official candidate.[60]

One curious episode regarding teachers and elections arose in 1868. Duruy received an anonymous letter complaining that the Abbé Bresson, headmaster at the *collège* of Dôle, had actively campaigned against the official government candidate for deputy from the Jura. When Duruy had the matter investigated, he learned that the allegation was unfounded. Somehow, however, Duruy discovered that the

58. Horvath, "Victor Duruy and French Education," 104–106, 445–47.

59. Victor Duruy to Napoleon III, September 9, 1866, copy of a letter in possession of Mme Albert Duruy; Duruy, *Notes et souvenirs*, I, 240; confidential circular, June 9, 1864, and Victor Duruy to the prefect of the Charente-Inférieur, January 27, 1867, copy of a confidential letter, F(17) 2682, AN.

60. Victor Duruy to the rectors of Bordeaux, Douai, Grenoble, and Montpellier and to the prefect of the Charente-Inférieur, copies of confidential letters, F(17) 2682, AN.

author of the anonymous letter was a priest because a few months later he commented in a letter: "I have the greatest respect for religion. This respect is one of my principles. It is also in my heart [the respect is emotional as well as intellectual]. [But I know] I have administered Jura in difficult times when they incite a priest to complain to me."[61]

If Duruy's main motivations in his many acts to improve the lot of teachers were to be distilled to their essence, they would be two in number—to improve the education of teachers and to make the teaching profession attractive. The former was necessary because normal school education was just catching hold in France and because, in the early 1850s, at a crucial moment in the development of the normal schools, conservatives had crippled them. The latter was necessary because there were not enough well-qualified teachers and because teachers generally did not enjoy a comfortable existence.

We have seen that Duruy made sincere efforts to improve normal school education and to lessen some of the major problems teachers faced—low and irregularly paid salaries, insufficient pensions, and inadequate opportunities for promotions. He also spent considerable energy on the dispute over military exemptions, attempting to see that justice was done. Duruy's successes overall were only partial; many excellent proposals, unfortunately, were reduced or made infeasible by budgetary considerations.

There were no dramatic changes in the normal schools, and reforms for teachers and the teaching profession were modest. Yet Duruy's reforms were considerable enough, given the history of the recent past, and the revival of the normal schools during the 1860s owes much to him. Also, the reinstitution of pedagogy courses and the emphasis on intelligence over memory in education were significant, playing as they did an important part in the pedagogical revolution Jean Hébrard discovered in France of the 1860s.[62] And we should not forget the important development Duruy gave to agricultural education, the numerous promotions in secondary education he effected, and the real if modest improvements in salaries for which he was responsible.

61. Undated note concerning elections in the Jura (probably August or September, 1868), in Duruy's hand, *ibid*.
62. Hébrard, "Ecole et alphabétisation," 76.

Doubtless the gap between what needed to be done and what was done for teachers was still wide when Duruy left office in 1869. But enough was attempted and achieved to trigger a new sense of optimism in the teaching profession.[63] And that was a truly important accomplishment.

63. Monod, "Victor Duruy," 487.

IX · Conclusion

If the future belongs to those who see far, the present often belongs to
those whose view is limited.
—Paul Painlevé, in *Le centenaire de Victor Duruy, 1811–1911*

On May 24, 1869, the imperial government held national elections for
the Corps législatif, the first since 1863. Staged against the background of rising political, social, and economic discontent, stimulated
particularly by the new laws on the press and public meetings and by
the confused and partial abandonment of the policy of official candidates, the elections represented a stunning repudiation of authoritari-
anism and the personal politics of Eugène Rouher. The government
still held a majority of the popular vote, but that majority had fallen
from a comfortable 73 percent (in 1863) to a troubling 62 percent,
and with the addition of disloyal official candidates to the recently
elected candidates of opposition parties, the opposition was now in
the majority in the Corps législatif.[1]

Among the opposition factions, none was as strong as the centrists,
a coalition of right centrists led by Emile Ollivier and left centrists, the
so-called Third party, led by Adolphe Thiers, Louis Buffet, and Napoleon Daru.[2] Although the centrists would soon divide over the question of whether the government should be continued as an empire
(greatly liberalized) or whether it should become a true parliamentary
regime, the message of the 1869 elections was clear: if the sickly
Napoleon III wished to salvage his throne for the Prince Imperial, he
would have to agree to major political concessions.

Most of these concessions would be hammered out in the political

1. Seignobos, *Le déclin de l'empire et l'établissement de la Troisième République*,
59–81; Theodore Zeldin, *The Political System of Napoleon III* (New York, 1971),
135–42; Henry Berton, *L'évolution constitutionelle du Second Empire* (Paris, 1900),
250, 259.
2. Seignobos, *Le déclin de l'empire et l'établissement de la Troisième République*, 46.

bargaining that took place in the months following the elections.[3] But the one that became immediately pressing was the demand that the emperor dismiss his current ministers and elevate new men from among the opposition. The first sign of Napoleon's willingness to do this came when he dismissed Rouher on July 12. During the next five days, however, he deliberated with the centrists and vacillated over further concessions.

That Napoleon had some hope of retaining Duruy, his most liberal minister, in the new and more liberal regime is suggested by a letter Duruy wrote to Pierre Magne, former minister of finances, on July 14, 1869: "I am held in reserve just in case," Duruy told him. "It is . . . the natural game of parliamentarianism which begins anew."[4] Actually, the emperor had no choice but to dismiss Duruy. Duruy was too tainted by the despotism of the past and too anticlerical to satisfy the Third party and the large number of clericals who supported it. Napoleon finally acknowledged this fact and dismissed Duruy on July 17, 1869. In Duruy's place, he elevated Louis Olivier Bourbeau, dean of the faculty of law at Poitiers, a moderate republican deputy and a member of the Third party. To console Duruy, Napoleon gave him a seat in the Senate, the traditional refuge for ministerial casualties.

Few newspapers paid any attention to Duruy's dismissal; most were too preoccupied with the larger political questions of the day. Only the continuously loyal *RIP* thought to eulogize Duruy and his many accomplishments.[5]

Duruy was not jolted by his dismissal. Since the very beginning he had known, as did other ministers, that tenure in office was subject both to the whims of the emperor and to the vicissitudes of politics. Consequently, on the day following his dismissal, he wrote the emperor a cordial letter, expressing approval of his successor and suggesting that because Bourbeau had applauded so many of his reforms, he did not expect him to destroy them. Duruy assured the emperor that in any case he would not oppose Bourbeau's ministerial initiatives as Rouland had done his.[6] And on that same day, Duruy pulled from the

3. *Ibid.*, 76–81.
4. Victor Duruy to Pierre Magne, July 14, 1869, copy of a letter in possession of Mme Albert Duruy.
5. *RIP*, 1869, pp. 257–58.
6. Victor Duruy to Napoleon III, July 18, 1869, copy of a letter in possession of Mme Albert Duruy.

shelf of his library at Villeneuve-Saint-Georges the old yellowed notes he had saved for succeeding volumes of his *Histoire des Romains* and settled down to work as if he had never been interrupted from his career as a professional historian.[7] Cincinnatus returned to his plow.

The almost idyllic life that Duruy enjoyed thereafter was rudely interrupted by the Franco-Prussian War. During the next several months, he was agonized by the barbarity of the invaders, who pillaged his home at Villeneuve-Saint-Georges, and was anxious for the return of peace. He had thought the war was inevitable and had faith that even if the French were defeated, they would recover quickly. But this faith did not minimize the sorrow he felt for his country, nor did it prepare him for the eruption of civil war in his beloved Paris in the spring of 1871. Long afterward, he would continue to have nightmares about both the war and the Commune.[8]

When life finally returned to normal, Duruy resumed writing. He completed the third and fourth volumes of his Roman history by 1877 and the fifth through seventh volumes by 1885. All seven volumes were soon translated into English, German, and Italian. Later, before he developed a cataract on one eye and went blind in the other, he finished a history of the Greeks. These Roman and Greek histories would become French classics.

The years 1873 to 1894, overall, brought Duruy a mixture of joys and sorrows. Politically, he fully accepted the Third Republic as a logical historical development. He saw no possibility for the creation of a third Napoleonic empire, which, as a liberal, he would have opposed. But he did believe that Bonapartism would continue to play a role in politics for some time. He made one bid for political office in 1876, when he ran unsuccessfully for the Senate from Seine-et-Oise. Otherwise, he confined himself to scholarly pursuits, his family, and occasional stints as an educational consultant. Professionally, he saw his scholarly works attain considerable renown. And he came to enjoy as a result the singular distinction of election to three chairs at the Institut: a chair at the Académie des Inscriptions et Belles-Lettres in 1873; a chair at the Académie des Sciences Morales in 1879; and a chair at the Académie Française in 1884. In the more personal realm, he suffered immensely from the loss of his two eldest sons and his remaining

7. Lavisse, "Victor Duruy," 78.
8. *Centenaire de Victor Duruy,* 22–23, 26 (speech of Paul Painlevé).

daughter. Only one son from his first marriage, George (the spelling a reflection of English ancestry in the family),[9] would survive him. But in 1873, he married an elementary schoolteacher who was a good friend of Eugénie's and a tutor to the Prince Imperial, and in the following year, at the age of sixty-three, he sired another son, Louis-Victor. This last son, raised in his adolescent years as a Catholic by his mother but nudged to a "more manly" scientific appreciation of the world by his father, would also survive him.[10]

After 1888, Duruy's activities were curtailed significantly. A bad fall on the steps of the Académie Française forced him to spend most of his final years bedridden. But he continued his intellectual pursuits almost to the end, boasting: "Despite the infirmities which have come with age, I am *un privilegié de la vie*. . . . because I am still able to study." [11] During the concluding months of his life, he grieved only rarely, complaining just once to Jules Simon, "I am dead." [12] Normally, however, as intimates attested, he continued to display the stoicism that he had cultivated in earlier life. He speculated on dying, death (to which he was resigned as the "rule of life"), and afterlife with his friends, but he determined that there was little profound that could be said on those matters: "It is wisest to say with the prophet, *in manus tuas Domine, commendo spiritum meum*." [13] Duruy never expected to see the end of 1892, but he lived until Christmas Day, 1894. After death, his body was returned to Villeneuve-Saint-Georges, given a Catholic blessing (as a result of his previous orders), and interred in the cemetery on the hill just above his country home.[14] A simple monument topped by a stone cross marks the final resting place of the man who was called one of the leading anticlericals of the liberal empire.

What can be said in conclusion about this man, about the regime he served, and about his influence on French education after the Second Empire?

Duruy can properly be called the major liberal of the empire in its

9. Interview with Mme Albert Duruy, August, 1975.
10. L. de Lanzac de Laborie, "Au fil de l'histoire," *Le Correspondant*, CCV (1901), 542.
11. Duruy, *Notes et souvenirs*, II, 311.
12. Victor Duruy to Jules Simon, December 10, 1879, Jules Simon Papers, 87AP 3, AN.
13. M. de Malarcé, "Journal de ma vie," *La Revue hebdomadaire*, March 30, 1901, 685.
14. Laborie, "Au fil de l'histoire," 542.

closing years. He was the only high official to promote liberal reforms consistently. Morny and Prince Napoleon had of course been the prominent liberals in the earlier days of the liberalizing empire, but they left the political scene in 1865. Thereafter, there were only the emperor and Persigny, and Frenchmen could never be sure of their genuine intentions. Duruy alienated a certain number of liberals on occasion by placing restrictions on some of his reforms and by refusing to hold firm on freedom of speech and thought in the cases of Renan and the doctoral student at the Parisian faculty of medicine. But he had to bend to the will of the emperor and political exigencies in some matters in order to promote liberal reforms that would have a broader and more enduring impact on society. In the end, however, his reputation as a liberal perdured. Emile Ollivier even briefly considered returning him to the Ministry of Public Instruction in 1870 when he was constituting a cabinet for the liberal empire.[15]

Duruy also was the leading anticlerical of the "liberal" regime. He was the only member of the Council of Ministers who publicly displayed hostility to reactionary Catholicism and to the machinations of such men as Louis Veuillot, and he was the only anticlerical minister charged with a portfolio that was of preeminent concern to the Church. The emperor had ordered him to limit the continuing progress of the religious congregations in education, and he accomplished this task not by attacking them head-on and trying to crush them—because Duruy genuinely believed that public schools needed the competition of private schools—but by forcing them to comply with the law and by strengthening state schools to meet the competition.[16] The line between what was done for pedagogical reasons and what was done out of anticlerical motivation, however, ineluctably became blurred. And as Duruy advanced each new program and reform, he earned increasing hostility from clericals, who began fearing for the security of religious institutions.

The battle of Mentana (November 3, 1867) was an important turning point in the story. It shifted more liberals into the opposition and

15. Liard, *L'enseignement supérieur en France*, II, 286; Ollivier, *Liberal Empire*, 13:307.
16. *AIP*, 357; Adrien Dansette, *A Religious History of France* (2 vols.; Freiberg, 1961), I, 277; Victor Duruy to Napoleon III, April 21, 1866, copy of a letter in possession of Mme Albert Duruy; Duruy, *Notes et souvenirs*, I, 255, 330.

provided clericals with hopes that they might be able to reforge the alliance they had enjoyed with the state in the 1850s. But Mentana was not the sole event that precipitated the unprecedented "clerical war" (or what Lavisse called *la guerre sainte*) against Duruy. Four slightly earlier developments also played a major role: the conflict over military dispensations for religious orders in 1866, the reappearance of the aggressive *L'Univers* (January, 1867), the confirmation of plans to hold a high Church council to consolidate the forces of the Church in an ever more hostile world (June, 1867), and the program of public secondary courses for young girls (circular, October 30, 1867). By the spring of 1868, "clerical" Catholics decided that Duruy was the chief obstacle to a *ralliement* with the regime, and they announced that they would side with opposition parties in elections until Duruy was removed. Thus, to paraphrase the *JGIP*, the electoral future of France had been thrown into doubt because of the activity of Victor Duruy.[17]

Yet curiously, in both his liberalism and anticlericalism, Duruy appears relatively moderate, especially when he is compared with the men of the opposition. He exhibited a mix of nineteenth- and twentieth-century liberalism, favoring strong state control over public education because the state alone had sufficient force to effect significant reform and progress but at the same time supporting and encouraging collaborative local and private initiatives in education. Moreover, his reforms were an amalgam of liberal and conservative ingredients. As a historian, Duruy was convinced that all enduring improvements in human life come only through evolution. From the beginning to the end, therefore, Duruy was a proponent of the only reform that has truly succeeded in France—incremental reform.[18]

Duruy's anticlericalism also was mild, particularly because he fervently respected differences among men and supported the principle of freedom of conscience. Had Duruy been a staunch anticlerical like the radical republicans of the day, he would never have curried the favor of Catholic liberals or supported a bill for *liberté de l'enseignement supérieur*. Nor would he have insisted that teaching in the schools be

17. Lavisse, "Un ministre," 60; *JGIP*, 1868, p. 210.
18. Crozier and Freidberg, *L'acteur et le système* (no pages given), cited in George Weisz, "The Anatomy of University Reform, 1863–1914," in Baker and Harrigan, *Making of Frenchmen*, 375.

respectful of the Catholic religion. An article in the liberal *Le Figaro* in May, 1868, correctly noted for its readers that Duruy's actions oftentimes were not anticlerical; at most, Duruy was "anticlerical in theory." Duruy's anticlericalism was so relatively tame that it made Catholics in the Ferry era look back wistfully. It could, Adrien Dansette argues, have provided France with an agreeable settlement of the religious question in education "if only Catholics could have accepted the fact that Frenchmen were deeply divided on religion." [19]

All of the programs Duruy promoted and supported and the extent to which he fostered them were, of course, based on his personal evaluation of the educational needs of his contemporary France. But all were likewise tempered by political considerations. When he dropped the principle of obligation in primary education, he did so to salvage the principle of gratuity but also to help stall the growth of political opposition to the regime from the right. The same consideration partially influenced him in dealing with the petitions on materialism that were sent to the Senate in 1867 and 1868. Despite his distaste for the "sins" of the past (especially the coup d'etat) and the fact that almost paradoxically he was the closest to being an opposition minister the regime had, Duruy consistently remained loyal to the emperor he had agreed to serve. Duruy was, in fact, the quintessential *honnête homme*.

Duruy's curious political situation casts more light on the nature of liberal reform in the Second Empire. Throughout the 1860s Napoleon III was engaged in a difficult balancing act between contradictory political, social, and economic forces. Following longstanding French tradition, he played his ministers off against each other and attempted to ensure that there were men in high office who, as a group, could offer something for everyone. His choice of Duruy in 1863 to assuage the liberals and anticlericals was clever. Yet if he ever really had a chance of appeasing liberals and anticlericals (and we recall here Ollivier's warning to Morny that the enemies of the empire would not be grateful for concessions; they would only use the concessions to fight the government more effectively [20]), he defeated himself by failing to give full support to Duruy's liberal initiatives. In the end, of course,

19. Excerpt from *Le Figaro* in *JGIP*, 1868, p. 354; Dansette, *Religious History of France*, I, 292, 291.
20. Berton, *L'évolution constitutionnelle du Second Empire*, 367.

he satisfied no one, and by 1869, as Eugénie vividly confided later, the regime was so trapped into immobility that it could not even "sneeze."[21]

Scholars seeking to rehabilitate the Second Empire have found little in its politics to praise, except perhaps the emperor's good intentions. But in its social and economic programs, they have found a wealth of redeeming features.[22] It has been one of the major purposes of this book to add to those appreciations by demonstrating that the contributions the regime made to French education under Duruy's administration were as significant as those that were made in other social, socioeconomic, or cultural realms. If Duruy's reforms were sometimes compromised by politics during the Second Empire, at least the basic ideas behind them were taken up by the Third Republic and subsequent regimes. Indeed, Octave Gréard correctly claimed that there was scarcely a reform in education over the next "forty years that did not recall the work of Victor Duruy."[23]

In primary education, the Ferry Laws of 1881 and 1882 installed free and compulsory education. By that time most school-age children were attending school and the majority (57 percent in 1876 as opposed to only 41 percent ten years earlier) were attending gratuitously, thanks considerably, as Ferry acknowledged, to the Duruy Law of 1867.[24] The Ferry Law of 1882 on compulsory education thus cor-

21. Duruy's liberalism won Napoleon new popular support (see John A. Rothney, "The Modernization of Politics and the Politics of Modernization," in *Proceedings of the Eighth Annual Meeting of the Western Society for French History*, VIII [1981], 375; and Patrice L. R. Higgonnet, *Pont-de-Montvert: Social Structure and Politics in a French Village, 1700–1914* [Cambridge, Mass., 1971], 111) but because this liberalism was circumscribed by various "considerations," it failed to be of substantive advantage against opposition forces on the left. Eugénie quoted in Lavisse, "Un ministre," 76.

22. Alan Spitzer, "The Good Napoleon III," *French Historical Studies*, II (1962), 308–29; and Stuart L. Campbell, *The Second Empire Revisited: A Study in French Historiography* (New Brunswick, 1978).

23. Institut de France, *Inauguration du monument élevé à la mémoire de Victor Duruy à Villeneuve-Saint-Georges*, 6.

24. Furet and Ozouf, *Lire et écrire*, I, 172; Prost, *Histoire de l'enseignement en France*, 94–95; Auspitz, *Radical Bourgeoisie*, 43. This statement should not be construed as a denial of the importance of social demand so well argued by Furet and Ozouf and illustrated in Thabault, *Education and Change in a Village Community*. But few would deny that certain education laws were important for removing various obstacles to *scolarisation*. See, for example, *ibid.*, 55; Pierre Chevallier, "L'évolution de l'enseignement primaire en France de 1850 à 1963," in Chevallier, *La scolarisation en France depuis un siècle* (Paris, 1974), 34–35; Desert, "Alphabétisation et scolarisation dans le Grand-Ouest," 149; Furet and Ozouf, *Lire et écrire*, I, 172; and Pasquet, "L'alphabétisation dans le départment de la Vienne au XIXe siècle," 266.

rected for that great problem that had regularly vexed Duruy—attendance—and helped to instill the republican notion that families had a
duty to send their children to school.[25] Illiteracy and the patois were no
longer major problems, thanks to the advance of primary education,
the improvement of teaching, and the decline of rural isolation. Night
schools for adults remained strong for fully twenty years after Duruy
left office, and *salles d'asile* thrived, especially where they were successful previously: cities and manufacturing centers.[26] The sole departure from the Duruy agenda for primary education was the securiza-
tion of the schools during the Ferry years.

In secondary education, Duruy's reform of the classical program was
continued by Third Republic educators. An *arrêté* in 1880 strengthened
the position of history in the curriculum, reduced the amount of Latin
and Greek, and gave expanded coverage to French language and literature, modern languages, and science. Duruy's special education was
also continued, at least into the 1870s, and it prospered, claiming by
1880 half of all students in the communal *collèges* and a quarter of all
students in the *lycées*. But beginning in 1881, republicans began to
give special education a more academic and theoretical character, and
by 1891 they ultimately repudiated it by replacing it with a pseudo-
classical program known as *enseignement moderne*. Terminated thus,
unfortunately, were Duruy's efforts to make the secondary schools responsive to the needs of agriculture, industry, and commerce.[27]

The program of public secondary education for young women fared
better. Under Duruy, we recall, it had had only modest success in that it
was implemented in fewer than fifty cities and attracted fewer than two
thousand students, although it did, as Françoise Mayeur rightly under-
scores, get parents to send their daughters for a liberal and disinterested higher education at a time when there were no careers for young
women.[28] After Duruy left office, the number of courses fell precipi-

25. Prost, *Histoire de l'enseignement en France*, 101, 109.

26. Jefferson, "Worker Education in England and France," 356–57; Matrat and Kir-
gomard, *Les écoles maternelles*, 44–45.

27. Gerbod, "La place de l'histoire dans l'enseignement secondaire," 130; Prost,
Histoire de l'enseignement en France, 250; Gréard, *Éducation et instruction, enseigne-
ment secondaire* (Paris, 1887), I, 4ff., as quoted in Piobetta, *Le baccalauréat*, 152;
Piobetta, *Le baccalauréat*, 154–55, 151; Day, "Development of Higher Primary and
Intermediate Technical Education in France," 57; Rambaud, "Victor Duruy," 491.

28. Mayeur, *L'éducation des filles en France*, 123–24, 130.

tously. But they never totally disappeared, and if Duruy had only limited success in the short run, he was ultimately victorious in the long run. The republicans of the late 1870s built on the precedents he established; they even ostentatiously invoked his name to reassure Frenchmen that public secondary education for women had already developed a respectable tradition. With the Sée Law of 1881, republicans established *lycées* and *collèges* (as day schools, not boarding schools) for young women and adopted the same curriculum Duruy had used for his secondary courses for girls. They also borrowed Duruy's concept of independent public secondary courses for places that could not sustain a women's *collège* or *lycée*, and they created sixty-four such courses in 1881, some of which were still in existence in 1931.[29]

Higher education during the Third Republic would see great change. Although achieved gradually and quietly, much of the change would follow the main lines Duruy had traced during the Second Empire, particularly because those most responsible, the directors of the division of higher education at the ministry, were all admirers of his ideas.

Liberté de l'enseignment supérieur, which Duruy had campaigned so hard for during the Second Empire, became law in 1875. *Cours libres*, Duruy's interim measure to accustom Frenchmen to the notion of *liberté* at the highest level, thus fell into decline. But they were revived after 1884 by Louis Liard, the greatest director of higher education in the nineteenth century, when need arose to introduce new subjects into higher education and to stimulate local interest in and financial support for advanced studies. The Ecole Pratique des Hautes Etudes continued to be an enormously important research institution, and it was well supported by men of the Third Republic. Indeed, it was within the framework of the Ecole Pratique that Gabriel Monod and associate historians developed the famous "new history." The experiment with *écoles normales secondaires*, which was related to the Ecole Pratique, faded after Duruy left office, but in 1877 republicans began offering scholarships for students in the faculties of letters and sciences and requiring students to have the same practical experiences that Du-

29. Françoise Mayeur, *L'enseignement secondaire des jeunes filles sous la Troisième République* (Paris, 1977), 37; H. Boiraud, "Sur la création par l'état d'un enseignement féminin en France," *Paedagogica historica*, XVII (1977), 30; Gréard, *Education et instruction*, II, 91–92, 150; Mayeur, *L'éducation des filles en France*, 142, 145.

ruy had planned for the *maîtres répétiteurs auxiliaires*. Duruy's efforts to revolutionize the teaching in the letters and sciences faculties were thus continued, with the exception of the hiatus between 1870 and 1877. Universities were also ultimately created in France, although they were given life in a piecemeal fashion through the gradual implementation of most of the ideas that had appeared in Duruy's 1870 bill on universities. Finally, in higher education, economics instruction came into its own. The Collège de France was given a chair of political economy, and the law of 1877 extended an earlier regulation of Duruy's and made the teaching of economics obligatory at all faculties of law.[30]

Duruy was not solely responsible for the great reform movement in French higher education during the Third Republic. Pasteur and Renan were important reformers in the 1860s, and after that decade, the shock of defeat in the Franco-Prussian War, the rise of the republicans (and especially the positivist republicans, who saw education as the chief vehicle for molding a new society), the strategic positioning of a number of academics in political posts, the great increase in the number of faculty and students after 1870, which exerted new pressures for change, and the work of the new higher education lobby, the Société pour l'Etude des Questions d'Enseignement Supérieur, all made significant contributions. In short, there was a favorable *conjoncture* for change. But according to Louis Liard, Duruy could claim most credit for having sent "shock waves" through the system and for having "kindled" the momentum for reform that bore fruit in the Third Republic.[31]

Finally, for teachers, Duruy's efforts to strengthen the position of the normal schools were assiduously continued by republicans in the 1870s. The first great school law of the Third Republic, the law of 1879, obliged all departments to maintain not only a normal school for men but also one for women. The "mistake of 1833" was thus rec-

30. Weisz, "The Academic Elite and the Movement to Reform French Higher Education," 278; Liard, *L'enseignement supérieur en France*, II, 294–95; Bruneau, "French Faculties and Universities," 23, 62, 192; Duruy, "Statistique de l'enseignement supérieur," 557; Le Van-Lemesle, "La faculté de droit de Paris et l'introduction de l'économie politique dans son enseignement," 334.

31. Philip A. Bertocci, *Jules Simon: Republican Anticlericalism and Cultural Politics in France, 1848–1886* (Columbia, Mo., 1978), 161; Weisz, "Anatomy of University Reform," 369; Fox and Weisz (eds.), *Organization of Science and Technology in France*, 19; Liard, *L'enseignement supérieur en France*, II, 286, 337.

tified. Then a series of decrees and other regulations complemented the law of 1879, corrected a number of continuing weaknesses in the normal schools, and secularized them. Pedagogy courses continued to be an important concern of educators, although no substantive changes were made until 1920, when the courses were further specialized.[32] Teachers' salaries also continued to attract the solicitude of republicans. In 1889, finally, the concept of *retribution scolaire* at the elementary level was suppressed and the state took full responsibility for paying the salaries of schoolteachers. And another major issue concerning teachers during the Duruy years, the question of military service for ecclesiastics, was resolved in 1889, during the height of the Opportunistic Republic, by making military service for ecclesiastics obligatory.

Thus the reforms and concerns of Victor Duruy during the 1860s were successful in the long run. One must not seek to appreciate Duruy's contributions solely by looking at what happened in the 1860s. Duruy's ideas and programs constituted a liberal program of reform for the Second Empire. But they also formed (minus the secularization promoted later) the republican agenda in education for the Third Republic.[33]

---

32. Gontard, *La question des écoles normales primaires*, 83, 85, 89, 114.

33. Readers may notice a similarity between my closing sentence and a sentence in Patrick Harrigan with Victor Neglia, *Lycéens et collégiens sous le Second Empire* (Paris, 1979), 159, and, indeed, I duly accredit this source. I would like, however, to call the attention of those readers to the fact that my choice of words is somewhat different.

Appendix A · Academic Jurisdictions Within the University of France

Academy	Constituent Departments
Aix	Basses-Alpes, Bouches-du-Rhône, Corse, Var, Vaucluse, Alpes-Maritimes *
Besançon	Doubs, Jura, Haute-Saône
Bordeaux	Dordogne, Gironde, Landes, Lot-et-Garonne, Basses-Pyrénées
Caen	Calvados, Eure, Manche, Orne, Sarthe, Seine-Inférieure
Chambéry	Savoie, Haute-Savoie *
Clermont	Allier, Cantal, Corrèze, Creue, Haute-Loire, Puy-de-Dôme
Dijon	Aube, Côte-d'Or, Haute-Marne, Nièvre, Yonne
Douai	Aisne, Ardennes, Nord, Pas-de-Calais, Somme
Grenoble	Hautes-Alpes, Ardêche, Drôme, Isère
Lyon	Ain, Loire, Rhône, Saône-et-Loire
Montpellier	Aude, Gard, Hérault, Lozère, Pyrénées-Orientales
Nancy	Meurthe, Meuse, Moselle, Vosges
Paris	Cher, Eure-et-Loir, Loir-et-Cher, Loiret, Marne, Oise, Seine, Seine-et-Marne, Seine-et-Oise
Poitiers	Charente, Charente-Inférieure, Indre, Indre-et-Loire, Deux-Sèvres, Vendée, Vienne, Haute-Vienne
Rennes	Côtes-du-Nord, Finistère, Ille-et-Vilaine, Loire-Inférieure, Maine-et-Loire, Mayenne, Morbihan
Strasbourg	Bas-Rhin, Haute-Rhin
Toulouse	Ariège, Aveyron, Haute-Garonne, Gers, Lot, Hautes-Pyrénées, Tarn, Tarn-et-Garonne

Source: *JGIP*, June 24, 1854 (law of June 14), and August 26, 1854 (decree of August 22).
* Added in 1860.

Appendix B · *Structure of the University in the* 1860s

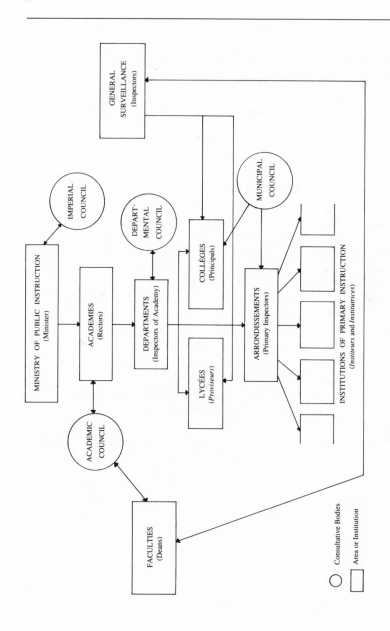

GENERAL SURVEILLANCE (Inspectors)

IMPERIAL COUNCIL

DEPARTMENTAL COUNCIL

MUNICIPAL COUNCIL

MINISTRY OF PUBLIC INSTRUCTION (Minister)

ACADEMIES (Rectors)

DEPARTMENTS (Inspectors of Academy)

COLLÈGES (Principals)

ARRONDISSEMENTS (Primary Inspectors)

LYCÉES (*Proviseurs*)

ACADEMIC COUNCIL

FACULTIES (Deans)

INSTITUTIONS OF PRIMARY INSTRUCTION (*Instituers and Institutrices*)

○ Consultative Bodies

▢ Area or Institution

Appendix C · An Agricultural Education Program for Young Girls

---

Instruction: Catechism, sacred history, religious music, reading, writing, a little history and geography

Calculations: Weights and measures, farm bookkeeping and household management

Hygiene: Care of children, the sick and wounded; home medicine; care of herbs; elements of veterinary medicine; gymnastics and swimming

Biology applied to agriculture: A knowledge of helpful and harmful beasts, application of the principles propagated by the society for the prevention of cruelty to animals

Work in the fields, practical agriculture: Seedlings, crops, manures, grape harvests, cultures, and harvests special to the diverse areas of France

Botany: Study of the simple and useful plants

Fruit orchards: Orchards, acclimation

Truck farming: Early vegetables, flowers to be sold, care of the garden and vegetable (kitchen) garden

Agricultural chemistry: Improvement of the soils, manures, fertilizers

Household chores: Washing, bleaching

Food preparation: Preparation of food for the master, the domestics, and the animals; canning of fruits and vegetables; preparation of jam, liqueurs, etc.; preparation of the *charcuterie*

Making bread and pastry

Creamery: Making cheese and butter

Cellar (Cave): The storeroom, the brewery

Fruit cellar: Preservation and wintering of fruits and vegetables

Care of animals, the cow barn: Raising of calves, yaks, etc.

Sheep pen: Raising lamb, washing and shearing of wool

Pig pen

Chicken yard: Incubation, raising and fattening of the hens, turkeys, geese, ducks, pigeons, etc., collection of their feathers and down; rabbits: raising of the young, collecting and selling the skins and feet; kennels

Pheasant preserve: Aviary, acclimation of new breeds

Pisciculture: Care of the ponds and breeding beds, multiplication and raising of fish

Apiculture: Beehives and honey

Sericiculture: Model menageries for productive experiences and educations; grain feeding the silkworms on mulberry trees, oak, and the castor oil plant

Manual Work: Ironing and creasing; sewing, knitting, crocheting, machine sewing; the art of tailoring, designing, and remodeling garments; maintenance of linen; dying of linen and hemp; spinning thread by bobbin or wheel; making embroidered slippers; making fishing line and mending fishing line; basket making, braiding straw; making straw hats; making tapered lace (*dentelles au fuseau*); bleaching and mending lace; unwinding and preparing silk; embroidery flowers for churches, etc.; and all other useful and lucrative women's crafts

Source: *BAIP*, no. 164 (1867), pp. 932–40.

Bibliography

PRIMARY SOURCES

ARCHIVES

Archives de la Seine, Paris.
    Acte de Naissance, 6314 (Victor Duruy).
Archives Nationales, Archives Privés, Paris.
    XIX AB 523 Dupanloup Papers.
    42 AP 268 François Guizot Papers.
    87 AP 3 Jules Simon Papers.
    114 AP Victor Duruy Papers (3 cartons).
Archives Nationales, Paris.
    F(17) series (Ministère de l'Instruction Publique).
    F(19) series (Ministère des Cultes).
Bibliothèque de l'Hôtel de Ville de Paris.
    Michelet, Jules. Correspondence. XIV.
    Michelet, Jules. Papers. 1.5.A.
    Michelet, Jules. Voyages. I.A.
Genealogical Society of the Church of the Latter Day Saints, Salt Lake City, Utah.
    Microfilm 312981 (Baptismal Register, Eglise Succursale de Saint-Médard, Paris, 1811–14).
Private Collections
    Holley-Darboy Collection. Mount Saint Mary's College, Emmitsburg, Maryland.
    Victor Duruy Collection, in possession of Mme Albert Duruy, Paris, France.

OFFICIAL PUBLICATIONS

Ministère de l'Agriculture, du Commerce et des Travaux Publics. *Enquête sur l'enseignement professionel ou recueil de dépositions faites en 1863 et 1864 devant la Commission de l'Enseignement Professionel.* Paris, 1864.
Ministère de l'Instruction Publique. *L'administration de l'instruction publique de 1863 à 1869.* Paris, 1870.
[———.] *Annuaire de l'instruction publique.* Paris, 1863–69.

————. *Bulletin administratif de l'instruction publique.* 1863–69.

————. *Rapports adressés à S. Exc. M. le Ministre de l'Instruction Publique par les membres de la commission chargées d'examiner les travaux d'élèves et les moyens d'enseignement exposés au ministère et au Champs-de-Mars.* Paris, 1867.

————. *Réponse de Son Excellence le Ministre de l'Instruction Publique à la petition des habitants de Maisons-Alfort pourtant demande d'une école laique de filles dans la dite commune.* Paris, 1865.

————. *Statistique de l'enseignement supérieur.* Paris, 1868.

NEWSPAPERS

Le Charivari, 1867–68.

Journal des Landes, October 21, 1866.

Journal général de l'instruction publique, 1863–69.

Moniteur universel, March 3, 1867.

L'Opinion nationale, October 25, November 15, 1866, November 23, 1867, November 6, 1868.

Revue de l'instruction publique, 1863–69.

Le Siècle, March, 1867, November 16, 1867, January 14, 1868.

INTERVIEWS

Duruy, Mme Albert, May 7, 1969, and August, 1975.

Prost, Antoine, October, 1968.

BOOKS AND PAMPHLETS

Adam, Juliette. *Mes sentiments et nos idées avant 1870.* Paris, 1905.

Arnold, Matthew. *Matthew Arnold on Education.* Edited by Gillian Sutherland. Baltimore, 1973.

————. *The Popular Education of France.* London, 1861.

Avenel, Joseph d'. *Le pape, prince italien réponse à la brochure Les papes, princes italiens.* Paris, 1860.

Berton, Henry. *L'évolution constitutionnelle du Second Empire.* Paris, 1900.

Le centenaire de Victor Duruy, 1811–1911. Cahors et Alençon, 1911.

Cochin, Augustin. *Paris: Sa population, son industrie.* Paris, 1864.

Darimon, Alfred. *Histoire d'un parti: Le tiers parti sous l'empire (1863–1866).* Paris, 1887.

Desraimes, Marie. *Les oeuvres complètes.* N.p., 1895.

[Dupanloup, Félix]. *Les alarmes de l'épiscopat justifiées par les faits.* Paris, 1868.

[————]. *La femme chrétienne et française, dernière réponse à M. Duruy et à ses défenseurs par Mgr. l'évêque d'Orléans.* Paris, 1868.

————. *Femmes savantes et femmes studieuses.* Paris, 1867.

[————]. M. Duruy et l'éducation des filles, lettre de Mgr. l'évêque d'Orléans à un de ses collègues. Paris, 1867.

————. Nouvelles oeuvres choisies de Mgr. Dupanloup. 7 vols. Paris, 1873.

[————]. Seconde lettre de Mgr. l'évêque d'Orléans sur M. Duruy et l'éducation des filles. Paris, 1867.

Duruy, Albert. L'instruction publique et la démocratie, 1879–1886. Paris, 1886.

Duruy, Victor. Histoire sainte d'après la Bible. Paris, 1863.

[————]. Les papes, princes italiens. Paris, 1860.

————. Leçon d'ouverture du cours d'histoire à l'Ecole Polytechnique pour les deux divisions réunies. Paris, 1862.

————. Notes et souvenirs, 1811–1894. 2 vols. Paris, 1901.

Duruy, Victor, Auguste Filon, Louis Lacroix, and Jean Yanoski. Italie ancienne. 2 vols. Paris, 1850–51.

Dutoit, Henri Edouard. Dupanloup: Choisir les meilleurs textes. Paris, 1933.

Evans, Thomas W. The Second French Empire. New York, 1905.

Gréard, Octave. Education et instruction. 4 vols. Paris, 1904.

Hanriot, Charles. Mgr. Dupanloup et l'enseignement secondaire. Troyes, 1873.

Institut de France. Inauguration du monument élevé à la mémoire de Victor Duruy à Villeneuve-Saint-Georges. Paris, 1900.

Laprade, Victor de. L'éducation homicide. Paris, 1867.

Lavisse, Ernest. Association des anciens élèves de l'Ecole Normale Supérieure. 49th annual general reunion. Paris, 1895.

————. Un ministre—Victor Duruy. Paris, 1895.

Legouvé, Ernest. Dernier travail, derniers souvenirs. Paris, 1898.

Liard, Louis. L'enseignement supérieur en France, 1789–1893. 2 vols. Paris, 1888–94.

Monod, Gabriel. Portraits et souvenirs. Paris, 1897.

Nisard, Desiré. Souvenirs et notes biographiques. 2 vols. Paris, 1888.

Ollivier, Emile. L'empire libéral. 18 vols. Paris, 1903.

[Pillet, Leon]. Mémoire remis à l'empereur par un de ses ministres des cultes sur la politique à suivre vis-à-vis de l'Eglise. Bourges, 1873.

Robert, Charles. Les ameliorations sociales du Second Empire. 2 vols. Paris, 1868.

————. Considerations générales sur le Group X. Paris, 1863.

————. De l'ignorance des populations ouvrières et rurales de la France et des causes qui tendent à la perpetuer. Montbéliard, 1868.

————. Instruction primaire. Strasbourg, 1863.

————. De la necessité de rendre l'instruction primaire obligatoire en France. Montbéliard, 1861.

————. *Plaintes et voeux présentés par les instituteurs publics en 1861*. Paris, 1864.

Roux, Ferdinand. *Histoire des six premiers années de l'Ecole Normale Spéciale de Cluny*. Paris, 1889.

M. Victor Duruy. N.p., 1876.

ARTICLES

Broglie, Albert duc de. "Victor Duruy." *Revue des deux mondes*, February 1, 1898, pp. 524–61.

Duruy, Albert. "La statistique de l'enseignement supérieur." *Revue des deux mondes*, 3rd period, 32 (April 1, 1879), 556–91.

[Duruy, Victor]. "Une conquête du féminisme sous le Second Empire." *Bulletin enseignement public au Maroc*, a. 41 (October–December, 1954), 51–61.

Ecolan, A.-M. "Une lettre de Victor Duruy." *L'éducation nationale*, November 27, 1952, p. 12.

Femmes diplômes. Special number 43, 1962.

Française, February 12, 1938.

Glachant, Victor. "Monseigneur Parisis et la ministère de l'instruction publique: D'après des documents inédits." *Quinzaine*, LXVI (1905), 223–32.

Laveleye, Emile de. "De l'instruction du peuple au dix-neuvième siècle." *Revue des deux mondes* (1865), 976–1012.

Lavisse, Ernest. "Victor Duruy." *Revue de Paris*, January 15, 1895, pp. 225–53; March 1, 1895, pp. 47–85.

Levasseur, Emile. "L'enseignement des jeunes filles et M. Duruy." *Revue internationale de l'enseignement*, XXX (1895), 549–56.

Malarcé, M. de. "Journal de ma vie." *La Revue hebdomadaire*, March 30, 1901, pp. 667–87.

Monod, Gabriel. "Victor Duruy." *Revue internationale de l'enseignement*, XXVIII (1894), 481–89.

Rambaud, Alfred. "Victor Duruy (1811–1894)." *Journal des savants*, September, 1904, pp. 485–98.

Robert, Charles. "Victor Duruy." *Bulletin de la Société de Participation aux Bénéfices*, XVI (1894), 173–78.

Roustan, M. "L'enseignement primaire de Fortoul à Duruy: Le ministère Rouland (1856–1863)." *Revue pédagogique*, LVIII (1911), 152–76.

Simon, Jules. "Notice historique sur la vie et les travaux de Victor Duruy." *Journal des débats*, Supplément, November 30, 1895.

Thamin, R. "Victor Duruy." *Revue pédagogique*, XLII (1903), 460–67.

Zévort, E. "Victor Duruy." *Revue pédagogique*, XXV (1894), 481–90.

SECONDARY SOURCES

BOOKS AND PAMPHLETS

Acomb, Evelyn M., and Marvin L. Brown, Jr. *French Society and Culture Since the Old Regime.* New York, 1966.

Actes du Colloque international d'histoire réligieuse de Grenoble des 30 Septembre–3 Octobre, 1971. *Les catholiques libéraux aux XIXe siècle.* Grenoble, 1974.

Anderson, Robert D. *Education in France, 1848–1870.* Oxford, 1975.

Artz, Frederick B. *The Development of Technical Education in France, 1500–1850.* Cambridge, Mass., 1966.

Audiganne, Armand. *Les populations ouvrières et les industries de la France.* 2 vols. Paris, 1860.

Aulard, Alphonse. *Napoleon 1er et le monopole universitaire.* Paris, 1911.

Auspitz, Katherine. *The Radical Bourgeoisie: The Ligue de l'enseignement and the Origins of the Third Republic, 1866–1885.* New York, 1982.

Baker, Donald N., and Patrick J. Harrigan, eds. *The Making of Frenchmen: Current Directions in the History of Education in France, 1679–1979.* Waterloo, Ontario, 1980.

Beauroy, Jacques, Marc Bertrand, and Edward Gargan. *The Wolf and the Lamb: Popular Culture in France from the Old Regime to the Twentieth Century.* Saratoga, Calif., 1977.

Bertier de Sauvigny, Guillaume de. *The Bourbon Restoration.* Translated by Lynn M. Case. Philadelphia, 1967.

Bertocci, Philip A. *Jules Simon: Republican Anticlericalism and Cultural Politics in France, 1848–1886.* Columbia, Mo., 1978.

Bouglé, Célestin. *The French Conception of Culture Générale and Its Influence upon Instruction.* New York, 1938.

Bourgain, Louis. *L'église de France et l'état au dix-neuvième siècle (1802–1900).* 2 vols. Paris, 1901.

Butler, Cuthbert. *The Vatican Council.* 2 vols. London, 1930.

Cacérès, Benigno. *Histoire de l'éducation populaire.* Paris, 1964.

Campbell, Stuart L. *The Second Empire Revisited: A Study in French Historiography.* New Brunswick, 1978.

Charlton, Donald G. *Secular Religions in France, 1815–1870.* London, 1963.

Chevallier, Pierre. *La scolarisation en France depuis un siècle.* Paris, 1974.

Chevallier, Pierre, Bernard Grosperrin, and Jean Maillet. *L'enseignement français de la Révolution à nos jours.* Vol. I. Paris, 1968. Vol. II by Chevallier and Grosperrin. Paris, 1971.

Cinquantenaire du Lycée Victor Duruy (1912–1962). Paris, 1963.

Cipolla, Carlo M. *Literacy and Development in the West.* Baltimore, 1969.

Dansette, Adrien. *A Religious History of France.* 2 vols. Freiberg, 1961.

Debidour, Antonin. *Histoire des rapports de l'église et de l'état en France de 1789 à 1870.* Paris, 1898.

Duveau, Georges. *Les instituteurs.* Paris, 1957.

———. *La vie ouvrière en France sous le Second Empire.* Paris, 1946.

Fourrier, Charles. *L'enseignement français de 1789 à 1945: précis d'histoire des institutions scolaires.* Paris, 1965.

Fox, Robert, and George Weisz, eds. *The Organization of Science and Technology in France, 1808–1914.* Cambridge, 1980.

Furet, François, and Jacques Ozouf. *Lire et écrire.* 2 vols. Paris, 1977.

Gagnon, Paul A. *France Since 1789.* New York, 1964.

Gerbod, Paul. *La condition universitaire en France au XIXᵉ siècle.* Paris, 1965.

———. *La vie quotidienne dans les lycées et collèges au XIXᵉ siècle.* Paris, 1968.

Gontard, Maurice. *Les écoles primaires de la France bourgeois (1833–1875).* Toulouse, 1964.

———. *La question des écoles normales primaires de la Révolution de 1789 à nos jours.* Paris, 1962.

Graff, Harvey J., ed. *Literacy and Social Development in the West: A Reader.* Cambridge, 1981.

Harrigan, Patrick J. *Mobility, Elites and Education in French Society of the Second Empire.* Waterloo, Ontario, 1980.

Harrigan, Patrick, with Victor Neglia. *Lycéens et collégiens sous le Second Empire.* Paris, 1979.

Hayes, Carlton. *France: A Nation of Patriots.* New York, 1930.

Higonnet, Patrice L. R. *Pont-de-Montvert: Social Structure and Politics in a French Village, 1700–1914.* Cambridge, Mass., 1971.

Irsay, Stephan d'. *Histoire des universités françaises et étrangères des origines à nos jours.* 2 vols. Paris, 1935.

Isser, Natalie. *The Second Empire and the Press: A Study of Government Inspired Brochures on French Foreign Policy in Their Propaganda Milieu.* The Hague, 1974.

Kurtz, Harold. *The Empress Eugénie, 1826–1920.* Cambridge, Mass., 1964.

Lebey, A. *La lutte scolaire en France au XIXᵉ siècle: Le ministre Duruy.* Paris, n.d.

Le Bras, Gabriel. *Etudes de sociologie religieuse.* 2 vols. 1955. Reprint, New York, 1975.

McManners, John. *Church and State in France, 1870–1914.* New York, 1972.

Marcilhacy, Christianne. *Le diocèse d'Orléans sous l'épiscopat de Mgr. Dupanloup, 1849–1878.* Paris, 1962.

Matrat, Marie, and Kergomard, Pauline. *Les écoles maternelles.* Paris, 1889.

Maurain, Jean. *La politique ecclésiastique du Second Empire de 1852 à 1869.* Paris, 1930.

Mayeur, Françoise. *L'éducation des filles en France au XIXᵉ siècle.* Paris, 1979.

————. *L'enseignement secondaire des jeunes filles sous la Troisième République.* Paris, 1977.

Mitchell, B. R. *European Historical Statistics, 1750–1970.* New York, 1975.

Moody, Joseph N. *French Education Since Napoleon.* Syracuse, 1978.

Ozouf, Mona. *L'école, l'église et la république, 1871–1914.* Paris, 1963.

Piobetta, J. B. *Le baccalauréat.* Paris, 1937.

Ponteil, Felix. *Histoire de l'enseignement en France, 1789–1965.* Paris, 1966.

Price, Roger. *The French Second Republic: A Social History.* London, 1972.

Prost, Antoine. *Histoire de l'enseignement en France, 1800–1967.* Paris, 1968.

Raphael, Paul, and Maurice Gontard. *Un ministre de l'instruction publique sous l'Empire autoritaire: Hippolyte Fortoul, 1851–1856.* Paris, 1975.

Rémond, René. *L'anticlericalisme en France de 1815 à nos jours.* Paris, 1976.

Ringer, Fritz. *Education and Society in Modern Europe.* Bloomington, Ind., 1979.

Roche, Daniel. *Ordres et Classes: Colloque d'histoire sociale saint-cloud 24–25 mai 1967.* Paris, 1973.

Rohr, Jean. *Victor Duruy, ministre de Napoleon III: Essai sur la politique de l'instruction publique au temps de l'empire libéral.* Paris, 1967.

Rousselot, Paul. *Histoire de l'éducation des femmes en France.* 2 vols. Paris, 1882.

Schapiro, Jacob Salwyn. *Liberalism and the Challenge of Fascism: Social Forces in England and France, 1815–1870.* New York, 1964.

Seignobos, Charles. *Le déclin de l'empire et l'établissement de la Troisième République.* Vol. VII of Ernest Lavisse, ed., *Histoire de France contemporaine.* 10 vols. Paris, 1921.

Smith, Robert J. *The Ecole Normale Supérieure and the Third Republic.* Albany, N.Y., 1982.

Stearns, Peter. *European Society in Upheaval: Social History Since 1750.* New York, 1975.

Stone, Lawrence, ed. *Schooling and Society: Studies in the History of Education.* Baltimore, 1976.

Taine, Hippolyte. *The Modern Regime.* 2 vols. New York, 1931.

Thabault, Roger. *Education and Change in a Village Community: Mazières-en-Gâtine, 1848–1914.* Translated by Peter Tregear. New York, 1971.

Thompson, James Westfall, and Bernard J. Holm. *A History of Historical Writing.* 2 vols. New York, 1942.

Trénard, Louis. *Salvandy en son temps: 1795–1856.* Lille, 1968.

Turner, G. L'E., ed. *The Patronage of Science in the Nineteenth Century.* Leiden, 1976.

Vignery, Robert J. *The French Revolution and the Schools.* Madison, 1965.

Weber, Eugen. *Peasants into Frenchmen.* Stanford, 1976.

Williams, Roger. *The World of Napoleon III.* New York, 1957.

Zeldin, Theodore. *The Political System of Napoleon III.* New York, 1971.

————, ed. *Conflicts in French Society: Anticlericalism, Education and Morals in the Nineteenth Century.* London, 1970.

ARTICLES

Anderson, Robert. "Secondary Education in Mid-Nineteenth Century France: Some Social Aspects." *Past and Present,* no. 53 (November, 1971), 121–46.

Baillaud, René. "L'insuffisance de la recherche scientifique en France sous le Second Empire." *P. V. M. Académie des Sciences et Belles-Lettres* (Besançon), CLXXVII (1968 [1966–67]), 77–96.

Beslais, Aristide. "Obligation, gratuité, laïcité." *Revue socialiste,* no. 159 (January, 1963), 61–70, and no. 160 (February, 1963), 176–84.

Boiraud, H. "Sur la création par l'état d'un enseignement féminin en France." *Paedagogica Historica,* XVII (1977), 20–36.

Dansette, Adrien. "Le corps enseignant au XIXᵉ siècle." *La revue de Paris,* October, 1966, pp. 117–20.

————. "Un grand ministre méconnu." *Revue de Paris,* December, 1967, pp. 50–60.

Day, C. R. "The Development of Higher Primary and Intermediate Technical Education in France, 1800 to 1870." *Historical Reflections/Réflexions historiques,* III (1976), 49–66.

Dejob, Charles. "Le réveil de l'opinion dans l'Université sous le Second Empire: *La revue de l'instruction publique* et Victor Duruy." *L'enseignement secondaire,* March 15–May 1, 1914, pp. 65–68, 82–85, 107–10, 120–24.

Forestier, Henri. "L'enquête de 1856 sur la désertion des campagnes." *Bulletin de la Société des sciences historiques et naturelles de l'Yonne* (Auxerre), XCVII (1959), 271–73.

Gagnon, Paul. "The French Lesson: The Right to Culture," *Change,* VII (December–January, 1975–76), 36–40.

Gerbod, Paul. "Les inspecteurs généraux et l'inspection générale de l'instruction publique de 1802 à 1882." *Revue historique* (July–September, 1966), 79–106.

————. "La place de l'histoire dans l'enseignement secondaire de 1802 à 1880." *Information historique,* XXVII (1965), 123–30.

Goldstein, Doris S. "'Official Philosophies' in Modern France: The Example of Victor Cousin." *Journal of Social History,* I (1968), 259–79.

Gontard, Maurice. "Une réforme de l'enseignement secondaire au xixe siècle: 'La Bifurcation' (1852–1865)." *Revue française de pédagogie*, no. 20, pp. 6–14.

Harrigan, Patrick J. "Secondary Education and the Professions in France During the Second Empire." *Comparative Studies in Society and History*, XVII (1975), 349–71.

———. "Social and Political Implications of Catholic Secondary Education During the Second French Empire." *Societas*, VI (1976), 41–59.

Hébrard, Jean. "École et alphabétisation au XIXe siècle (Approche psycho-pédagogique de documents historiques)." *Annales: Economies, sociétés et civilisations*, XXXV (1980), 66–80.

Horvath, Sandra A. "Victor Duruy and the Controversy Over Secondary Education for Girls." *French Historical Studies*, IX (1975), 83–104.

Huckaby, John K. "Roman Catholic Reaction to the Falloux Law." *French Historical Studies*, IV (1965), 203–13.

Isambert, François André. "Religion et développement dans la France du XIXe siècle." *Archives de sociologie des religions*, VIII (January–June, 1963), 63–69.

Jacquin, R. "Hippolyte Fortoul a-t-il banni la philosophie?" *Revue des sciences religieuses* (Strasbourg), a. 31, n. 4 (1957), 383–87.

Janet, Paul. "L'éducation des femmes." *Revue des deux Mondes*, 3rd period, LIX (1883), 48–85.

Jefferson, Carter. "Worker Education in England and France, 1800–1914." *Comparative Studies in Society and History*, VI (1964), 345–66.

Johnson, Richard. "Educational Policy and Social Control in Early Victorian England." *Past and Present*, no. 49 (November, 1970), 96–119.

Kulstein, David I. "Economics Instruction for Workers During the Second Empire." *French Historical Studies*, I (1959), 225–34.

Laborie, L. de Lanzac de. "Au fil de l'histoire." *Le correspondant*, October–December, 1901, pp. 533–45.

Marlin, Roger. "La dernière tentative électorale de Montalembert aux elections législatives de 1863." *Revue d'histoire moderne et contemporaine*, XVII (1970), 999–1018.

Mayeur, Françoise. "Les évêques français et Victor Duruy: Les cours secondaires de jeunes filles." *Revue d'histoire de l'église de France*, LVI (1971), 267–304.

Oberlé, Raymond. "Etude sur l'analphabétisme à Mulhouse au siècle de l'industrialisation." *Bulletin du Musée Historique de Mulhouse*, LXVII (1959), 99–110.

O'Boyle, Lenore. "The Problem of an Excess of Educated Men in Western Europe, 1800–1850." *Journal of Modern History*, XLII (1970), 471–95.

Palmade, Guy. "Le Journal des economists et la pensée libérale sous le Second

Empire." *Bulletin de la Société d'histoire moderne et contemporaine*, no. 22 (1968), 9–16.

Planté, Louis. "Une rencontre de César: Victor Duruy, ministre de l'instruction publique." *Revue bleue*, May 2, 1931, pp. 270–75.

Rothney, John A. "The Modernization of Politics and the Politics of Modernization." *Proceedings of the Eighth Annual Meeting of the Western Society for French History*, VIII (1981), 368–77.

Royle, Edward. "Mechanics Institutes and the Working Classes, 1840–1860." *Historical Journal*, XIV (1971), 305–21.

Schwab, Marguerite. "Victor Duruy et les premiers pas de l'enseignement laique," *Cahiers Laiques*, Brochure no. 73 (January–February, 1963).

Secondy, Louis. "Place et rôle des petits séminaires dans l'enseignement secondaire en France au XIXe siècle." *Revue d'histoire de l'église de France*, LXVI (1980), 243–59.

Sherman, Dennis. "The Meaning of Economic Liberalism in Mid-Nineteenth Century France." *History of Political Economy*, VI (1974), 171–99.

Spitzer, Alan. "The Good Napoleon III." *French Historical Studies*, II (1962), 308–29.

Spivak, Marcel. "Le développement de l'éducation physique et du sport français de 1852 à 1914." *Revue d'histoire moderne et contemporaine*, XXIV (1977), 28–38.

Sutherland, Gillian. "The Study of the History of Education." *History*, LIV (February, 1969), 49–59.

Tersen, Emile. "L'instituteur de la Ière République à l'aube de la IIIe." *Europe*, nos. 372–73 (April–May, 1960), 8–19.

Vigier, Philippe. "Diffusion d'une langue nationale et résistance des patois en France au XIXe siècle." *Romanticisme*, XXV–XXVI (1979), 191–208.

Vincent, Gérard. "Les professeurs de l'enseignement secondaire dans la société de la 'Belle Époque.'" *Revue d'histoire moderne et contemporaine*, XIII (1966), 49–86.

Weisz, George. "Le corps professoral de l'enseignement supérieur et l'idéologie de la réforme universitaire en France, 1860–1885." *Revue française de sociologie*, XVIII (1977), 201–32.

Zehr, Howard. "The Modernization of Crime in Germany and France, 1830–1913." *Journal of Social History*, VIII (Summer, 1975), 117–41.

Zeldin, Theodore. "English Ideals in French Politics." *Historical Journal*, II (1959), 40–58.

———. "Higher Education in France, 1848–1940." *Journal of Contemporary History*, II (1967), 53–80.

DISSERTATIONS

Anderson, Robert D. "Some Developments in French Secondary Education During the Second Empire." Ph.D. dissertation, Oxford University, 1967.

Bruneau, William Arthur. "The French Faculties and Universities, 1870– 1902." Ph.D. dissertation, University of Toronto, 1977.

Harrigan, Patrick J. "Catholic Secondary Education in France, 1851–1882." Ph.D. dissertation, University of Michigan, 1970.

Horvath, Sandra A. "Victor Duruy and French Education, 1863–1869." Ph.D. dissertation, Catholic University of America, 1971.

Weisz, George David. "The Academic Elite and the Movement to Reform French Higher Education, 1850–1885." Ph.D. dissertation, State University of New York at Stony Brook, 1976.

UNPUBLISHED PAPERS

Langlois, Claude. "Women, Religious Orders, and Education in Nineteenth-Century France." Translated by Timothy Tackett. Paper given at the Sixty-first Annual Meeting of the American Catholic Historical Association, Washington, D.C., December 28, 1980.

Index